# After Poststructuralism

GU00496618

In the last decades of the twentieth century, French poststructuralist 'theory' transformed the humanities, not least literary studies and philosophy. However, theory also met with resistance and the claim that French thought is obscure, jargon-ridden nonsense has never quite subsided. In a time when the death of theory is frequently proclaimed, this book returns to the debates around theory and offers an original take on the question posed by so many critics: what next?

Colin Davis argues that in order to move forward we need to reassess the past and potential contribution of theory to the understanding of ourselves and the world. Having diagnosed significant misreadings on both sides of what are often called the 'Theory Wars', he undertakes careful new readings of the work of Jean-François Lyotard, Emmanuel Levinas, Louis Althusser and Julia Kristeva. Organized around the fundamental issues of knowledge, ethics, hope and identity, these readings reveal the real intellectual challenge of French thought, which Davis argues has been undervalued. He then addresses current debates on the death of theory and outlines a new way of understanding its practice and its limitations. The book closes with a convincing case for theory's survival: its presence may be denied and its nature may be transformed, but it has not gone away. After poststructuralism, then, comes the *afterlife* of poststructuralism.

*After Poststructuralism* is a wonderfully accessible account of the past and present fortunes of theory, suitable for anyone researching, teaching or studying in the field. However, it offers much more than this, by tracing the real contribution of poststructuralist thought to core philosophical and critical issues. Most importantly, Colin Davis's stunning, original study offers a way forward for the humanities – a way forward in which theory will play a crucial part.

**Colin Davis** is Professor of French Studies at the University of Warwick. His publications include *Levinas: An Introduction* (1996), *Ethical Issues in Twentieth-Century French Fiction* (2000) and *French Fiction in the Mitterrand Years* (with Elizabeth Fallaize, 2000).

# After Poststructuralism

Reading, stories and theory

Colin Davis

Routledge
Taylor & Francis Group

LONDON AND NEW YORK

First published 2004
by Routledge
11 New Fetter Lane, London EC4P 4EE

Simultaneously published in the USA and Canada
by Routledge
29 West 35th Street, New York, NY 10001

*Routledge is an imprint of the Taylor & Francis Group*

© 2004 Colin Davis

Typeset in Goudy by The Running Head Limited, Cambridge
Printed and bound in Great Britain by
TJ International Ltd, Padstow, Cornwall

*British Library Cataloguing in Publication Data*
A catalogue record for this book is available from the British
Library

*Library of Congress Cataloging in Publication Data*
Davis, Colin, 1960–
After poststructuralism : reading, stories and theory / Colin
Davis.
  p cm
Includes bibliographical references and index.
1. Structuralism (Literary analysis) 2. Structuralism.
3. Poststructuralism. 4. Criticism—20th century.
5. Literature—history and criticism—Theory, etc. I. Title.
PN98.S7D38 2003
801'.95'09045—dc21
                                          2003008592

ISBN 0–415–31609–X (pbk)
ISBN 0–415–31608–1 (hbk)

# Contents

# Acknowledgements

Some of the material in chapters 5 and 6 has previously appeared in *Textual Practice* and *Sites* respectively. I am grateful for permission to reprint. Further information on both journals can be found on http://www.tandf.co.uk. I would like to thank the following for advice, encouragement, and assistance in various forms during the preparation of this book: Sarah Kay, Emma Wilson, Michael Worton, Christina Howells, Robert Eaglestone, Mireille Rosello. I am grateful to the Universities of Oxford and Warwick for supporting my research, and to the Arts and Humanities Research Board for awarding an extra term's leave during which the book was completed. I would also like to thank the anonymous readers who commented so generously and constructively on earlier drafts of the book.

# Introduction

A series of damaging allegations is repeatedly made against post-war French thought, and more specifically poststructuralism and postmodernism. They celebrate a 'decentring of the subject' or 'death of man' which denies human agency and freedom; their anti-foundationalism condemns them to a sterile relativism; they are nihilistic and irrationalist; they can provide no basis for an ethics because they do not accept the universality of any values; they are concerned with the abstractness of 'theory' to the point that they allow no place for 'practice' and no conceivable application to the world which common sense tells us we inhabit; they denigrate and undermine all knowledge, belief and serious intellectual endeavour; they are elitist, stylistically baroque and intellectually shallow; politically, they are ineffectual and reactionary; and their rhetorical and terminological complexity only serves to mask their lack of real substance. French theory is too hard to read and too trivial to bother with. It has more to do with fashion than serious intellectual enquiry, and it is of more interest to literary critics than to real philosophers.

These charges have been made so often now that for some they can be taken as proven. Often, though, the hysterical or anxious denunciations of French thought are based on little or no knowledge of primary texts, and they dumbly replicate more or less gross misreadings seasoned with a hint of xenophobia.[1] For basic standards of reading and critical responsibility to have been flouted so blatantly, more must be at stake than is to be found in routine academic disagreements. From its earliest reception in British and North American universities, poststructuralism seemed to its supporters to renew the scope and nature of intellectual enquiry and to its opponents to undermine the values of evidence and argumentation. This book examines some of the claims and counter-claims made about French theory and suggests some of the ways it has contributed positively to our interminable project of self-understanding.

There is no point in claiming that any account of these matters can maintain a purely neutral stance towards them. For better or worse, and more or less consciously, poststructuralism is part of the background of most of us working in the humanities today. This is certainly true in my own case. When I read Jacques Derrida's *De la grammatologie* in 1983 I had just begun my first term as a graduate student. At the time I knew that deconstruction and poststructuralism gave rise to both passionate enthusiasm and deep opposition, but I had had little direct contact with them. Reading *De la grammatologie* was an exhilarating experience. Here was a heady mix of detailed interpretation and daring generalizations about meaning, truth and the history of philosophy. Derrida succeeded in raising the stakes of reading to an extraordinary degree. He suggested that close attention to relatively neglected texts such as Rousseau's *Essai sur l'origine des langues* might turn out to reveal the fault lines of Western thought and undermine deeply entrenched habits of thinking. Jürgen Habermas, who is generally neither a sympathetic nor a careful reader of Derrida, is right in his assessment of the appeal of Derrida's approach to people working in literature departments. At a stroke, we were no longer engaged in the respectful and humble task of serving Great Works; rather, literary criticism could take on 'an almost world-historical mission with its overcoming of the metaphysics of presence and of the age of logocentrism'.[2] Derrida showed that reading mattered.

The fact that the work of Derrida and others aroused such evident anxiety and distaste in some quarters only added to the appeal. Allegiances in the so-called Theory Wars were not difficult to detect. Theorists and anti-theorists could easily be seen through the enthusiastic approval or scornful hostility with which they greeted buzzwords such as anti-humanism, the death or decentring of the subject, difference (or differance), and dissemination. Was Derrida's infamous claim that '*there is nothing outside the text*' (*il n'y a pas de hors-texte*) arrant nonsense or did it represent an important insight into textuality, experience and the world? Views often differed more on grounds of quasi-tribal allegiance than on the basis of any sustained attempt to understand what Derrida might be getting at. But in any case, some argued that there was no reason to think Derrida was getting at anything at all, since to assume that he might have 'meanings' which he intended to communicate to his readers would undermine his general thesis, according to which meaning is always fractured and differed. Why bother to read Derrida when you could rely instead on grotesque caricatures of his thought to rebut him?

Discussions of theory no longer raise the same passions. The scandal caused in the United States by the discovery of Paul de Man's wartime journalism shortly after his death in 1983 was used to discredit the man, his work and, by association, theory in general. Moreover, many of the thinkers associated with the rise of theory have died. In France, which was the immediate source of most of the ideas which stoked controversy in British and North American universities, no new generation of comparable stature (or at least notoriety) has emerged to replace thinkers such as Barthes, Althusser, Lacan, Foucault, Deleuze and Lyotard. Reports of the death of theory can be traced back to at least the early 1980s. So whilst I was blissfully reading *De la grammatologie*, some commentators already considered that the theoretical movement for which it was a key text was either moribund or dead. The rise of cultural studies in its various forms entailed a renewed focus on the political, the concrete and the culturally specific in comparison with which theory could be characterized as elitist, patriarchal, universalizing and Eurocentric. Theory, which had set out to demystify work in the humanities, now appeared to be precisely what most needed demystifying.

There is undoubtedly an element of simplification in the opposition between theory and cultural studies, partly because it obscures the extent to which cultural studies grew out of and is informed by debates in theory, and partly because it relies on a false account of the claims of theory.[3] In the title essay of *Lob der Theorie* (*In Praise of Theory*), the German philosopher Hans-Georg Gadamer suggests two senses of theory, both derived from its Greek etymon. It is a form of seeing, 'Sehen dessen, was ist' (seeing that which is), as Gadamer puts it. This does not mean 'seeing that which is' simply in the sense of observing ambient phenomena, rather it involves seeing things of fundamental importance, catching a glimpse of the secrets beneath the surfaces of the visible.[4] At the same time, *theoria* refers to the functions of an envoy sent to participate in, for example, a religious ceremony or communal games. Since the envoy is an official representative of his home city, his role has a political aspect.[5] The *theoros* is both witness and participant, and his presence is also a mode of intervening in public affairs. Theory, then, is not disinterested, disengaged contemplation of immutable truths; it is a form of involvement which alters the context in which it appears. Theorists are inevitably tempted to claim greater powers and knowledge than they actually have. However, as a form of participation, theory cannot stand dispassionately outside the field in which it intervenes; so its failure to achieve the neutrality of the fully knowing, fully objective gaze is one of its essential characteristics. Using Lacanian vocabulary, Rabaté describes theory not as the discourse of the Master, but as the discourse of the hysteric, which is 'a quest for truth that always aims at pointing out the inadequacies of official, serious, and "masterful" knowledge'.[6] Rather than imposing its own authority definitively, it is engaged in a quest for understanding which is interminable because it can never occupy a final, assured position.

This book focuses on French theory, especially poststructuralism. It discusses the controversies to which it has given rise and the work of some of its most interesting exponents. Chapters 1 and 2 analyse the arguments and rhetoric which have been deployed in the repudiation of French theory and the kinds of anxiety which lie behind them. Chapter 1 discusses the charge of imposture made against French theory in two intellectual rows which attracted wide publicity, one in the 1960s and the other in the late 1990s; chapter 2 examines Habermas's rebuttal of poststructuralism and the dispute over the meaning and legacy of the Enlightenment. If attacks on French theory are more often than not based on false or caricatural depictions of the theorist's views, misreading is by no means restricted to one side of the argument. The claims and counter-claims are consistent and depressingly repetitive, and the co-implication of opponents through the shared rhetoric of controversy suggests that they have more in common than they wish to accept. These chapters are both a defence of French theory against its detractors and an attempt to identify what is at stake in the anxious patterns of misreading, or of refusal to read, which characterize the various controversies.

The central chapters of the book examine aspects of the work of four thinkers who have played a crucial role in fixing the image of French theory outside France: Jean-François Lyotard, the archetypal postmodernist; Louis Althusser, whose brand of Marxism revitalized political thought in the 1960s but whose later work remains relatively unexplored; Emmanuel Levinas, whose ideas were a key influence on the ethical turn taken by poststructuralism from the 1980s onwards; and Julia Kristeva, whose work has had a major impact on thinking in semiotics, feminism and psychoanalysis. Each of the chapters on these thinkers revolves around one of what Kant identified as the four fundamental questions of philosophy. The first three of these are formulated in Kant's *Critique of Pure Reason*, and the fourth is added in his *Logik*:[7]

1  What can I know?
2  What ought I to do?     }
3  What may I hope?
4  What is the human being?

In each of these chapters Kant's questions and his own treatment of them serve as a touchstone to indicate the continuity of concern and the differences of approach in the work of the French thinkers. Poststructuralism appears here, not as an outright rejection of its own philosophical roots, but as a continuing reflection on the major issues identified by Kant; and like it or not, the refraction of the Kantian questions through the poststructuralist lens vitally informs our own intellectual context.

The final chapter considers some of the changing ways in which theory has been understood, and it examines recent discussions of the 'death of theory' and the 'post-theoretical' condition. The title of this chapter, 'Spectres of theory', alludes to Derrida's book *Spectres de Marx*, in which Derrida analyses the surprising extent to which ghosts figure in Marx's writing. Ghosts are never quite avowed nor ever fully relinquished, they are both present and absent; they are the trace of something dead but which in some sense lives on. The final chapter concludes by examining how the personification of theory and the announcement of its death enable it to survive and to return in just such a ghostly manner. Its presence may be denied, its nature may be transformed, but it has not quite gone away. Its death is not its end, it is merely a prelude to its *afterlife*.[8]

As its title implies, this book is about aspects of being 'after poststructuralism'. One sense of this involves *going after* poststructuralism as hunters goes after their prey, to catch it and to catch it out. Chapters 1, 2 and 7 illustrate ways in which some of those who felt threatened or offended by poststructuralism or other theoretical practices have gone after it in this sense. But being after poststructuralism also entails being still being bound up with it, still concerned to come to terms with its legacy. The book returns to poststructuralist texts and other French theoretical works in the anticipation that they may still speak to us if we are prepared to listen to them. We may come after them but we are not yet over them. It is in this sense that *after* may be understood in the titles of chapters 3, 4, 5 and 6: 'After knowledge', 'After ethics', 'After hope', and 'After identity'. In none of these cases does *after* mean that the following term has been simply superseded and consigned to the past. On the contrary, the central chapters of the book suggest that the problems of knowledge, ethics, hope and identity are of pressing concern. The terms are still to be used, even if they also require to be re-thought and displaced.

The place of Kant in this book requires some comment. Kant appears in most chapters, though there is relatively little direct discussion of his thought. Chapter 2 considers different responses to one of his best-known essays, 'An Answer to the Question: What is Enlightenment?', and to varying extents he also figures significantly in chapters 3, 4, 5 and 6. The role Kant plays here is partly due to his status as a touchstone of philosophical legitimacy for anyone trained in philosophy in France. Reference to Kant is commonplace in work which aspires to be taken seriously as philosophy, and thinkers such as Deleuze, Lyotard, Foucault and Lacan all engage with him explicitly and repeatedly. As Derrida, himself a persistent and respectful reader of Kant, puts it, 'Whether one follows it or whether turns aside from it, Kant is the norm'.[9] The reference to Kant is what 'guarantees, authentifies, legitimizes the philosophical dignity of a discussion'.[10] This does not mean that Kant is to be slavishly followed. On the contrary, Derrida insists, the point of reading him is to question and to displace the effects of his philosophical authority. Derrida describes how attempting to bypass Kant altogether runs the risk of falling under his influence all the more surely:

> If one were happy to 'turn the page', to sidestep Kant, no longer to name him, to act as if he himself, that is his legacy, were no longer there, one would risk reproducing him all the more effectively, naïvely, secretly, unconsciously. This is because the irrigation of the common philosophical discourse by Kantian philosophemes, words, procedures and axioms is most often subterranean. Its routes are so complicated and indirect that it passes unnoticed. So, at the risk of returning again to Kant to add to the surplus value of his critical over-evaluation, isn't it *better*, isn't it *necessary* to read and therefore to situate Kant otherwise?[11]

In Derrida's account, reference to Kant serves both an institutional and an intellectual purpose. Institutionally, it is what marks out one's own work as philosophically serious; and intellectually, it is through engagement with Kant that his legacy can be recognized and contested. It is one of the purposes of this book to demonstrate that poststructuralist thinkers contributed significantly to transforming our understanding of the grand philosophical problems of knowledge, meaning, ethics and identity. But Kant's importance here is also tied to an ambiguity inherent in his legacy, and in the very notion of legacy. Again, Derrida has written eloquently and persuasively about how a legacy always requires to be read and re-read. What one inherits is, according to Derrida, 'always a secret – which says "read me, will you ever be able to?"'.[12] A legacy is a legacy *because* it is ambiguous, still to be decided. If it were unequivocal, there would be no disagreement about what it was and to whom it properly belonged. So it is the nature of the legacy to be in dispute; and this is as true of Kant's legacy as it is of the legacy of poststructuralism, which we have still not settled.

Derrida's account of the constitutive ambiguity of legacies concludes with the injunction *to read* and the warning that it may not be possible. Reading, Derrida suggests, will not settle the legacy once and for all; rather, it will keep the dispute alive, providing new resources with which to preserve and to re-interpret the monuments of our intellectual history. The key texts are not so familiar that they no longer have anything new to offer. The following chapters attempt to show that the texts of poststructuralism are still worth reading. In fact, reading is a key issue of this book. At a very basic level, the assaults on theory charted in chapters 1 and 2 derive from bad reading, caused either by ineptitude and impatience or by a complete failure to engage with the texts in any sustained way. My criticism of this does not imply, however, that reading could ever be a straightforward matter. Each of the chapters in the book is concerned in one way and another with reading as a deeply problematic activity. This is illustrated by the ways in which supporters and opponents of theory read and misread one another and by the problems of making sense out of history, of our own lives, of a patient's symptoms, and of theoretical texts. Stories and storytelling figure in several chapters of the book because they foreground the difficulties of establishing meaning with particular clarity. Stories fascinate and irritate because they explain too much whilst keeping their secrets to themselves. They can be told differently and interpreted differently. In distinctive ways, Levinas, Althusser and Kristeva all tussle with narrative as it both enables and obstructs the endeavour to find meaning in texts, life and the world. Of the three, only Kristeva actively welcomes the ability of stories, with all their obscurities and gaps, to make sense out of traumatized lives.

One of the connections between stories and theory lies in the challenge to reading which they both represent. When we read stories, we know – largely because theory has taught us – that we should attend to their irregularities, obscurities, blind spots and ambiguities in the expectation that these also signify in their way, even if we do not know exactly what they signify. The thinkers discussed here require of their readers that the same forms of attention should be brought to theoretical texts. Their work is intensely self-reflective, and their awareness of the problems of language and textuality inevitably impinges on the way they write. Their texts can be difficult and rebarbative, sometimes obscured by points of detail, as they enact the entanglement of the theoretical endeavour in its own textuality. As Rabaté argues, theory aims at the most general questions but 'it cannot avoid being enmeshed in the letter of the text, in partly untranslatable signifiers'.[13] In other words, the letter of the text may be as important in theoretical writing as it is in literature, and it is for this reason that much of the following chapters is taken up with detailed reading of theoretical texts. This does not mean that the distinction between theory and story is abolished and that theory is treated merely as another literary genre. Theory attempts to attain a general level of validity even as it remains entangled with its own signifiers. The following chapters are studies (and perhaps examples) of reading and misreading, of theory's necessary worrying at the borders of sense and nonsense.

# Chapter 1

# Impostures of French theory

> It is constantly surprising how skilful some commentators are at not reading.[1]

The first two chapters of this book trace some of the controversies sparked by French theory and examine the arguments and rhetoric used to repudiate it. This chapter looks at two widely publicized intellectual rows in which theory was stigmatized as a form of imposture. The first was provoked by the publication in 1965 of a polemical pamphlet entitled *Nouvelle Critique ou nouvelle imposture* by Sorbonne professor and Racine expert Raymond Picard. That work was an attack on what at the time was being called *la nouvelle critique* (the new criticism), a blanket term grouping together literary critics such as Jean Starobinski, Jean-Pierre Richard, Charles Mauron, Lucien Goldmann and Serge Doubrovsky who were exploring new protocols of reading based on existentialism, Marxism, psychoanalysis, semiology and anthropology. In particular Picard directed his invective against Roland Barthes, whose book *Sur Racine* (1963) was taken to epitomize the sloppy intellectual practices of *la nouvelle critique*. The second controversy erupted in 1997 around the publication of a book by two physicists, Alan Sokal and Jean Bricmont, entitled *Impostures intellectuelles*. The book had a restricted ambition and a more general one. It purported to demonstrate how a host of major intellectual French figures (Jacques Lacan, Julia Kristeva, Luce Irigaray, Bruno Latour, Jean Baudrillard, Paul Virilio, Gilles Deleuze and Félix Guattari) misuse scientific terminology, and thereby claim for their work an intellectual prestige and rigour that it does not actually have; more generally, Sokal and Bricmont aimed to discredit postmodernism, to show, as they put it, that the king is naked.[2]

One of the points that connects these two controversies is the massive media interest which they aroused beyond the portals of academia. They occasioned a public airing of the value and validity of advanced intellectual research; and a large contingent of academics, journalists and readers were all too grateful for the opportunity to sound off about thinkers and texts they had probably not read and had almost certainly not understood. The discovery that the king was naked was received less as a regal disgrace than as an excuse for complacency: why bother to read the works of Barthes, Lacan *et al.* now that they have been demonstrated to be little more than empty verbiage? The demi-gods of the French intellectual scene turned out to be paltry divinities, clothed only in their incomprehensible jargon, and potentially pernicious in their influence on younger critics. Denunciation thus appears as both an intellectual and a moral undertaking. Moreover, whilst the media response to the two controversies displayed significant parallels, there were also close similarities between the nature of the accusations made against *la nouvelle critique* on the one hand and postmodernism on the other. Postmodernist texts have allegedly duped us by their surface difficulty into thinking that they are profound. Sokal and Bricmont set out to debunk this mistake: 'In particular, we want to "deconstruct" the reputation that certain texts have of being difficult because the ideas in them are so profound. In many cases we shall demonstrate that if the texts seem incomprehensible, it is for the excellent reason that they mean precisely nothing' (5). More than thirty years earlier, Picard had come to much the same conclusion about Barthes:

> Monsieur Barthes's jargon has quite different effects: its function, perhaps artless but nevertheless effective, is – we've already seen it a dozen times – to give a 'scientific' prestige to absurdities, to place commonplaces in a flattering light, to hide (fairly badly) the indecision of thought. With his terms which are themselves obscure, which aren't defined and which are used – without any warning – in different senses, with his elastic notions and his too open concepts, this jargon is no more than the instrument of an *impudent criticism* [*critique à l'estomac*].[3]

This chapter traces some of the major strands of the two *imposture* controversies, emphasizing the similarities between them. Together, they illustrate the range and nature of the accusations repeatedly made against French theory. The earlier of the controversies is in part a struggle for the soul of literary criticism. It revolves around questions of authority and interpretation, and it sets the parameters of debate in lit-erary critical circles for decades to come. It also forms a template for the assault on thinking which is difficult to understand and apparently con-trary to common sense. The allegations made by Picard would be levelled at French thinkers virtually unchanged, as the *Impostures intel-lectuelles* affair showed over thirty years later. In both cases, the key charge is that the theorists under attack are impostors, they do not have the right to claim authority over their subject. Despite serious reserva-tions about the manner in which these attacks are conducted, the chapter concludes by suggesting that the charge may nevertheless con-tain the germ of an important insight. Imposture may after all play an essential role in the practice and performance of theory.

## Racine and *la nouvelle critique*

In 1956 Picard had established himself at the centre of French literary scholarship with the publication of his *thèse d'état*, the monumental (and monumentally dull) *La Carrière de Jean Racine*. In 700 pages it meticulously surveys every known document dealing with the French playwright Jean Racine's career from birth to death. The period during which Racine was active in the theatre, 1664–77, forms a small part of that career, and it is not Picard's intention to offer anything like a com-prehensive interpretation of the plays. He is interested only in their place in the development of Racine's career. Devoting himself to patient, painstaking scholarship, Picard pays no attention to the rapid changes which were taking place in literary criticism at the time when he was writing. Of most direct importance here is the reassessment of Racine undertaken in two very different books, one appearing shortly before and one shortly after the publication of Picard's thesis: Lucien Goldmann's *Le Dieu caché* (1956), which gives a Marxist sociological reading of Racinian tragedy, and Charles Mauron's *L'Inconscient dans l'œuvre et la vie de Racine* (1957), which offers a Freudian psychoanalytic reading of Racine's plays. In 1961, when Picard's *La Carrière de Jean Racine* was reissued, he added a brief Foreword in which he alluded to the works of Mauron and Goldmann, but he excluded them from the ranks of 'serious publications' (*publications sérieuses*), and he insisted that he has got nothing from them other than a heightened insight into 'the disarray of our time' (*le désarroi de notre temps*).[4] The combination of intellectual dismissal and moral distaste is already evident here, but Picard did not yet feel it was necessary to enter into fully-fledged re-buttal. In 1963, however, Barthes grouped together three previously published articles under one cover in *Sur Racine*, and in the following year he published his *Essais critiques*, which included two essays – 'Les Deux Critiques' and 'Qu'est-ce que la critique?' – which dismissed the finest fruits of French academic scholarship as reactionary and outdated. Things had gone far enough. Picard published a hostile review of *Essais critiques* in *Le Monde*, and then consolidated the attack on Barthes and *la nouvelle critique* in *Nouvelle Critique ou nouvelle imposture*. A massive media battle ensued, with critics and intellectuals taking sides in the press and journals; and in 1966 Barthes riposted in his *Critique et vérité*.[5]

At the beginning of *Nouvelle Critique ou nouvelle imposture* Picard recorded that he had originally thought that Barthes's work on Racine was intellectually negligible but relatively harmless.[6] That Picard's initial disregard should turn in the space of four years into virulent opposition suggests that he had at first misunderstood the stakes and dangers of these heretical readings of Racine. The disarray of the intellectual scene came to appear to be a threat to established critical and academic values. Part of what outraged Picard was that *la nouvelle critique* had undertaken to analyse Racine, the central canonical playwright of the French tradition, and an author who therefore should be treated with the greatest respect and learning. Picard's own immense scholarship was devalued if irresponsible amateurs were to be taken seriously. Moreover, whereas his work was patient and judicious, carefully avoiding hasty interpretations and generalizations, the new critics moved rapidly from particular details to global assertions, regarding Racine's plays as a coherent, unified *œuvre* rather than as a set of individual texts that should be treated on their own terms.

Although the studies of Goldmann, Mauron and Barthes are in most respects very different – and straightforwardly contradictory of one another on important points – they share the project of finding an interpretative framework which will explain both the structural coherence and the variations in Racinian tragedy. Goldmann locates this framework in what he calls a 'vision of the world' (*vision du monde*):

> The vision of the world is in effect the *conceptual extrapolation* to the point of *extreme coherence* of the real, affective, intellectual and even activating tendencies of a group. It is a *coherent* ensemble of problems and responses which is expressed, in literature, by the creation through words of a concrete universe of beings and things.[7]

Racine's vision derives from Jansenism, which envisaged the world as irremediably corrupt, with God either absent or silent (hence the 'hidden god' of Goldmann's title *Le Dieu caché*). Goldmann presents Racine's plays as engaged in the struggle to resolve the tension within Jansenist ideology which arises when Man (Goldmann's *l'Homme* includes some female characters) finds himself caught between a fallen world on the one hand and a silent God on the other.

Mauron also looks for a coherent pattern underlying Racine's writing. His equivalent of Goldmann's 'vision of the world' is what he calls 'a field of forces' (*un champ de forces*), which accounts for both fixity and dynamism in psychic life; it is compared to a magnet which causes iron filings to form recognizable shapes when they come under its influence: 'A structure is, in summary, the result of a history. The past, it seems, seeks to live again: it haunts us. The way it haunts us is through situations, let us say family situations, with various poles of sympathy and antipathy, desire and fear.'[8] Once the psychic field of forces has been formed, everything that comes from the outside – feelings, impressions, ideas, new situations – is inflected so that it is modelled around pre-existing patterns. Racine's plays are therefore analysed in terms of psychic forces – specifically the struggle of the male subject with a dominating, incestuous mother – which are ultimately located in the unconscious of the author.

In *Sur Racine* and particularly in 'L'Homme racinien', the first and most substantial of the three essays collected in that volume, Barthes shares Goldmann's and Mauron's desire to find the unity of Racinian tragedy; but unlike them, he denies that it should be located outside the texts themselves, in ideological or psychological forces. Rather, Barthes's study proposes a sort of structural anthropology of the Racinian world, as he analyses the signifying system underlying each of the plays. He finds in them a consistent setting – the antechamber posed between an inner sanctuary and the outside world – and a consistent set of characters playing out variants of what Barthes describes as a 'fundamental relationship' (*la relation fondamentale*). He provocatively represents this relationship in the form of what he calls 'a double equation':

A has all power over B.
A loves B, who does not love A.[9]

Pushing the analysis ever further, Barthes shows how Racine's plays revolve around the same drama of authority, involving the father and his son, the king and his subject, and ultimately God and his creature.

Even on this cursory account of new critical readings of Racine, it should be apparent how very different they are in tone and content from the cautious modesty of the Picardian scholar who humbly endeavours to unearth some solid facts about Racine. Moreover, despite their similarities, the projects of Goldmann, Mauron and Barthes are very different from one another, and perhaps even irreconcilable. In seeking the systematic coherence of Racine's plays, each of them looks for it in a different place. The systems they elaborate may be rigorous and persuasive in themselves (though by no means all would concede even this point), but when compared with one another they are barely compatible. Goldmann, Mauron and Barthes disagree, for example, about the number and identities of the true agents in Racinian tragedy. For Goldmann there are three, God, Man and the World; for Mauron there are two, the son and the mother; for Barthes there are also two, but they are God and his creature. So Agrippine, the dominant mother of *Britannicus*, is a relatively minor character in the play for Goldmann, representing no more than one of the voices of the World; for Mauron, on the contrary, her position is central and determining, since she is the possessive mother against whom the son must rebel; and Barthes, who isn't very interested in mothers (or at least this is how he appeared, until he described his response to a photograph of his own mother in *La Chambre claire*), integrates her into his own version of the Racinian system by including her in his roll call of *fathers*.

One of the crucial issues raised by these readings, then, is the question of competing readings, and how to decide between them. How can the same set of texts produce such variant interpretations? Should we just dismiss some or all of them as wrong, or is there some way of reconciling them? Barthes addresses precisely this problem in his Foreword and the final essay of *Sur Racine*, 'Histoire ou littérature?'. Barthes poses the question, 'Why speak about Racine today?':

> Racine's work has been associated with all the critical endeavours of some importance which have been undertaken in France over the last ten or so years: sociological criticism with Lucien Goldmann, psychoanalytical criticism with Charles Mauron, biographical criticism with Jean Pommier and Raymond Picard, depth psychology with Georges Poulet and Jean Starobinski; to the point that, by a remarkable paradox, the French author who is probably most linked with the idea of classical *transparency* is the only one to succeed in attracting all the new languages of the century.

(6)

The point is, for Barthes, that Racine's transparency is fundamentally ambiguous:

> it is that about which there is nothing to say and about which there is the most to say. It is then, definitively, his very transparency which makes Racine a commonplace in our literature, a sort of degree zero of the critical object, an empty place, but one which is eternally offered up to meaning.
>
> (6–7)

What makes Racine the greatest French writer is not any particular signification or virtue, but 'an unequalled art of availability, which allows him to be eternally present in the field of any critical language' (7).

The aim of the critic, then, is not to give a definitive account of Racine, but through Racine to engage 'all the language through which our world speaks to itself and which is an essential part of the history which it tells itself' (8). In 'Histoire ou littérature?' Barthes argues that criticism is based on assumptions and preferences which are normally not openly confronted; it is subjective, hypothetical and experimental. And this is just as true, he insists, of traditional scholarship as it is of his own writing, however much the scholars might dislike the fact. The point for Barthes is not to deny the situation, but to push it as far as it will go, to try out a critical language with as much rigour as possible, in the full knowledge that its findings tell us as much or more about ourselves and our intellectual tools as they do about the texts we are studying. In his own reading of Racine, Barthes fully accepts this risk.

*Sur Racine* concludes by underlining the possibility of using different critical discourses to interpret Racine: 'Racine lends himself to various languages: psychoanalytical, existential, tragic, psychological (others may be invented, others will be invented); none is innocent. But to recognize this inability *to tell the truth* on Racine [*cette impuissance à dire vrai sur Racine*] is precisely to recognize the special status of literature' (156). *Sur Racine* can be seen, then, as Barthes's exercise in practising what he preaches and theorizing his own practice. He pushes as far as he can a particular reading of Racine, whilst fully acknowledging that what he is offering is not the final truth of his subject. Throughout his career and certainly in *Sur Racine* Barthes seems comfortable with the evaporation of assured meaning from the literary text. It is if anything the source of his continuing interest in it. Ultimately, then, the status of Barthes's book is as floating, as ambiguous, as the texts he analyses; it both offers meaning, in the form of coherent interpretation,

and lets it evaporate in front of our eyes, as he tells us that we cannot
'*tell the truth* on Racine'. Barthes seems happy that his own practice,
and his own appropriation of Racine, should not be tied to a discourse
of truth. It is, he suggests, the elusiveness of meaning which ensures the
special status of literature, and which no doubt therefore explains its
interest and part of its pleasure. But Barthes's critics were not so happy
that the truth claims of both his and their practice should be so seduc-
tively undermined.

## The defence of truth

Picard's *Nouvelle Critique ou nouvelle imposture* and some of the supportive articles which followed it are characterized by a rather shocking
violence of tone, as Barthes underlines at the beginning of his response
in *Critique et vérité*.[10] 'Such a book has got what it takes to turn your
stomach', declares Picard of *Sur Racine* (57). As the title of his book
indicates, the new critics are not merely wrong-headed, they are impostors; hence to denounce them is not simply a matter of self-interest, it is
a positive moral duty: 'It seemed to me that it was a duty, however
painful it might be to fulfil, not to remain at such a superficial level'
(86). The struggle for the meaning of Racine, which is the local cause
of the controversy, thus gets bound up in a discourse of rights and
duties, pressing intellectual dangers and urgent remedies. Picard makes
a number of specific criticisms of Barthes's reading of Racine and, in the
later parts of his pamphlet, of *la nouvelle critique* more generally: Barthes
misunderstands Racinian vocabulary and does not know the secondary
literature sufficiently well; his terminology is elastic to the point of
being meaningless, and his jargon is merely obfuscation; he is obsessed
with sex; he makes general claims on the basis of one or two examples;
his readings are unverifiable; more generally, *la nouvelle critique* dissolves
the literary work by locating its meaning in some external source, and
thereby it fails to respect the specificity of the individual text. The
moral language adopted by Picard suggests not merely that these are
*errors* that can and should be corrected, but that Barthes and the new
critics are wilfully deviant and aberrant; their mistakes flout basic rules
of critical responsibility:

> No one has the right [*On n'a pas le droit*] to see an evocation of
> water in the formula *to return to port*, nor a precise allusion to respi-
> ratory mechanisms in the expression *to breath at your feet* . . . no
> one has the right to say either that Titus . . . is acting and making

*theatre* . . . because he says to Paulin: 'I propose a more noble theatre': the term *theatre* has nothing to do here with the idea of a dramatic representation.

(66–7)

Of his various criticisms, Picard insists most forcefully on the unverifiability of Barthes's interpretations: 'All these affirmations are evidently to be taken or to be left: they are beyond (or short of) verification' (16). No principle of legitimation is established, so there is no means of distinguishing between correct and aberrant interpretations. In reference to Barthes's insistence on the 'impossiblity of *telling the truth* on Racine', Picard asserts that this is tantamount to saying, '*One can say anything at all*' (*On peut dire n'importe quoi*) (66). Having thus pinpointed what Barthes is 'really' saying, Picard has no trouble pointing out where he is right and wrong: 'He is right in so far as no one could conceive what the total, absolute, definitive truth of Racine would be, but he is wrong in so far as one cannot say anything at all' (66).

Here, Picard makes the claim that will consistently be made of advanced critical methods in following years, namely that they endorse a sort of interpretative free-for-all without rules and constraints. Picard's procedure, however, is every bit as disreputable as the practices he imputes to *la nouvelle critique*: he puts words into Barthes's mouth, and then declares those words to be utterly wrong. In effect, Barthes is wrong to have said what he never said. In later years Derrida categorically denied that deconstruction gives the critic the right to say *anything at all*.[11] Barthes is equally adamant that his approach does not remove all constraints from critical discourse. In fact, in the Foreword to *Sur Racine* he had insisted that 'we must respect certain rules' (7); and in *Critique et vérité*, he agrees with Picard that 'The critic cannot say "*anything at all*"' (64). He describes the constraints that a critic must respect: the need to establish the comprehensive grammar of a work which explains every part of it, the symbolic logic governing variants and transformations, the nature of the critic's own language. These constraints may not be the same as those imposed by Picard, but they are constraints nonetheless.

Some of Picard's points are challenging and well made; others are based on weak reasoning, crude misreading, misrepresentation and direct insult. Picard lifts quotations from Barthes's text and makes little apparent effort to understand the context of the argument from which they are taken. In other words, he does to Barthes pretty much what he accuses Barthes of doing to Racine. The virulence and self-blindness of the attack are signs that much more is at stake in this exchange than the interpretation of literary texts. Barthes, it seems, has not just insulted scholars of Racine's work, he has launched an assault on truth itself; and Picard's defence of critical objectivity attempts to dispel this dangerous doctrine:

> There is a truth of Racine, on which everyone can finally agree. By relying in particular on what we know for certain about language, on the implications of psychological coherence, on the imperatives of generic structures, the patient and modest researcher manages to draw out self-evident things which to some extent determine zones of objectivity: it is from here that he can – very cautiously – attempt interpretations.
>
> (69)

Interpretation, if it is to take place, should come after scholarship, though in fact Picard is not massively keen on interpretation at all: 'Isn't it better to determine in a solid way such and such a little fact about Racine rather than to construct a grandiose interpretation of the tragedies, which collapses as soon as it is examined seriously?' (79). Any assured fact, however small, is better than any hypothetical interpretation, however far-reaching.

The Picard–Barthes debate makes it unmistakably apparent that specific critical disagreements, about Racine for example, are also and most crucially disagreements about fundamental values. What is at stake is not just correct and incorrect interpretation, but also rights and duties, truth and lies. By attacking the very grounds which might support critical validity and intellectual authority, in Picard's eyes Barthes is *worse than* wrong, he is ethically flawed. Not content to perpetrate crude misreadings of texts, he corrodes the very criterion of truth, muddying the waters through which any intellectual clarity might be achieved:

> This work [*Sur Racine*] flouts the elementary rules of scientific or merely articulate thought: on almost every page, in the disarray of a rampant systematization, the part is given for the whole, the several for the universal, the hypothetical for the categorical; the principle of non-contradiction is mocked; the accident is taken for the essence, the chance for a law; and all this confusion is covered in a language of which the ostentatious precision is a mirage.
>
> (58)

The controversy allows an airing of basic beliefs about literature, authority, truth and verifiability. It also brings into question the very nature of humankind. Barthes denies the individuality of specific characters: 'there are no *characters* in Racine's theatre . . . there are only situations, in the almost formal sense of the term: everything draws its being from its place in the general constellation of strengths and weaknesses' (18–19). In other words, characters are made who they are by the situation they find themselves in, by the place they occupy in a particular relation of authority. For Picard, on the other hand, Racine's characters are all individuals who deserve to be regarded and analysed as such. And this fundamental belief in the individual as the source of his or her own meanings and intentions is one of the most crucial stakes in this whole dispute. It has vital consequences for the status of the author and his or her relationship to the literary work. Picard accuses the new critics of making literature little more than an outlet for delirium: 'Possessed by automatic responses of which he is unaware, the writer is a brilliant robot whose controls are elsewhere' (123; see also 108–9). For Picard, on the contrary, literature is the triumph of voluntary, conscious creation (91). Even if an author draws on dreams, like Nerval, he or she is not simply a dreamer, but someone who gives his dream intelligible form: 'What separates a poet of dream from a simple dreamer is literature, that is, the lucid activity of a man who engages, with reference to norms and demands which he has made his own, in a work of expression' (138). To understand and to appreciate literature properly is not to plumb the depths of what authors did not know they had put in their works, not to pursue unconscious psychic or ideological structures, but to respect conscious meaning, and the effort of expression that turns chaos into order:

> The writer's truth is in what he has chosen, not exclusively in what has chosen him. What is most important to me in the literary work is not the obscure world of anarchic tensions which it surpasses by the very exercise of coherent language, it is the work itself, what it says and what it brings to us in the effort of seeking expression.
>
> (136)

The new criticism is not just wrong, it is dangerous: 'What I have tried to indicate are not so much the ridiculous aspects of the "new criticism" as its dangers' (148). At its most pernicious, it undermines the value of truth and our respect for the conscious works of humankind in favour of an anarchic free play of interpretations which valorizes the unconscious and the unverifiable. The 1960s in France was a time when, from a variety of points of view – Marxist, anthropological, psychoanalytic, structuralist – many thinkers and critics were exploring the ways in which the subject is chosen as much as it chooses, spoken as much as it speaks. Picard wants to close all that down and return to a more comforting world where the subject is master of its own meanings, and the Sorbonne is the final judge of academic endeavour.

## Barthes and Picard

*Nouvelle Critique ou nouvelle imposture* was in effect an attempt at intellectual censorship; ironically it is long out of print, whilst *Sur Racine* is still available in paperback. Even so, the accusations made by Picard against *la nouvelle critique* bring to light the sorts of anxiety and resistance to which the difficulty of avant-garde French thought has continued to give rise. So the interest of this controversy is not only historical; it also raises still pertinent questions about interpretative validity and academic authority, and it reveals aspects of the structure of intellectual controversy which we will find repeated very precisely in relation to *Impostures intellectuelles*. One of the most intriguing aspects of all this is the entanglement of opposing discourses. As we have seen, Picard repeats some of the failings of which he accuses Barthes: misreading, generalizing from limited evidence, quoting out of context, making dogmatic assertions rather than reasoned arguments. If Barthes is a poor reader of Racine, Picard is certainly a poor reader of Barthes, and the similarities here look too consistent to be merely a product of chance. It is as if the discourses of the opponents are fatally bound up with one another, despite everything that opposes them. Each denounces and repeats the error of the other, and each is irritated by the polemical exaggeration and intellectual self-assurance of the other. In relation to the specific accusation of imposture, particular problems arise when an opponent is ventriloquized in the attempt to tease out what he is really saying. Picard puts himself in Barthes's shoes in order to parody his style, and to tell us what he means even when he doesn't say it. The risk here, though, is that Picard becomes the author of the views which he ascribes to Barthes, even if he has authored them only in order to refute them. Occupying even for a moment the position of the impostor makes of him the impostor of the impostor, and may obstruct his comfortable return to the position of authority and expertise.

But if the positions of Barthes and Picard are thoroughly imbricated with one another, there is also a crucial difference between the two sides.

Barthes never denies that his perspective is precisely that, a perspective, not a view from nowhere. He never claims that his view is the only correct or permissible one, despite the tendency to dogmatism that Picard finds in him. It is hard to imagine the critical and moral assurance of Picard's repeated 'no one has the right' (*on n'a pas le droit*) coming from Barthes's pen. Picard invests all authority in his own approach whereas Barthes makes no exclusive and definitive claims for his position. Picard resists the entanglement of his discourse with Barthes's, but Barthes exploits it, using it to suggest that both of their perspectives are situated, historically and ideologically, even if one of them wishes to deny it. Picard's belief in the greater objectivity of his approach is deluded, and his critical discourse entails as many questionable choices as Barthes's. So each side is condemned to participate in the war of words and of opinions, however much one party might present its views as having a higher, more assured sanction. By entering into the polemic with Barthes, Picard made the fatal mistake of disclosing his interdependence with him. Wanting to re-establish the solid authority of scholarly criticism, he inadvertently made its fragility and historical situatedness all the more visible. The more he distanced himself from Barthes, the closer he got.

If the *nouvelle critique* controversy came to an end, it was more because the media had lost interest than because anything had really been resolved. Controversy seems to lead to little advance in mutual understanding, and in consequence there is no internal reason why it should come to an end until it finally becomes dull to all involved. But, remaining unsettled, it can also reappear in new guises which, for all their novelty, repeat in uncanny fashion the stakes, the terms and the mutual entanglements of its earlier forms. More than quarter of a century after the publication of *Nouvelle Critique ou nouvelle imposture*, Sokal and Bricmont's *Impostures intellectuelles* took up essentially the same struggle against the new impostor: postmodernism.

## Sokal, Bricmont and postmodernism

In 1996 the American physicist Alan Sokal published an article entitled 'Transgressing the boundaries: toward a transformative hermeneutics of quantum gravity' in *Social Text*, a journal dedicated to the social sciences. The article purports to meet the challenge of postmodern thought to science; it is heavily referenced, with numerous quotations from prominent French and American thinkers. The second paragraph gives a flavour of the author's apparent opinions and argument:

But deep conceptual shifts within twentieth-century science have undermined this Cartesian–Newtonian metaphysics; revisionist studies in the history and philosophy of science have cast further doubt on its credibility; and, most recently, feminist and post-structuralist critiques have demystified the substantive content of mainstream Western scientific practice, revealing the ideology of domination concealed behind the façade of 'objectivity'. It has thus become increasingly apparent that physical 'reality', no less than social 'reality', is at bottom a social and linguistic construct; that scientific 'knowledge', far from being objective, reflects and encodes the dominant ideologies and power relations of the culture that produced it; that the truth claims of science are inherently theory-laden and self-referential; and consequently, that the discourse of the scientific community, for all its undeniable value, cannot assert a privileged epistemological status with respect to counter-hegemonic narratives emanating from dissident or marginalized communities.[12]

Shortly after its publication, Sokal revealed in a follow-up article that the previous piece was a hoax.[13] Although the quotations and references are authentic, the science is bogus, and in some details laughably wrong. The article was written as a sort of experiment, to see if a journal which was favourable to postmodernism would publish an essay expressing views apparently sympathetic to the editorial line, even if they were devoid of any intellectual merit. The media got hold of the story, and many commentators took it as discrediting the most difficult exponents of modern thought and indicating a profound malaise in humanities departments in general. Since one of Sokal's targets is the influence of French thought on American academics, the controversy spread across the Atlantic to France, partly via the internet where many of the key articles are posted. In 1997, Sokal published a book in French, written together with a Belgian physicist, Jean Bricmont, entitled *Impostures intellectuelles*. The book takes some of the best known modern French thinkers and claims that their numerous references to science are almost entirely meaningless, or at best ridden with error. This is taken in turn, though to some extent Sokal and Bricmont deny this, to throw doubt on their thought in general, and to justify an attack on the dangerous influence of postmodernism in modern universities, especially in the United States. The book was fiercely attacked in France by some as being anti-French, anti-intellectual, and anti-philosophical; but it was welcomed by others as a timely defence of genuine intellectual values against contemporary fads and fashions. Outside France the book also met with a mixed reception. Translated in the UK as *Intellectual Impostures* and in the US with the even more strident title *Fashionable Nonsense*, it was dismissed by some, but greeted by others for showing that modern French philosophy is 'a load of old tosh',[14] and for possibly heralding 'the beginning of the end of the dark ages in the humanities'.[15]

In *Critique et vérité* Barthes gave a nice summary of the accusations made against *la nouvelle critique*:

> So now the movement has been sharply accused of imposture, its works (or at least certain amongst them) have been the target of prohibitions which ordinarily, by repulsion, define every avant-garde movement: it is discovered that they are intellectually empty, verbally sophisticated, morally dangerous, and that they owe their success only to snobbery.[16]

Barthes could well have been referring to comments made in the Preface to the second edition of *Impostures intellectuelles*, in reference to someone who declares a lecture by a famous intellectual to have been brilliant, even though he did not understand a word of it; it might be, Sokal and Bricmont suggest, that the lecturer is simply a poor pedagogue: 'But it is equally possible that the lecture is nonsense or banalities skilfully hidden behind an obscure jargon.'[17] There is little doubt that this is Sokal and Bricmont's preferred explanation since they repeatedly accuse French thinkers of talking nonsense. The charges laid at the door of postmodernism echo quite uncannily those made by Picard against *la nouvelle critique*: its obscure jargon masks the banality or senselessness of its ideas; it uses terms drawn from science for their prestige value, though they are not properly explained or understood; it is driven by fashion rather than the search for truth; it is relativistic and subjective because it denies any objective truth; it gives excessive importance to language rather than to reality; it is nihilisitic and irrationalist. It is characterized by

> a fascination with obscure discourses; an epistemic relativism linked to a generalized scepticism toward modern science; an excessive interest in subjective beliefs independently of their truth or falsity; and an emphasis on discourse and language as opposed to the facts to which those discourses refer (or, worse, the rejection of the very idea that facts exist or that one may refer to them).

(173–4)

Finally, and perhaps most importantly, the intellectual shortcomings of postmodernism are envisioned as moral flaws. Postmodernism is dangerous and corrupting. Students should be protected against it: 'What is worse, in our opinion, is the adverse effect that abandoning clear thinking and clear writing has on teaching and culture. Students learn to repeat and to embellish discourses that they only barely understand' (194). Sokal and Bricmont deplore the pernicious influence of postmodernism on modern youth as Picard had deplored the effects of moral relativism on the young readers of Gide's *Les Nourritures terrestres*.[18] In both cases, intellectual censorship is pursued in the name of and for the benefit of the young. Our poor students are apparently so impressionable that they have to be protected against nefarious postmodern ideas.

What, though, are these postmodern ideas? The problem of defining postmodernism will be discussed in chapter 3 of this book; for the moment, it is worth noting that *Impostures intellectuelles* does little to define what it nevertheless characterizes as its principal target. In fact, Sokal and Bricmont openly fudge the issue of definition:

> Over the past two decades, much ink has been spilled about postmodernism, an intellectual current that is supposed to have replaced modern rationalist thought. However, the term 'postmodernism' covers an ill-defined galaxy of ideas – ranging from art and architecture to the social sciences and philosophy – and we have no wish to discuss most of these areas.
>
> (173; see also 12)

Even Picard, whose restricted range of references leads one to think that his knowledge of *la nouvelle critique* was hardly extensive, did better than this. Who holds the view that postmodernism has supplanted modern rationalist thought? The phrase *that is supposed to have replaced* avoids specifying who is doing the supposing. A footnote to the first sentence quoted above does little to dispel the air of fudge here:

> We do not want to get involved in terminological disputes about the distinctions between 'postmodernism', 'poststructuralism' and so forth . . . For simplicity, we shall use the term 'postmodernism', while emphasizing that we shall be concentrating on the philosophical and intellectual aspects and that the validity or invalidity of our arguments can in no way depend on the use of a word.
>
> (173)

So although they are attacking postmodernism, they are not much interested in what postmodernism is; and even if the word is inappropriate they claim that this does not in any sense invalidate their argument. In as far as postmodernism is defined at all, it is characterized by a rejection of the rationalist tradition of the Enlightenment, theoretical constructs which cannot be tested empirically, and cognitive and cultural relativism (see 1 and 11–12). But there is no attempt to apply this fairly sketchy definition to the thinkers attacked in *Impostures intellectuelles* who represent disciplines as diverse as psychoanalysis, philosophy, the sociology of science, and literary theory. None of them except Lyotard is normally considered to be straightforwardly a postmodern thinker, so it is at the very least problematic to suggest that their attack on selected French philosophers can *also* be taken as discrediting postmodernism.[19]

Given that postmodernism poses enormous problems of definition, Sokal and Bricmont can perhaps be forgiven for avoiding the issue; but in the context of their call for greater intellectual integrity and rigour, their ignorance of the history and use of the term is less understandable.[20] In an interview, Bricmont suggested that the word *postmodern* first appeared in Lyotard's *La Condition postmoderne*.[21] Given that a passage from this book is discussed in *Impostures intellectuelles*, Bricmont's comment is not just ignorant, it suggests that he has not actually read the book he is nevertheless happy to discredit, since a footnote to the first sentence of Lyotard's first chapter gives a number of references to earlier works which use the word *postmodern*. Postmodernism for Sokal and Bricmont is little more than a catch-all term for everything they dislike; as Yves Jeanneret puts it, 'What is postmodern is the composite negative of the values in which they believe: a mixture of excessive pretention, intellectual laziness and cognitive relativism'.[22]

Most, but by no means all, critics of *Impostures intellectuelles* have assumed that Sokal and Bricmont are basically right when they draw attention to specific instances of the misuse of scientific terminology.[23] Without a solid scientific training, it would be hard to dispute their assertions. But the question of what consequences a thinker's scientific incompetence may have for the rest of his or her work remains open. Sokal and Bricmont repeatedly insist that they are not competent to judge, or even to understand, the works of the authors they discuss. However, on numerous occasions they insinuate much more general conclusions about the texts which they are scrutinizing. In the passage already quoted earlier in this chapter, they claim that 'In many cases we shall demonstrate [*démontrer*] that if the texts seem incomprehensible, it is for the excellent reason that they mean precisely nothing' (39). The use of the words *demonstrate* and *precisely* suggest that this is done with a scientific rigour and patience, so that no reader of good faith could fail to be convinced. Throughout their book, however, what they tend to do is quote a long, difficult passage and *assert* its meaninglessness, leaving the unqualified reader simply to accept their assertion as true.[24]

The chapter on Deleuze and Guattari is a particularly dramatic example of this. The chapter is fourteen pages long. Well over half the chapter is made up of quotations with footnotes added by Sokal and Bricmont to draw attention to abuses and confusions relating to science. There is very little detailed commentary and no attempt at all to understand or explain the passages in context. Instead, the long quotations are prefaced or concluded with blunt assertions of their meaninglessness:

> And a specialist reader will find their statements most often meaningless, or sometimes acceptable but banal and confused.
>
> (146)

> This passage contains at least a dozen scientific terms used without rhyme or reason, and the discourse oscillates between nonsense . . . and truisms.
>
> (148)

> With a bit of work, one can detect in this paragraph a few meaningful phrases, but the discourse in which they are immersed is utterly meaningless.
>
> (149)

> The beginning of this text has the aura of a deep remark . . . but the end . . . is totally devoid of meaning.
>
> (150)

> Again, the end of the passage is meaningless, even if the beginning alludes vaguely to the philosophy of science.
>
> (150)

> Once again, this paragraph . . . is stuffed with technical terms; but apart from a banal observation that a cell communicates with the outside world through its membrane, it is devoid of both logic and sense.
>
> (156)

Sokal and Bricmont make no real effort to *read* the texts they are criticizing. The discovery of errors in them inhibits, or serves as an excuse to ignore, any presumption that they may contain anything worth saying. And Sokal and Bricmont repeatedly insinuate general conclusions about the work of the authors they discuss. It is suggested that Lacan is founding a new religion rather than a therapeutic practice; that Irigaray falls into a mysticism harmful to feminism, that there may be nothing to the thought of Baudrillard once its verbal veneer is stripped away. These suggestions are made on the basis of passages lifted out of their context, without any consideration of why and how they might fit into a broader argument. In this respect, Barthes's comment on Picard is curiously apposite: 'It's a strange lesson in reading, to contest every detail in a book without suggesting for one moment that one has seen its overall project, that is, quite simply: its meaning.'[25]

## Imposture and authority

In the Epilogue to *Impostures intellectuelles* Sokal and Bricmont draw the lessons to be learned from their study, the very first of which is the rule that 'It's a good idea to know what one is talking about'; anyone who wants to speak about the sciences 'needs to be well informed and to avoid making arbitrary statements [*éviter de dire n'importe quoi*] about the sciences or their epistemology' (176). The implication that postmodernists say *n'importe quoi* precisely repeats Picard's allegation about *la nouvelle critique*. However, if Sokal and Bricmont's principle seems reasonable enough, they are happy to flout it when talking of philosophy and the social sciences, as they themselves concede: 'We shall limit ourselves to explaining our point of view, without justifying it in any detail. It goes without saying that we claim no special competence in history, sociology, or politics; and what we have to say must, in any case, be understood as conjectures rather than as the final word' (173). We see here another instance of the mutual entanglements already observed in the Picard–Barthes exchange; failings, here the manifest lack of expertise, are denounced and repeated in the same texts, as Sokal and Bricmont commit the error in relation to philosophy which they accuse French thinkers of committing in relation to science.

Even the claim of *imposture* is double-edged, since the only unambiguous case of imposture in this whole affair was the article initially submitted to *Social Text*, in which Sokal masqueraded as holding views which he in fact did not hold. It takes an impostor to catch an impostor, apparently, but this also means that imposture cannot be ascribed uniquely to the pernicious Other. Entrapment involves playing the Other's (postmodernist's) game, and thus ensuring that imposture inheres in the possibilities and practice of the Self. To put it bluntly, the price to be paid for attacking 'the admittedly nebulous *Zeitgeist* that we have called "postmodernism"' (4) is that you enter into it, become part of it. As the title of Lyotard's *La Condition postmoderne* implies, postmodernism is not simply a set of beliefs which any individual may or may not hold. It is a condition, and as such part of a shared context. Some may prefer to be elsewhere, but they have little choice in the matter. In other words, as an attack on postmodernism, *Impostures intellectuelles* is a symptom of what it diagnoses.

One sign of this postmodernism is the burgeoning controversy around Sokal's original *Social Text* article and the later *Impostures intellectuelles*. Rather than putting an end to the babble of 'fashionable nonsense', Sokal and Bricmont found themselves increasingly engulfed in a media Babel, as the meaning and significance of their work were wrested from them. What they intended to demonstrate was not what they are taken to have demonstrated. The position of Derrida in the controversy is interesting in this respect. The *Social Text* article contained only one quotation from him, and he is entirely spared the attacks of *Impostures intellectuelles* on the grounds, as Sokal and Bricmont have acknowledged, that his references to science are rare and cautious (see 7). Yet in the articles and internet exchanges provoked by the controversy, Derrida is widely cited as being incriminated in the affair, with only Lacan being referred to more frequently.[26] Moreover, the original reference to Derrida in the *Social Text* article has also revealed a surprising after-life apparently not anticipated by Sokal. In a commentary on the article, Sokal and Bricmont state that the Derrida quotation introduces 'a gradual crescendo of absurdity', as Sokal refers to the 'ineluctable historicity' of $\pi$, this being 'a parody of confused discourses on non-Euclidean geometry'.[27] However, one commentator has pointed out that the view that $\pi$ has a constant and universal value was in fact refuted in the nineteenth century, so that 'this mathematical statement that Sokal attributes to the "postmodern" masters is in fact accepted by mathematicians, physicians and engineers'.[28]

Sokal's absurdity turns out to be someone else's banal truth. The stability of the text's meaning and its author's command over it are both shaken when the parodic falsehood turns out to be unwittingly accurate; and readers without competence in science and mathematics are likely to be left uncertain over how to position themselves in relation either to the text or its self-authorized interpreters. The grounds on which Sokal distributes praise and blame are less secure than they had seemed, and the barriers between parody and truth are not so clear-cut that they can be assumed to be definitively established. Who should we trust here? Slavoj Žižek adds a further twist to the already convoluted problem of reading *Impostures intellectuelles*. After hearing of Sokal's *Social Text* parody he considered how easy it would be to write, as a sort of companion piece, a parodic commonsensical rejection of postmodernism from a scientist's perspective; but after reading *Impostures intellectuelles* Žižek realized that the book had already been written: 'it struck me that this book, although meant to be taken seriously by its authors, already *is* this parody (does its characterization of opponents not as a rule amount to a caricaturalized version of what postmodern Theory is?).'[29] All in all, when a parody is taken seriously and the serious work reads like a parody, the situation is highly postmodern.

Of course, Sokal and Bricmont are hardly content to be caught up in the postmodern erosion of intellectual authority, particularly when it affects their ability to direct the reception of their own texts. So, repeatedly, they seek to bring back under control the discursive juggernaut that they have released. Sokal's article 'A physicist experiments with cultural studies' was published shortly after the original *Social Text* piece and revealed it as a hoax. This is his first attempt to take command of the founding text of the controversy and to show its 'real' significance, but it will not be his last, as the gesture of recontainment needs repeating again and again in subsequent articles: 'Pourquoi j'ai écrit ma parodie', 'What the *Social Text* affair does and does not prove', Bricmont's 'La Vraie Signification de l'affaire Sokal', and so on.[30] This need to contain an unruly text recurs in *Impostures intellectuelles*, which reproduces in an appendix the *Social Text* article together with, as a second appendix, a detailed commentary on it. But each new act of containment produces new misunderstandings and a renewed need to assert the meaning of the inaugural event in the controversy.[31] The text cannot be trusted to speak for itself, it requires supplements and commentaries which fragment it at the very moment they endeavour to shore up its unity. Thus, *Impostures intellectuelles* has an Epilogue written 'principally to avoid having ideas attributed to us against our will (as has already been done) and to show that our position on many issues is quite moderate' (173). But this attempt to avoid or to control all possible misunderstandings, or readings contrary to the intentions of the authors, seems to have failed, so they wrote a new Preface for the second French edition of the book and a Preface for the English edition which attempt once again to spell out how the book should and should not be read.

Referring to two misreadings of the first edition, they aim to put the record straight: 'We would like to explain briefly why neither is the case, and to answer both our critics and our over-enthusiastic supporters. In particular we want to dispel a number of misunderstandings' (ix).

*Impostures intellectuelles*, then, is a postmodern text ill at ease with itself. It gives voice to contrary views but attempts to eradicate them; and the very effort of eradication ensures their survival. Like Tweedledee and Tweedledum, reading and misreading are inseparable and irreconcilable, yet so closely associated that they can barely be told apart. The situation is exacerbated by the role of the internet in the controversy. Sokal's home page contains links to numerous documents and sites where diverse views are thrown back and forth; favourable and hostile reviews stand side-by-side; texts and counter-texts, arguments and counter-arguments can be summoned at the click of a mouse button. All opinions are available, ready formed, repudiated and re-iterated before being repudiated again. The truth is out there, but so is falsehood. How should we decide which is which? Click on a link and take your pick. Though one thing is certain: no one will have the final word. This is, I suspect, the postmodern form of controversy. Its drawback is that the near-immediate, near-total availability of all materials and opinions is bewildering as much as informative. It is impossible to read through all the articles and sites that can be readily accessed, and there is no authoritative means of deciding in advance between what is or isn't worth the effort.

The fundamental weaknesses of *Impostures intellectuelles* are thus the weaknesses of postmodernism itself. By endeavouring to shout loudest in the marketplace of opinions, Sokal and Bricmont serve only to raise the volume so that no one can hear anything. The attacks on Lacan, Kristeva and others amount to an incitement not to read them, to reproduce Sokal and Bricmont's own exemplary acts of non-reading by selecting their opinions from the range on offer. The pernicious postmodernism of *Impostures intellectuelles* lies in its singular contribution to a culture in which reading is either impossible or redundant.

## The imposture of theory

In *Homo academicus* Pierre Bourdieu discusses the Picard–Barthes controversy and describes the interdependence of their opposed positions in terms of the sociology of academia: ancients and moderns, insiders and outsiders, defenders of orthodoxy and licensed heretics are lined up against one another according to pre-set patterns.[32] Politically, right-wing is opposed to left; institutionally, Picard's traditionalist Sorbonne is opposed to Barthes's more progressive Ecole des Hautes Etudes; in disciplinary terms, literary studies are opposed to the social sciences. Bourdieu argues that there is a 'structural complicity between the different powers and the different expressions, orthodox and heretical'[33] because each side is playing a role in a drama which is fixed in advance: 'This conflict shows up a divide which preexists it . . . the roles seem to be handed out in advance by the logic of the field.'[34] Bourdieu finds prefigurations of the controversy in the Dreyfus affair and struggles within the Sorbonne at the end of the nineteenth century, and he finds later echoes of it in the events of May 1968.

In the furore surrounding *Impostures intellectuelles* the same effects of polarization and entanglement of opposing positions can be observed. Hostility is an aspect of structural interdependence and occluded indebtedness that neither side of the controversy might want to acknowledge. It is possible to see operating in these polemics a stereotype of controversy in which accusation and counter-accusation alternate according to a predictable pattern. The heretical theorists are accused of using obscure jargon, of promoting fuzzy thinking which flouts the rules of rigorous rational thought and constitutes an outrage to authentic intellectual or scholarly values; what they say is modish, unverifiable, fit to be treated as poetry or even religion rather than thought, and finally it is pernicious, a danger to the young. In response the orthodox traditionalists are accused of being reactionary and repressive, of trying to close down creative, subversive thought in acts of authoritarian censorship.[35] The trumping move available to all sides at all moments is to say: you've misread or misunderstood the text. Everyone accuses everyone else of failing to read the texts of Racine or of each other with sufficient care, attention or good faith. Locked in this structural complicity, opponents depend upon one another to provide the arms which will ensure the other's defeat; but this dependence also gives both sides an interest in the survival of what was supposed to be eliminated. The Picard–Barthes controversy turned out to be a wonderful career move for both Picard and Barthes; one critic argues that 'Barthes seems to have derived nothing but profit from Picard's attack',[36] and were it not for Barthes, Picard might today be all but forgotten. Similarly, *Impostures intellectuelles* did wonders for the public profiles of Sokal and Bricmont, giving them a much broader audience than they would normally expect for their academic work.

The common stakes of the two imposture controversies are relatively clear. In the name of responsible values of objectivity and truth, an array of French thinkers are denounced for their obscure jargon, relativism, scepticism, intellectual shoddiness and implicitly the corruption of youth. Yet Sokal and Bricmont, like Picard, employ a rhetorical virulence bordering on overkill, which suggests that something is going on here which exceeds simple academic infighting. Barthes is not just sadly misguided, he is aberrant, absurd and frightening;[37] thinkers associated with postmodernism are not merely wrong, they are vacuous or banal, deliberately obscure, charlatans, irrationalist or nihilistic.[38] This rhetorical extravagance certainly does nothing to raise the level of the debate. Moreover, the emphatic distancing of Self from Other (I am rigorous, you are shoddy; I am rational, you are irrational; I am responsible, you are dangerous; I am genuine, you are an impostor) looks more like an implicit acknowledgement of proximity than a marking out of real differences. Without resemblance between the genuine and the false, imposture would not be possible; but that resemblance also disturbs the secure position from which the distinction can be confidently maintained. Moreover, the situation becomes more complex when the expert adopts the techniques of the impostor. When Picard puts words into Barthes's mouth in order to refute them, or Sokal parodies postmodernism in order to ridicule it, they bring to light the element of imposture in their own procedures. And so the question is raised: who has the authority to say who is and isn't an impostor? The biggest impostors may be the ones who maintain most virulently their own expertise and their right to adjudicate; and once the possibility of imposture has been raised, there can be no player in the game who is entirely above suspicion. The accusation of imposture is therefore not a simple move, nor one to be taken lightly, since it can rebound on the accuser. Imposture turns out to be a dialectical process which may consume its authentic counterpart and confine opponents to the vortex of simulacra from which it was meant to save them.

In *Sur Racine* Barthes characterized Racine's plays as a sort of semantic cipher through which critics could explore the languages of their own epoch. The variety of responses triggered by *Impostures intellectuelles*, ranging from enthusiastic acceptance to bitter rejection, suggests that Sokal and Bricmont's text is itself a sort of void which readers either find totally persuasive or deeply flawed according to the views they bring with them. Neither of the controversies discussed in this chapter gives much reason to believe in a model of intellectual debate as a responsible exchange leading to the final resolution of differences. Whether it be Barthes reading Racine, or Picard reading Barthes, or Barthes reading Picard, or Sokal and Bricmont reading Lacan or Kristeva or Baudrillard,

all are fuelling a circulation of discourse which is in principle interminable, and in which the very notion of the final word makes no sense.
Barthes's 'inability *to tell the truth* on Racine' is echoed in each party's
failure to put an end to the dispute, as successive attempts to impose
clarity serve only to add to the confusion. And the impossibility of
securing an exclusive claim on intellectual authority is rehearsed
throughout both the controversies that have been discussed here. The
mirroring which can be observed in the debates, as each side replicates
the methods and errors of the opponent, ensures that there no position
outside the exchange, no 'truth' or final ground that can be definitively
occupied. Once summoned, the spectre of imposture haunts every available position.

Barthes is accused of knowing nothing, or not enough, about Racine;
Sokal and Bricmont's targets know nothing, or not enough, about science. The king is naked. In making these accusations, Picard, Sokal and
Bricmont are demanding that we should only speak when we know
what we are talking about. Their opponents are scandalous and incomprehensible to them because they do not share this apparently
self-evident principle. If practising criticism or doing theory is imposture
as soon as it is not based on established prior knowledge and unquestionable shared values, then criticism and theory for Barthes and his
successors are, fundamentally and essentially, forms of imposture. Knowledge, for them, comes after the act of writing – if at all. The theorist is
not someone who knows more than others; on the contrary, he or she is
someone who never quite knows enough, and who is dissatisfied with
forms of knowledge which have become comfortably established. So in
a sense Picard, Sokal and Bricmont are absolutely correct to be outraged: the king is indeed naked, theory is imposture. Worse still, it is a
form of imposture which corrodes the authority of experts because it
insinuates that they too know less than they claim.

## Chapter 2

# Enlightenment/
poststructuralism

After the media-fuelled controversies which raged around the Picard and Sokal affairs, this chapter looks at the more specific and intellectually significant accusation that poststructuralism represents a betrayal of what was best about the project of Enlightenment. Here, the most powerful voice has been the German philosopher Jürgen Habermas, who sees poststructuralism (or what he calls neostructuralism) as undermining reason, destroying universality and renouncing the hope for emancipation. It is certainly not hard to find disparaging comments on the coercive or mystified aspects of the Enlightenment in texts by authors of a broadly poststructuralist or postmodernist persuasion. Adorno and Horkheimer's *Dialectic of Enlightenment* often lies behind such comments, as it mercilessly tracks how the advances of Enlightenment are inevitably shadowed by new forms of repression. Adorno and Horkheimer describe the Enlightenment as totalitarian; it is bound up with the mythology it claimed to repudiate; its appeal to reason is racist and imperialist.[1]

However, references to the Enlightenment legacy in poststructuralist texts tend to be more nuanced than opponents (and some supporters) of poststructuralism imply. In *Limited Inc.*, for example, Derrida associates deconstruction with what he calls 'a respectful homage to a new, very new *Aufklärung*'.[2] Even as he reiterates the newness of what he is doing, Derrida reclaims the heritage which some of his critics see him as repudiating. Similarly, in *Spectres de Marx* Derrida links deconstruction to the ideals of democracy and emancipation and to work undertaken 'in the name of new Enlightenment [*nouvelles Lumières*] for the century to come'.[3] Habermas envisages his own work as continuing (and perhaps even completing) what he has called the 'unfinished project' of Enlightenment, but so, it seems, does Derrida.[4] Understandably confused, commentators come to quite opposed conclusions. One asserts that for Derrida (at his best) 'there is no question of simply revoking the Kantian paradigm and declaring a break with that entire heritage of enlightened critical thought',[5] whereas another argues that Derrida (at his best) writes texts which do not fit within any conceptual scheme previously used in philosophy.[6] In one account there is no common ground between Derrida and the Enlightenment legacy defended by Habermas; in the other their projects are not so very far apart, despite differences in approach.

What, then, is the Enlightenment legacy which is in dispute here, and what does it mean to repudiate or to reclaim it? In 1784 Kant explained what he understood by Enlightenment in an article entitled 'An answer to the question: What is Enlightenment?'. In 1984, in the final months of his life, Michel Foucault delivered a lecture, later published as 'Qu'est-ce que les Lumières?', in which he discussed what he believed to be the significance of Kant's essay. Shortly afterwards, in a sympathetic memorial address published as 'Taking aim at the heart of the present: on Foucault's lecture on Kant's *What is Enlightenment?*', Habermas welcomed Foucault's late recognition of the values of Enlightenment. These three short texts clearly cannot provide an exhaustive account of the nature of the Enlightenment, but they can be used to indicate some of the stakes in the dispute over the Enlightenment legacy. This chapter begins by outlining Habermas's critique of post-structuralist thought as laid out in his influential book, *The Philosophical Discourse of Modernity*; it then looks at the different ways in which Habermas and Foucault interpret Kant's 'What is Enlightenment?'; the final sections of the chapter discuss Derrida's response to Habermas's criticisms of his work, and more generally the reasons why the dialogue between Habermas, Foucault and Derrida never truly gets off the ground. Finally, Derrida's treatment of the notion of legacy offers an account of why the significance of Kant's writing has yet to be settled, and therefore why it is still at issue for poststructuralist philosophers.

## Habermas, the Enlightenment and poststructuralism

*The Philosophical Discourse of Modernity* is in part a powerful philosophical critique of poststructuralism. Its analysis of the failure of Derrida and Foucault to provide norms for judgement and action lies behind the common criticism that in political terms poststructuralism is ineffectual or even reactionary. Rather than depicting poststructuralism as a radical innovation or break within the history of philosophy, Habermas places the thought of Derrida and Foucault in an intellectual tradition stretching back to the eighteenth century. *The Philosophical Discourse of Modernity* is organized along broadly historical lines, as it analyses philosophical developments from the eighteenth century to Habermas's own time. In an earlier lecture Habermas describes the project of modernity as consisting in the effort 'to develop objective science, universal morality and law, and autonomous art according to their inner logic', the aim of this being 'the enrichment of everyday life'.[7] In the fuller account given in *The Philosophical Discourse of Modernity* Habermas tells a story of promising beginnings and wrong turns. Hegel plays a key role as he is credited with being the first to develop a clear concept of modernity. For Hegel, 'modernity' is not just the moment which we currently occupy; it is an epochal concept which marks the separation of the contemporary world from the Middle Ages and Antiquity. Modernity represents 'the last stage in History',[8] distinguished by the new possibilities and problems it brings with it. Habermas endorses what Hegel isolates as the fundamental problem of the present age: 'Modernity can and will no longer borrow the criteria by which it takes its orientation from the models supplied by another epoch; *it has to create its normativity out of itself*' (7).

Hegel inaugurates the discourse of modernity and defines what will be its central question: if the validity of existing norms is no longer accepted, how can new ones be established? Philosophy now assumes a key role in what Habermas calls the 'self-reassurance' (*Selbstvergewisserung*) of modernity because it is instrumental in the critique of the modern world; it is centrally involved in the endeavour to ground a new normativity and to overcome the divisions of the present. Kant had installed reason in the supreme seat of judgement, but he had in the process also consolidated the rift between belief and knowledge, and divided knowledge itself into the separate domains of science, morality and art. For Hegel, Kant makes the mistake of not perceiving these formal divisions as fissures and hence of failing to see the need for re-unification. Hegel will endeavour to establish reason as the force of re-unification through which the subject bends back on itself and draws its new normativity from this act of rational self-reflection. Hegelian absolute knowledge represents the reconciliation of the divisions of modernity brought about through the unifying force of reason.

For Habermas, Hegel's analysis of modernity and its problems is itself an epochal event. But even as he inaugurates the philosophical discourse of modernity, Hegel takes a wrong turn. In Hegel's early writings Habermas finds traces of a theory of communicative reason which foregrounds intersubjectivity rather than subjectivity and which anticipates philosophical positions which Habermas himself would elaborate nearly two centuries later. Hegel, however, did not follow up this promising line of thought. Instead, he conceived modernity as marked by the self-relation of subjectivity, which carries with it individualism, the right to criticism, autonomy of action and the idealistic philosophy which addresses these issues (see 16–17). The subject is both the source of the divisions which beset the modern world and the agent which, through rational self-reflection, may solve them. The problem for Habermas here is that Hegel's philosophy of the subject, in which the rational self-reflective subject is both the problem and its solution, overcomes the problems of modernity too effectively. One of the principal concerns of Enlightenment critique had been to improve the conditions of everyday life; the prospect of absolute knowledge diminishes the importance of the present and so impairs the original critical impetus of the use of reason:

> But as absolute knowledge, reason assumes a form so overwhelming that it not only solves the initial problem of a self-reassurance of modernity, but solves it *too well* . . . For reason has now taken over the place of fate and knows that every event of essential significance has *already* been decided. Thus, Hegel's philosophy satisfies the need of modernity for self-grounding only at the cost of devaluing present-day reality and blunting critique. In the end, philosophy removes all importance from its own present age, destroys interest in it, and deprives it of the calling to self-critical renewal.
>
> (42)

If Habermas does not accept Hegel's too-powerful solution to the divisions of modernity, he does not question the underlying historical narrative which conceives the eighteenth-century Enlightenment as heralding a new epoch and setting a new philosophical agenda. Hegel is pivotal both in enunciating the key problem of modernity as the search to find its norms within itself and in addressing this problem through a philosophy of the rational self-reflective subject. The subsequent story of the discourse of modernity compounds Hegel's inaugural error by failing to escape the perspective of subjectivity. Later in the nineteenth century, Nietzsche takes a further, even more disastrous, false turn. Having seen the failure of successive attempts by assorted left and right Hegelians to retrieve the concept of subject-centred reason, Nietzsche decides to give up on the Enlightenment project altogether, 'with the goal of exploding modernity's husk of reason as such' (86). Reason is displaced from its pedestal and revealed as merely a mask for the new supreme principle: the will to power. For Habermas, modernity promised progress and emancipation, even if its theorists had not yet solved its inherent problems. Nietzsche now signals the dawning of postmodernity, which denies progress in knowledge or morality and promises only discord and the struggle for dominance. For Habermas, Nietzsche oscillates between two strategies: a disabused scepticism which does not believe in truth and contemplates the world as a work of art, and the conviction of being a uniquely privileged initiate to the secrets of the world, the last disciple of Dionysus. These two strategies characterize the intellectual trends which will culminate, particularly in France, in the latter part of the twentieth century:

> The sceptical scholar who wants to unmask the perversion of the will to power, the revolt of reactionary forces, and the emergence of subject-centered reason by using anthropological, psychological, and historical methods has successors in Bataille, Lacan, and Foucault; the initiate-critic of metaphysics who pretends to a unique kind of knowledge and pursues the rise of the philosophy of the subject back to its pre-Socratic beginnings has successors in Heidegger and Derrida.
>
> (97)

In the rest of *The Philosophical Discourse of Modernity* Habermas analyses in detail the erroneous paths taken by the assailants of the Enlightenment project, such as Adorno and Horkheimer, Heidegger, Bataille, and especially Derrida and Foucault. Habermas argues that Derrida's critique of metaphysics has not shaken itself free from the search for foundations, and in the end it resembles nothing more than Jewish mysticism; at the same time it relegates philosophy to being merely, as Richard Rorty puts it, 'a kind of writing',[9] and thereby it levels the distinction between philosophy and literature, it relieves philosophy of the duty of solving problems, and so it dulls the sword of the critique of reason (210). Foucault is indicted on the triple charge of being presentistic (unable to move beyond his own starting position), relativistic (the claim that all discourses are no more than the effects of power they unleash undercuts the validity of his own analysis), and cryptonormative (he covertly relies on norms but can provide no justification of their foundations) (276).[10] Throughout this analysis Habermas is especially keen to demonstrate that Derrida and Foucault are never as successful in discarding the Enlightenment legacy as their radical rhetoric sometimes implies. Derrida is accused of being locked within a 'performative contradiction' because he uses the tools of reason to convict reason of being authoritarian in nature; he thereby implicitly re-affirms the pertinence of what he allegedly sets out to undermine (185).

Like Derrida, Foucault is also accused of being philosophically inconsistent. In Habermas's account, he is unable to think through the aporias of his own approach well enough to provide a persuasive alternative to the philosophy of the subject, and he does not provide a convincing justification for the privileged place accorded to his own genealogical approach. In general, the thinkers of postmodernity who affirm the death of Man and aspire to explore the 'other of reason' find themselves trapped within the habits of thought which they had wanted to abandon:

> Those who would like to leave all paradigms behind along with the paradigm of the philosophy of consciousness, and go forth into the clearing of postmodernity, will just not be able to free themselves from the concepts of subject-centered reason and its impressively illustrated topography.
>
> (309)

So in the main body of *The Philosophical Discourse of Modernity* Habermas demonstrates how modern thought has taken a number of wrong turnings in its endeavours to correct the shortcomings of the Enlightenment. In the penultimate of the main chapters, entitled 'An alternative way out of the philosophy of the subject: communicative versus subject-centred reason', Habermas finally outlines his own solution. His aim is not to abandon the Enlightenment and its ideals of reason, morality, freedom and progress. On the contrary, Habermas endorses those values. To make progress with the unfinished project of modernity entails confronting the problems posed by Hegel and solving them better. As Habermas puts it, his work hopes to recall that of other post-Enlightenment thinkers who 'pursued the goal of enlightening the Enlightenment about its own narrow-mindedness' (302). This involves picking up an element in the writings of the early Hegel and replacing subject-centred reason by communicative reason. 'Pure reason' is now rejected as a meaningless concept. Reason is situated and embodied, it finds its validity in the endeavours of responsible participants to achieve consensus with one another. In other words, rather than subject-centred and self-validating it is intersubjective. Habermas rejects 'the paradigm of self-consciousness, of the relation-to-self of a subject knowing and acting in isolation', and proposes instead 'the paradigm of mutual understanding, that is, of the intersubjective relationship between individuals who are socialized through communication and reciprocally recognize one another' (310). With this paradigm, Habermas reinstates the project of Enlightenment whilst suggesting that its goals can be achieved only by modifying the claims made for the guiding principle of reason. And perhaps unsurprisingly, his own work turns out to provide the tools to complete the project.

## Philosophy and/as literature

In Habermas's account philosophy plays a key role in the endeavour to further the Enlightenment project. The need to preserve the distinctive mission of philosophy lies behind the long excursus (185–210) in which Habermas criticizes Derrida for levelling the distinctions between philosophy and literature (though, as we shall see later in this chapter, Derrida vigorously rejects this charge). According to Habermas, Derrida treats works of philosophy as if they were literary texts and thereby relieves them of their duty to confront and to resolve problems. Reading philosophy as literature entails adopting the standards of rhetorical success rather than logical consistency (188). Habermas is uncomfortable with the deconstructive suspicion that, whilst logic and rhetoric are not identical, they may also not be entirely separable. This does not mean that for him rhetorical or formal considerations are always irrelevant in the discussion of philosophical works. He describes Adorno and Horkheimer's *Dialectic of Enlightenment* as 'an odd book' (106), and its oddness extends to its composition: 'It comprises an essay of something over fifty pages, two excursuses and three appendixes. The latter take up more than half the text. This rather unperspicuous form of presentation renders the clear structure of its train of thought almost undiscernible at first glance' (107). So the form of the text actually interferes with the intelligibility of its argument. Habermas is anxious to ensure that his book escapes this fate so that, at least in his own case, there is no conflict between argumentative coherence and rhetorical success. Philosophy, for him, must not be confused with literature, and the philosopher's rhetoric should remain in the service of reason.

So Habermas's formal concern in *The Philosophical Discourse of Modernity* is to ensure that the design of his text serves his philosophical intentions. Even if Habermas's admirers would not claim that his prose is notable for its clarity, *The Philosophical Discourse of Modernity* has a distinct structure and argument.[11] Its main body consists of twelve lectures which follow a largely chronological progression from Hegel, through the attempts of left and right Hegelians to revise Hegel, to Nietzsche, the aporias of postmodernity, and finally to the 'alternative way' of Habermas himself. Habermas concedes that two of the lectures are in a sense 'fictitious' (xix) in that they were not part of the original lecture series which forms the basis of the book; but this fictitiousness is apparent only because Habermas admits to it, and it does not noticeably disrupt the coherence of the argument. There are hitches in the linear progression of the book, however, as the developing argument is slowed down, if not interrupted, by the five Excursuses which *The Philosophical Discourse of Modernity* also contains. In the context of Habermas's comments on the excursuses which obscured the structure and the train of thought of Adorno and Horkheimer's *Dialectic of Enlightenment*, Habermas may risk disrupting the clarity of his work by adopting them himself. The very term *excursus* suggests a departure from the proper path, with the consequence that the structure of Habermas's book interestingly mirrors his account of post-Enlightenment thought which serially deviates from the most satisfactory route to the resolution of its key problems. But Habermas's wager is that his excursuses, unlike those of Adorno and Horkheimer, can be kept in check so that they do not unbalance his text and confuse its argumentative line. The surplus they introduce should not overwhelm the coherence and shape of the whole.

Habermas, then, resists the contamination of rational argument by formal and rhetorical factors. He attempts to maintain a clear and rigorous distinction between philosophy and other forms of writing, particularly literature and literary criticism; and he rejects the postmodern assault on reason on the grounds that it occupies 'the no-man's-land between argumentation, narration, and fiction' (302). However, in the light of his concern to keep his own work resolutely outside this no-man's-land, it is striking that the narrative element of *The Philosophical Discourse of Modernity* is so prominent, and Habermas shows a firm grasp of the power of narrative to organize and to make sense of his material. The argument of the book is held together by a global account of the directions taken by philosophy over the last 200 years, entailing promising beginnings and numerous false paths before the correct way forward is finally discovered. This narrative echoes that of Spirit's coming to self-consciousness in Hegel's *Phenomenology of Spirit*, though in more modest mode: the prospect of understanding and agreement between responsible individuals replaces the more outrageous dreams of absolute knowledge. Even so, Habermas turns out to be the hero of this 200-year narrative, appearing as the nursemaid of communicative reason just as Hegel had been the nursemaid of absolute knowledge. The account of the unfinished project of modernity configures the history of philosophy in a way which ensures the prominence of Habermas's own position within it.

Habermas's narrative, then, offers a strong reading of the history of philosophy since the Enlightenment. Habermas is both the narrator and the story's endpoint, since it is he who sees the pattern in the whole, perceives the error which the philosophical discourse of modernity has taken (its concentration on subject-centred reason), and finally redis-covers the solution (communicative reason) which Hegel had briefly glimpsed but discarded. Part of what makes Habermas incompatible with his postmodern adversaries is the degree of authority with which the narrative is invested. This is a grand narrative of the sort that Lyotard famously rejected because its claims are totalizing, it is a story which wants to be more than one possible story amongst others. And in the light of this story, Habermas assesses the thought of other phil-osophers by measuring how close it comes to his own.[12]

Another feature of the power of Habermas's story is its simplicity. It entails essentially only three stages: a beginning full of promise (the Enlightenment and modernity as theorized by Hegel), a protracted period of quest and error (from Hegel to Foucault), followed by a final return to the inaugural moment to recognize its true significance and to realize its promise (Habermas and communicative reason). Of course, to call this a story is not in itself to argue against its validity. Nevertheless, the neatness with which it leads from Hegel to Habermas might at least raise suspicion that the pattern of error and recognition it entails is to some significant extent self-serving. Moreover, Habermas uses this nar-rative paradigm more than once. As we shall see in the next section, it also underlies his memorial address to Foucault which depicts Foucault's return to the Enlightenment fold after years of trying to destroy it.

## What is Enlightenment?

Foucault was unable to reply to Habermas's criticisms of him in *The Philosophical Discourse of Modernity* because, by the time the book was published, he was dead. Habermas, though, did revise his view of Fou-cault in a memorial address which discusses one of Foucault's final texts, a lecture on Kant's 'An answer to the question: What is Enlightenment?'.[13] In 'Taking aim at the heart of the present: on Foucault's lecture on Kant's *What is Enlightenment?*' Habermas concedes that he may not have understood Foucault well on their only meeting.[14] His address represents a softening of his attitude to Foucault, in large part because in his account Foucault's lecture displays a much more positive attitude towards Kant. For the early Foucault of *Les Mots et les choses* (1966) Kant was, in Habermas's words, 'the epistemologist who thrust open the door to the age of anthropological thought and the human sciences with his analysis of finiteness' (174). In the 1984 lecture, Foucault's Kant has now become the thinker who inaugurates modernity by making philosophy address the significance of the present moment: 'transforming thought into a diagnostic instrument, he entangles it in the restless process of self-reassurance which to this day has kept modernity in ceaseless motion within the horizon of a new historical consciousness' (176). By characterizing the significance of Kant's thought in this way, Foucault can now portray himself as a thinker in the Enlightenment tradition.

Other commentators agree with Habermas that the Kant of Foucault's late lecture is different from the one encountered in *Les Mots et les choses*. In the earlier text, as Schmidt and Wartenberg put it, 'Kant had the dubious honour of awakening philosophy from its "dogmatic slumber" only to lull it back into what Foucault dubbed "the anthropological sleep" – the belief that all philosophy's questions could ultimately be reduced to the question "*Was ist der Mensch?*"'.[15] However, if Kant is depicted in *Les Mots et les choses* as laying the philosophical foundations of an empty humanism, Foucault's attitude to him even in that book is by no means one of unequivocal rejection. Although Foucault suggests that the epoch dominated by the anthropological question '*Was ist der Mensch?*' is drawing to a close, there is for him no point in simply denouncing that epoch because we are still part of it, it still defines the questions we ask and the way we answer them, so we could not simply stand outside it even if we wanted to. Moreover, Foucault acknowledges that the confusion of the empirical and the transcendental that occurs in the age of the human sciences (with Man as the empirico-transcendental doublet) cannot be blamed on Kant, who had on the contrary demonstrated that the empirical and the transcendental were irremediably separate.[16] Habermas overemphasizes Foucault's earlier antagonism towards Kant in order to underscore the significance of his later change in attitude. In a series of rhetorical questions Habermas suggests that Kant's philosophy of history should provoke the scorn of Foucault, whose 'stoic gaze' has frozen history into 'an iceberg covered with the crystalline forms of arbitrary discursive formations', allowing it to be merely 'a senseless back-and-forth movement of anonymous processes of subjugation' (176–7). By making Kant and Foucault appear utterly irreconcilable, Habermas escalates the drama of the turnabout revealed in Foucault's late account. He confesses himself to be 'surprised':

> In spite of these precautions it is a surprise to find that Foucault now presents the subversive thinkers who try to grasp the contemporary relevance of their present as the legitimate heirs of the Kantian critique. Under the altered conditions of their own times, they once again pose the diagnostic question of a modernity engaged in self-reassurance, the question that Kant was the first to pose. Foucault sees himself as carrying on this tradition.
>
> (178)

The later Foucault has completely revised his evaluation of the will to knowledge:

> Whereas, however, Foucault had previously traced this will to knowledge in modern power formations only to denounce it, he *now* displays it in a completely different light: as the critical impulse that links his own thought with the beginning of modernity, an impulse worthy of preservation and in need of renewal.
>
> (178)

The italicized *now* stresses the completeness of this turnaround. Foucault has shifted from denunciation of the Enlightenment tradition to a late recognition of his place within it; Kant is rehabilitated as a philosopher of history, and Foucault's earlier apocalyptic proclamations of the end of Man and of philosophy have given way to an acknowledgement of the value and persistence of the Enlightenment project. In Habermas's account, at the end of his life Foucault is drawn back 'into a sphere of influence he had tried to blast open, that of the philosophical discourse of modernity' (179).

The story Habermas tells about Foucault reproduces on a smaller scale the grand narrative of *The Philosophical Discourse of Modernity*: in Foucault's intellectual trajectory the Enlightenment is misrecognized, attacked, abandoned, but finally rediscovered. The rehabilitation of Foucault does not lead Habermas to revise his view of the French thinker's earlier work. Rather, it is motivated by the appearance of a late text which is depicted almost as a recantation or deathbed conversion. At the end Foucault is deemed to be retrievable because he has changed his mind, not because Habermas has changed his mind about him. The dead Foucault can now be depicted as a rather less lucid version of Habermas himself, a politically engaged intellectual in the Enlightenment tradition. There is a grudging edge to this generous reassessment, since its condition is that Foucault be deemed to have renounced his earlier positions in favour of an acceptance of the importance of Kant and the Enlightenment. In all this, Habermas sets himself up as the authentic mouthpiece of the Enlightenment, uniquely placed to perceive and to correct its shortcomings.

It has been suggested that one of the differences between Habermas and Foucault is that Foucault acknowledges, but dissents from, Habermasian critique, whereas Habermas fails to acknowledge the claims of Foucaldian genealogy.[17] In this may be seen one of the points of fundamental incompatibility between poststructuralism and Habermas's modernist critique: whereas the former understands its own approach as one of a range of possibilities, Habermas presents his position as exclusive and authoritative. However, his version of the Enlightenment and his assimilation of the late Foucault to the Enlightenment project entail an appropriation of the meaning of Enlightenment, and of the respective essays of Kant and Foucault on the subject, which is by no means unquestionable. Habermas claims for himself the right to identify and to speak for the Enlightenment project, but the essays of Kant and Foucault take up positions which cannot necessarily be assimilated to Habermas's reading, or to one another.

## Foucault's Enlightenment

In the opening paragraph of 'What is Enlightenment?' Kant answers his title question with a clear, simple and authoritative definition which might seem to make the rest of the essay redundant:

> *Enlightenment is man's emergence from his self-incurred immaturity. Immaturity* is the inability to use one's own understanding without the guidance of another. This immaturity is *self-incurred* if its cause is not lack of understanding, but lack of resolution and courage to use it without the guidance of another. The motto of enlightenment is therefore: *Sapere aude!* Have courage to use your *own* understanding![18]

Two hundred years later, however, in 'Qu'est-ce que les Lumières?' Foucault observes that Kant's text cannot be considered 'as being able to constitute an adequate description of the *Aufklärung*'.[19] The essay is 'not always very clear despite being short' (564), and on key points it proves to be either ambiguous or problematic. It has been suggested that the same comment could be made of Foucault's essay, as it hesitates between systematicity and irregularity.[20] Foucault's essay is certainly closely entangled with Kant's at all levels. The very fact that Foucault's title repeats Kant's 'What is Enlightenment?' suggests that the question of the Enlightenment remains pertinent and that the answer has not yet been given. In his opening comments Foucault explains that Kant's essay marks the introduction into philosophy of one of the defining problems of modernity: 'A minor text, perhaps. But it seems to me that with it there enters discreetly into the history of thought a question which modern philosophy has not been able to answer, but from which it has never managed to disentangle itself' (562).[21] The question 'What is Enlightenment?' is still pertinent and urgent because the Enlightenment is an event 'which has determined, at least in part, what we are, what we think, and what we do today' (562). Its significance is a matter of dispute and of the utmost importance, to the extent that Foucault suggests it may even be the defining question of modern philosophy. Foucault indicates this when he formulates a possible response to the question 'What is modern philosophy?': 'modern philosophy is the one which attempts to answer the question posed, two centuries ago so imprudently: *Was ist Aufklärung?*' (562–3).

Foucault underlines four areas of difficulty raised by Kant's analysis of Enlightenment: it can be achieved only if the relations between the will, authority and the use of reason are fundamentally modified; it is both a process which is under way, and a duty of the individual requiring personal courage; it is unclear whether the Enlightenment affects the social and political existence of all humanity, or whether it represents a change in what constitutes the humanity of the human being; and since it is not only an obligation on the individual, it raises the problem of how the private use of reason can take public and political forms (564–6). For Foucault the key novelty of Kant's essay is that it sketches a philosophical approach to actuality which does not treat the present as part of an epoch, or as a repository of signs for the future, or as a point of transition leading towards a new world. Rather, Kant tries to understand the present as the site on which his own philosophical project is being played out; and his Enlightenment consists in binding together in unprecedented closeness the philosophical significance of his work and the specific moment in which and because of which he is writing. Whereas for Habermas modernity is an historical period, Foucault draws on Kant (and subsequently Baudelaire) to characterize it as an attitude: 'a mode of relation with regard to actuality; a voluntary choice made by some; finally, a way of thinking and feeling, also a way of acting and behaving, which at the same time marks a belonging and is presented as a task' (568).

This conception of modernity and of the role of Kant's essay in defining it allows Foucault to situate his own work in the Enlightenment lineage. This does not entail 'fidelity to elements of doctrine' but rather 'the permanent reactivation of an attitude, that is, of a philosophical *ethos* which could be characterized as the permanent critique of our historical being' (571). The final part of Foucault's essay further defines this ethos, which entails the careful analysis of ourselves as historically determined beings, perpetually aiming to find the contingencies underlying apparent necessities, and endeavouring to test and to cross boundaries in the search to extend the possibilities of being free and being human. Foucault summarizes this ethos as 'a philosophical life in which the critique of what we are is at the same time the historical analysis of the limits set on us and a testing of the possibility of crossing them' (577).

So in 'Qu'est-ce que les Lumières?' Foucault claims for himself a role in continuing the project of Enlightenment. Characterizing this project in terms of ethos rather than doctrine makes it possible for him to identify his work as undertaken in the space opened up by Kant's essay even when he describes its problems as quite distinct from those addressed by his German precursor. Rather than seeking to establish the universal conditions of knowledge and ethics, Foucault proposes to analyse the historical constitution of the discourses in which we articulate what we think and do; and whereas Kantian epistemology sought to draw up the limits which knowledge could not cross, Foucault argues that we should constantly seek out ways of transgressing the frontiers imposed on us (574). Foucault's deviation from Kant is implied in his slight misquotation of Kant's motto of Enlightenment, *sapere aude*. Foucault reverses the order of this, quoting it as *aude sapere* (565), perhaps thereby stressing the daring and transgression involved in 'Dare to be wise' rather than the wisdom achieved through such daring.[22] Revising the Enlightenment project in the light of his own concerns, he endorses a critique which will be genealogical in its aims and archaeological in its methods (574). He thereby appropriates the Enlightenment by turning it into something which Kant would not have recognized.

Christopher Norris has demonstrated how Foucault interprets Kant as mistaking culture-specific truth claims for a priori truths. On the basis of this revisionist reading, Foucault can take up his place in the Enlightenment tradition: 'In short, Foucault's wager is that we can in some sense keep faith with the project of enlightened critique, whilst acknowledging that in another sense – on the strong universalist or transcendental reading – that project has long since run its course and relinquished all claims to validity or truth.'[23] The return to Kant is also a turn away from him.

This does not in itself invalidate Foucault's reading of 'What is Enlightenment?', even if Norris has described it as a 'strong-revisionist (not to say downright perverse) misreading'.[24] Indeed, the fact that Foucault returned to Kant's essay repeatedly in the last decade of his life suggests that he perceived in it insights which were genuinely important for his own project; and in some respects, as commentators have pointed out, Foucault's departures from Kant nevertheless remain within the intellectual space opened up by the German philosopher. In particular, both Habermas and Foucault follow Kant's conception of Enlightenment at least in as far as they stress its unfinished, ongoing nature. Kant insists that the decisions of one age cannot bind those of its successors, and that this is the very nature of Enlightenment:

> One age cannot enter into an alliance on oath to put the next age in a position where it would be impossible for it to extend and correct its knowledge, particularly on such important matters, to clear up errors, or to make any progress whatsoever in enlightenment. This would be a crime against human nature, whose original destiny lies precisely in such progress.[25]

Progress here is *Fortschreiten*, a process without final point, rather than *Fortschritt*, a single identifiable event. And in so far as human nature is identified with this 'stepping forward', both it and the process of Enlightenment remain open-ended, without final destination. So Kant suggests that the present age, and perhaps any other age, cannot be described as *enlightened*, once and for all: 'If it is now asked whether we live in an *enlightened* age [*in einem* aufgeklärten *Zeitalter*], the answer is: No, but we do live in an age of *enlightenment* [*in einem Zeitalter der* Aufklärung].'[26] The careful distinction between an enlightened age and an age of Enlightenment hinges on the difference between the completion implied in the past participle (enlightened, *aufgeklärt*) and the openness of the noun (the process of enlightenment or enlightening, *Aufklärung*).

Kant's time is an age of Enlightenment because it provides favourable political and intellectual conditions for progress in knowledge and freedom. The wrong conditions would impede the process, but not even ideal conditions would ever allow it to be completed once and for all. If Enlightenment is, as Kant puts it in his opening sentence, 'man's emergence from his self-incurred immaturity',[27] maturity is not yet achieved, and it is by no means clear that Kant thinks that it is finally achievable.[28] Foucault concurs on this point when he poses the question of Enlightenment 200 years later: 'I don't know if we will ever become mature. Many things in our experience convince us that the historical event of the Aufklärung has not made us mature, and that we are not yet mature' (577).

If the process of Enlightenment is not – and can never be – complete, then neither is its meaning settled once and for all. So although Habermas is correct to observe that the later Foucault places his work within the Enlightenment lineage, this does not necessarily justify the rapprochement between Foucault and Kant which underlies Habermas's more generous appraisal of the French philosopher. If Habermas and Foucault agree about the importance of Kant, they disagree about the significance of his account of the Enlightenment, and Kant's Enlightenment is not the same as Habermas's or Foucault's. Ashenden and Owen have neatly summed up how Habermas and Foucault revise the Kantian account of Enlightenment in quite different ways: 'Consequently, whereas Habermas seeks to rearticulate Kant's project in terms of a weak transcendental argument grounded in a reconstruction of our communicative competences, Foucault offers a reworking of what it is to think "today" as difference in history'.[29]

The superficial agreement about the importance of the Enlightenment masks deep, perhaps irreconcilable, differences over its significance. Julie Candler Hayes suggests that the struggle for the meaning of the Enlightenment is part of our modern situation, so that 'Defining Enlightenment has become crucial to defining ourselves'.[30] If this is the case, the competition of interpretations and the proliferation of readings, misreadings, revisions and re-revisions would seem to be endemic in the contemporary search for self-understanding. The Habermasian telos of consensus turns out to be just another piece in the postmodern jigsaw, and there is little apparent prospect of reaching consensus about consensus itself. Foucault's Enlightenment is not the same as Habermas's, and there is no clear way of reconciling their positions.

## Missed encounters

In the early 1980s it was proposed to hold a conference in the US to bring together Foucault and Habermas. Foucault died before arrangements for the conference could be finalized; but the failure to stage an encounter between Habermasian critique and Foucaldian genealogy is perhaps not only due to circumstantial reasons. Habermas and Foucault even differ in their accounts of how the conference came to be proposed and what was to be its subject.[31] The failure to agree on the details of an encounter that never took place serves as a fitting emblem of the controversies discussed in this and the previous chapter.[32] Habermas's critique of poststructuralism avoids genuine dialogue; and the meeting of minds, or at least the softening of opposition, which occurs in Habermas's appreciation of Foucault's essay on 'What is Enlightenment?' turns out to be one more missed encounter. The debate never quite takes place, as opponents simplify and misread each other, and they end up refuting imaginary adversaries. In the case of Foucault and Habermas, Dreyfus and Rabinow argue that a genuine debate was impossible because of their fundamentally incompatible understanding of key terms.[33] Even when they seem to agree, the agreement between them is based on the false assumption that they are using words in the same way.

The dialogue between Habermas and Derrida is no more successful. In long footnotes in his books *Limited Inc.* and *Mémoires pour Paul de Man*, Derrida has expressed his anger at Habermas's misrepresentation of his views with unusual frankness.[34] Derrida is particularly angered by the second of the two chapters on him in *The Philosophical Discourse of Modernity* (described as an 'Excursus' in Habermas's book) in which Habermas refutes the levelling of the distinction between philosophy and literature which Derrida allegedly promotes. Derrida bitterly retorts that in the entire chapter the views Habermas imputes to him are not justified by a single reference or quotation; in fact, in *Limited Inc.* he makes this point seven times in the space of four pages. In particular Derrida is stung by the charge that he inverts the traditional primacy of logic over rhetoric, and he responds with surprising directness and simplicity: 'That is false.'[35] And anticipating the response of some of his critics who assert that Derrida does not believe in truth and falsehood, he underlines the point: 'I do indeed say *false*, as opposed to *true*.'[36]

Habermas accuses Derrida of a 'performative contradiction' because he uses the tools of subject-centred reason in order to convict it of being authoritarian.[37] Derrida in turn finds a performative contradiction in Habermas in that he purports to give a rational discussion of Derrida's views without any apparent effort to find out what they are or to understand them.[38] The philosopher of reason, argumentation and consensus does not put his values into practice when it comes to reading the work of those he attacks. Derrida acknowledges that Habermas's other chapter on him in *The Philosophical Discourse of Modernity* does contain some evidence of first-hand reading, but Derrida suggests that this by no means guarantees a higher standard of argumentation.[39] However, Derrida also replicates Habermas's failure to engage by refraining from a more detailed self-defence or repudiation of Habermas. This is particularly interesting since it appears in Derrida's *Limited Inc.*, a text which contains Derrida's responses to the criticisms of the American speech-act philosopher John Searle. *Limited Inc.* both thematizes and instantiates the missed encounter, perhaps even the impossible encounter, between poststructuralism and analytic philosophy. The exchanges between Habermas and his French adversaries illustrate once again this conspicuous absence of real dialogue.

The absence of a shared discourse or common ground on which opponents might meet is characteristic of what Herman Rapaport calls 'the theory mess'; Rapaport implies that some of the causes for this mess may be contingent and therefore in principle remediable, such as the current poor state of intellectual community which rewards academics for promoting public controversy rather than for patient intellectual engagement.[40] I would suggest, though, that the controversies discussed here also indicate the persistence of an intellectual tribalism which could not easily be overcome by reform to the conditions of academic employment. Instances where participants on either side of a controversy are persuaded by the arguments of their opponents are rare enough to be negligible. Even retractions on points of detail are hardly commonplace. It may be that misreadings are regrettable or correctable in detail, but their recurrence also appears to be predictable and inevitable, and misunderstanding remains one of the principal motors of intellectual debate.

There is at work in Habermas's repudiation of poststructuralism a further factor also seen in chapter 1. A key component of the rhetoric of controversy is the dismissal of one's opponent on ethical or political grounds. Derrida describes how the attack on theory consistently claims for itself the moral high ground:

> It's *always* in the name of ethics, of an ethics of discussion which is supposedly democratic, it's always in the name of transparent communication and 'consensus' that the most brutal breaches of the

> elementary rules of discussion (nuanced reading or listening to the other, proof, argument, analysis and quotation) occur. It's *always* the moralist discourse of consensus – at least the one which pretends to appeal sincerely to consensus – which in fact produces the indecent transgression of the classical norms of reason and democracy. To say nothing of elementary philology.[41]

As we saw in the previous chapter, attacks on theory are based on moral objections as much as on detailed or procedural disagreements. Moreover, it is striking that the moral objections are not enunciated through detailed, informed consideration of poststructuralist work in ethics, such as Derrida's essays on Levinas; rather, opponents take issue with what are depicted as shoddy intellectual practices, failings of the elementary rules of scholarship and argumentation, and the pernicious example which is set to the impressionable young. Since these objections are themselves almost invariably founded in an abysmal failure to read the texts which are being criticized in any intelligent way, they backfire onto their authors. It is particularly revealing when Habermas, the philosopher of communicative reason, so conspicuously fails to live up to his own standards when criticizing the work of others. Whilst aiming at consensus, he risks discrediting any possibility of achieving it through the absence of constructive engagement with the people whose work he repudiates. Replicating precisely the shortcoming he denounces in others, he adds to the postmodern cacophony which he had wanted to silence.

## The Kantian legacy

Habermas's reading of Foucault and Derrida attributes to them an unnuanced hostility to the Enlightenment. However, in 'Qu'est-ce que les Lumières?' Foucault insists that there can be no simple choice between embracing or rejecting our intellectual context, of which the Enlightenment constitutes an important element:

> But that does not mean that we have to be for or against the *Aufklärung*. What it means is precisely that we must refuse everything that might be presented in the form of a simplistic and authoritarian alternative: either you accept the *Aufklärung* and you remain in the tradition of its rationalism (which some consider to be positive and others on the contrary consider to be a reproach); or you critique the *Aufklärung* and you attempt to escape from its principles

of rationality (which again can be taken to be a good or a bad thing). And you don't escape this blackmail by introducing 'dialectical' nuances and seeking to determine what might have been good or bad in the *Aufklärung*.

(571–2)

Foucault is fully aware that his account of the Enlightenment entails a strategic deviation from its Kantian version, even as he insists upon the pertinence of the questions raised by Kant. Habermas's memorial address tries to force Foucault into a pattern of binary choices by seeing him first as the implacable opponent of Kant and the Enlightenment in *Les Mots et les choses* and then as undergoing a last-minute conversion in 'Qu'est-ce que les Lumières?'. Although, as commentators largely agree, there were shifts in emphasis in Foucault's treatment of Kant, to characterize those shifts in such dramatic terms misses the nuance of Foucault's discussions and imposes on them a requirement to be 'for or against' which he rejects. Indeed, in some respects there is a strong continuity between Foucault's depiction of Kant in *Les Mots et les choses* and in the late lecture. In the earlier book Kant is already described as a founding figure in the discourse of the modernity to which we still belong; the questions he posed are still pertinent, even if Foucault anticipates an imminent transformation of the intellectual agenda which Kant helped to establish. Kantian critique marks 'the threshold of our modernity', and modern thought still belongs in its dynasty.[42] Foucault's debt to Kant is fully conscious, even if it is also ambivalent. So it is a simplification to read Foucault's lecture on 'What is Enlightenment?' as demonstrating that he had straightforwardly changed his mind about Kant and the significance of his philosophy. As Schmidt and Wartenberg argue, Foucault's lecture should not be read as 'a deathbed conversion'.[43] Rather, it is the final evidence of Foucault's long-term engagement with Kant, who has been described as 'a thinker who never ceased to inspire and provoke Foucault'.[44]

The position of Kant in all this is fraught and pivotal. Associated with reason, universality, the transcendental conditions of knowledge and humanism, Kant appears to be the very epitome of everything Foucault *et al.* reject. But even a moderately intelligent reading of the work of thinkers such as Foucault, Derrida, Lacan, Deleuze or Lyotard shows that they have read Kant carefully and are aware of their debt to him. Foucault worked on the French translation of Kant's *Anthropologie in pragmatischer Hinsicht*; one of Deleuze's first books, *La Philosophie critique de Kant*, was an introduction to Kantian critique; and Kant is a constant point of reference in Lyotard's work on the sublime and Lacan's seminar on the ethics of psychoanalysis. It is hard to find instances in works by the thinkers described as structuralist, poststructuralist or postmodernist where the work of Kant is *simply* dismissed, even if it is also not *simply* embraced.

Derrida gives a particularly lucid account of the status of Kant for him and his contemporaries in *Du droit à la philosophie*.[45] Derrida describes the relation to Kant in ironic terms as being 'as if tattooed' (82) on academic philosophers because of the professional formation which they have undergone. The presence of Kant can be seen behind the modes of argumentation they learn, the norms they internalize and the exercises (such as a scholarly thesis) they undertake. To try to get around Kant by ignoring him runs the risk of reproducing his influence all the more surely. The way forward according to Derrida is to analyse why Kant has acquired his position as a philosophical touchstone, and this means reading him all the more carefully and intensely: 'we must still read Kant, turn to him, thematize the phenomenon of his authority, and therefore over-canonize him' (83). The excess implied in *over-canonize* (*sur-canoniser*) suggests that Kant will be better understood by paying him too much respect rather than too little. Reading here is of paramount importance: 'it is no doubt necessary to read Kant otherwise, but we must not stop reading him' (84).

Like Foucault, Derrida does not endorse the prospect of any abrupt liberation from Kant; rather, he proposes to question the claims of philosophy by staying in touch with the great texts of the past and finding within them the moments of excess which make it possible to envisage a transformation of the intellectual programme. Christopher Norris has argued that Derrida cannot be understood as abandoning the ground of post-Kantian critical thought, and that Habermas misrepresents Derrida as much as he misreads Foucault.[46] Like Foucault, if Derrida questions the Enlightenment, it is with a vigilant respect for its founding texts and values. And like Foucault, Derrida claims his part of the Kantian heritage, whilst also problematizing the identity of that heritage:

> The Kantian legacy is not only the Kantian legacy, something self-identical; it oversteps itself, as does every legacy, to obtain (or to lay claim to) the analysis of that legacy, and better still the instruments by which any legacy might be analysed. We must take account of this 'supplementary' structure. A legacy always bequeaths to us surreptitiously the means of interpreting it.

(82)

It is the nature of this legacy that it contains its own excess and thereby it enables us to interpret it differently. So it is with Kantian means that Kant must be read. Derrida's move is typically double-edged: he stresses the importance of the Kantian heritage whilst denying that it can ever be straightforwardly identified. It is open to, indeed it consists in, its availability to revision and appropriation. The legacy, Derrida claims, is always a *secret* which calls for further interpretation: 'If the legibility of a bequest were given, natural, transparent, unequivocal, if it did not call for and at the same time defy interpretation, there would be no need ever to inherit it.'[47]

The legacy is at once everyone's and no one's since all have a share but none can claim possession of it. Here again, we see a fundamental incompatibility between Habermas's desire to tell and to 'own' the single story of the Enlightenment, and the implication that there are always other ways of reading and configuring the founding texts of our modernity. For Derrida, to attend to Kant's legacy means to read and to re-read his texts in the belief that their claim upon us has not yet been exhausted. Their capacity to challenge, to intrigue and to surprise is unabated, otherwise the Kantian legacy would have been liquidated once and for all. The following chapters are written in the belief that this is as true of the work of some of the most exciting French thinkers of the past thirty years as it is of Kant.

# Chapter 3

# After knowledge
## Lyotard and the postmodern condition

In chapter 1 we saw that Sokal and Bricmont describe postmodernism as 'an intellectual current that is supposed to have replaced modern rationalist thought'.[1] In this account postmodernism represents the end of the Enlightenment project, a descent from reason to irrationality, from consensus to irreconcilable difference, from the prospect of assured knowledge to a nightmare of free play and unsupported opinion, from civic and ethical responsibility to an anarchic, subject-less domain of irresponsible relativity. According to this view, postmodernism answers Kant's first question, 'What can I know?', with a flippant, 'Not much'.

However, the previous chapter suggested that thinkers such as Derrida and Foucault are intensely aware of their indebtedness to the philosophical tradition. Even at its most radical, their ambition it not to *abandon* their intellectual heritage, but to find ways of making it more habitable. The first two chapters of this book have discussed some of the consistent charges made against French thought. The next four chapters deal more positively with ways in which some of the best known thinkers of recent decades have addressed and sought to inflect major philosophical problems. Kant's fundamental questions (What can I know? What ought I to do? What may I hope? What is the human being?) provide the starting point for discussion. The current chapter, on Lyotard and the problem of postmodern knowledge, also returns to the relationship between modern French thought and the Enlightenment. It shows that postmodernism, at least in Lyotard's version of it, does not abolish knowledge, or at least no more than Kant does. The chapter begins by sketching Kant's response to the question of knowledge; this is then contrasted with Lyotard's treatment of the same question. Finally, the chapter considers the extent to which postmodernism can be understood as being in some respects Kantian, just as Kant can be read as being in some respects postmodern.

## The Kantian dinner party

Reading Kant, one sometimes has the impression of being confronted with a boundless intellect, as his work ranges with bewildering complexity over epistemology, ethics, aesthetics, religion and politics. Kant's readiness to treat such diverse areas is sustained by the conviction that each of them, like each of his four fundamental questions, is interconnected; the philosopher aspires to progress towards the systematic unity which links together empirical knowledge. Insight in one domain may generate understanding in others. This can be illustrated by a passage which may seem to be incidental to Kant's more ambitious philosophical preoccupations, but which nevertheless illustrates the linkage between apparently unrelated areas of interest. The passage comes from Kant's *Anthropologie in pragmatischer Hinsicht*, the book which sets out to answer the fourth of his fundamental questions, 'What is the human being?'. The first part of the book ('On the manner of cognizing the inside and the outside of the human being') deals extensively with issues of cognition, pleasure and desire, but ends rather surprisingly with Kant's recommendations for how to hold a successful dinner party. He does not offer any recipes, but he does suggest five rules of conduct:[2]

(a)  A topic for conversation should be chosen which interests everyone, and allows everyone to contribute.
(b)  No deathly silences should be allowed, only momentary pauses in the conversation.
(c)  The topic of conversation should not be changed until it has been nearly exhausted; if the conversation falters, an individual may take the lead by suggesting a related topic without arousing attention or envy.
(d)  Any disputatious dogmatism [*Rechthaberei*] should be deflected by a skilful injection of humour.
(e)  When serious disagreements arise, a tone of mutual respect and goodwill should be maintained so that guests should not fall out with one another.

This passage may seem trivial in the light of Kant's massive contribution to nearly every field of intellectual enquiry. At the same time, the very comprehensiveness of the Kantian endeavour is part of its essential design, as Kant sought not to *add* to knowledge but to sketch its systematic unity. Reason may be used to elucidate issues as diverse as the conditions of empirical experience, the foundations of scientific knowledge, the dilemmas of ethics or the nature of social relations. These are different aspects of a single intellectual enterprise; every insight, every aspect of theory or practice, each modulation of doctrine or text, should have its place in the completed system. So Kant's interest in dinner parties may be less philosophically redundant than it first appeared. The section of *Anthropologie in pragmatischer Hinsicht* which concludes with the rules for a successful dinner party begins by describing the essentially human, even if ultimately unsuccessful, project of uniting physical and moral well-being. Sociability (*Umgänglichkeit*), as long as it does not become excessive, may be a virtue favourable to this project. The point is that the dinner party is *not just* a dinner party, it is also a place where a fundamental human drama is taking place. Moreover, joined together around a single table, the dinner guests are also enacting a political ideal. Their conversation is continuous, everyone participates, disagreements inevitably arise but do not disrupt the unity of the group; the person who chooses the initial subject of conversation is effectively the leader of the group, but that person may be discreetly replaced without rivalry or hostility as the topic changes. This is, in miniature, the very model of a successful civic society. Elsewhere, Kant describes the constitution of the ideal republican state: 'A *republican constitution* is founded upon three principles: firstly, the principle of *freedom* for all members of a society (as men); secondly, the principle of the *dependence* of everyone upon a single common legislation (as subjects); and thirdly, the principle of legal *equality* for everyone (as citizens).'[3]

The leader of this ideal state may well be a king (hence, Kantian republicanism is not incompatible with monarchy), but the king rules only in so far as he represents the united will of the people, which should also be the will of reason.[4] As free, dependent and equal, the dinner guests are united – literally, around a single table – despite their differences, participating in a single conversation, obeying the same civilities and led only to the extent that the host or his surrogate anticipates what will most interest, entertain and bring together his fellow guests. So the dinner party has philosophical and political resonance beyond its apparently modest context. Moreover, this picture of guests who are free agents, *different* but not *divided*, participating in distinctive but equal ways, consenting in the common endeavour to secure the success of their encounter, acquires a further level of significance through the purchase which it allows on Kantian epistemology. Like the successful dinner party, the whole project of knowledge requires a coalition of agencies – or faculties[5] – which alone can achieve nothing. A brief consideration of the *Critique of Pure Reason* can demonstrate the link between the Kantian dinner party and the doctrine of faculties.

Kant opens the Preface to the first edition of the *Critique of Pure Reason* by describing the peculiar dilemma of human reason: 'it is troubled by questions that it cannot dismiss, because they are posed to it by the nature of reason itself, but that it also cannot answer, because they surpass human reason's every ability'.[6] Reason relies on principles which it cannot avoid using, but which cannot be verified because they go beyond the boundary of all possible experience. The aim of critical philosophy is a self-cognition of reason by which baseless pretensions of thought will be dismissed and the rightful claims of reason assured (8); so *Critique of Pure Reason* essentially sets out to answer the first of Kant's fundamental philosophical questions, 'What can I know?'. Stanley Cavell gives a succinct summary of Kant's argument:

(1) Experience is constituted by appearances. (2) Appearances are of something else, which accordingly cannot itself appear. (3) All and only functions of experience can be known; these are our categories of the understanding. (4) It follows that something else – that of which appearances are appearances, whose existence we must grant – cannot be known. In discovering this limitation of reason, reason proves its power to itself, over itself. (5) Moreover, since it is unavoidable for our reason to be drawn to think about this unknowable ground of appearance, reason reveals itself in this necessity also.[7]

In terms of the foundation of knowledge, what Cavell calls the Kantian 'philosophical settlement'[8] is double-edged. On the one hand, in the realm of appearances knowledge may be absolutely assured. According to the doctrine of faculties this is achieved by sensibility, understanding and reason each fulfilling their own specific task in collaboration with the other faculties: through sensibility objects of experience are apprehended; through understanding they are given sense and unity as they are subsumed under the rules which make them into possible objects of experience in the first place; and reason gives unity to the manifold cognitions of understanding through the establishment of a system of concepts and principles (353).[9] On the basis of this coalition of faculties, Kant is able to anticipate a complete and unsurpassable success for the critical project of reason:

Once metaphysics has been brought by this critique onto the secure path of a science, it is able to encompass completely the entire realm of the cognitions pertaining to it. Hence it can complete its

work and put it aside for the use of posterity, as capital that can
never be increased.

(26)

However, this optimism has a reverse side. The prospect of assured
knowledge in the realm of experience is countered by an essential and
unalterable ignorance of what lies beyond that realm. Because we know
that appearances are precisely *appearances*, we can fairly assume that
they are appearances *of* something which by definition does not itself
appear (otherwise it would itself be merely another object of experience). If we know everything of the appearance, we know nothing of
the thing in itself, and we can never know anything of it because it can
never be made into an object of experience. Kantian epistemological
hubris, which hopes to provide a 'capital that can never be increased', is
counterbalanced by humility: Kant offers no knowledge and no possibility of knowledge of what cannot be directly experienced. This is
distressing for reason because it is its destiny and inclination to enquire
into what lies beyond experience. According to Kant, pure reason ultimately has three objects: the freedom of the will, the immortality of the
soul and the existence of God (730). Of these, freedom at least in its
practical (i.e., in this context, moral) implications, can be adequately
dealt with by reason, as Kant would endeavour to demonstrate in the
second critique, his *Critique of Practical Reason*. The two remaining concerns of pure reason remain intransigent, as Kant insists in response to
his own question, 'What can I know?'. He suggests that '[we] have (as I
flatter myself) exhausted all possible answers to this question' (735), but
he adds that his answers do not provide further knowledge about the
existence of God and the immortality of the soul:

> From the two great purposes, however, to which this entire endeav-
> our of pure reason was properly directed we have remained just as
> distant as if we had – from love of leisure – refused this job at the
> very beginning. Hence if our concern is knowledge, then at least
> this much is certain and established: that we shall never be able to
> partake of knowledge regarding those two problems.
>
> (736)

This is a surprisingly teasing, playful moment in the *Critique of Pure
Reason*. Eight hundred pages into his monumental work on the foundations and limits of knowledge, Kant informs us that, at least on the two
issues which might interest us most, we are no better off and never will

be any better off than if – 'for love of leisure' – we had not bothered at all. The austere philosopher and his exhausted reader are no further advanced than the idler who stayed at home watching television.

In the realm of experience, knowledge is assured through the coalition of sensibility (intuition), understanding and reason. Each plays its own distinctive role without which the whole process would falter: without intuition, reason would have no access to the world of experience, and hence all knowledge would be merely hypothetical; without understanding, the data provided by intuition would be chaotic and nonsensical, utterly useless for ensuring knowledge; without reason, there would be no final systematic unity to the manifold of experience. This coalition no longer operates when reason seeks to pass beyond the limits of experience. Even so, matters are perhaps not entirely hopeless, as Kant indicates in a well-known comment from the Preface to the second edition of the *Critique of Pure Reason*:

> For in order to reach God, freedom, and immortality, speculative reason must use principles that in fact extend merely to objects of possible experience; and when these principles are nonetheless applied to something that cannot be an object of experience, they actually do always transform it into an appearance, and thus they declare all *practical expansion* of reason to be impossible. I therefore had to annul *knowledge* in order to make room for *faith*.
>
> (31)

Once again, the comment is fundamentally double-edged: reason falters, knowledge is placed within bounds, but this also leaves space for faith in a way that the limitless expansion of knowledge would not. For *annul* Kant uses the verb *aufheben*, which is rendered, in what was for a long time the standard English translation, as *destroy*. Whilst Kant's use of *aufheben* may not yet have the specific sense that it would have for Hegel (describing a process of both preserving and surpassing), *destroy* is altogether too strong in that it implies that even the knowledge that was already established must now be abandoned. *Aufheben* is less dramatic and less final, suggesting an adjournment or curtailment rather than a complete destruction. Kant's point is that where knowledge ends, faith begins. In some domains faith cannot match the assurance achieved by reason, but in others faith can comprehend what reason cannot know. So *aufheben* does not suggest a conflict between reason and faith; rather it characterizes their potentially mutually supportive coexistence in that they have purchase over different domains: one patrols the limits of possible experience from the inside; the other ventures beyond those limits.

Whatever the area with which it deals, Kantian thinking is commanded by the search for the proper and peaceful collaboration of separate but related agencies. Although Kant shares the Hobbesian view that the natural state of man is the war of each against all, he also draws up what he hopes will be a viable programme for perpetual peace amongst states.[10] And although the title of *The Conflict of the Faculties* draws attention to a contemporary situation of academic strife, Kant's aim is not to demonstrate how the conflict might be resolved by the victory of one faculty over another, but rather to suggest how different faculties should acknowledge and respect the different roles of each in both the university and the state. In a whole series of different areas, then, Kant describes how autonomous agencies work together under the umbrella of a common endeavour or shared values: the coalition of intuition, understanding and reason serve to assure knowledge of objects of experience; reason and faith relay one another in the passage across the limits of experience; states which respect the principles of public right will coexist in peace; the faculties of philosophy and theology will not seek to trespass into each other's areas of competence. Far from disabling philosophical, religious, political or moral harmony, the recognition of barriers and limits is the founding condition of peace between and within subjects, nations and faculties.

This pattern of harmony achieved through respect for difference within unity, for separate capabilities within a single overarching scheme, becomes a more general intellectual structure which also governs the Kantian dinner party. Kant's rules for the successful dinner party are also rules for successful civic society, epistemological enquiry, the organization of universities, the preservation of religion and the establishment of peace between nations. Kant concedes that serious dispute (*ernstlicher Streit*) between guests is unavoidable, but insists on self-discipline and mutual respect, 'so that none of the fellow guests [*Mitgäste*] returns home from the gathering [*Gesellschaft*] in conflict [*entzweiet*] with another'.[11] Kant's language is careful and resonant here: the guests are not just *guests* (*Gäste*), they are *fellow* guests (*Mitgäste*); the prefix *mit-* suggests a togetherness which must not be *entzweiet*, literally split in two; and together the guests form a *Gesellschaft*, which may be a social gathering, but also a partnership, a community or a society.

So Kant is concerned both with the proper functioning and with possible dysfunctions in social, cognitive or institutional systems. Indeed, one way of describing the project of his critical philosophy would be as the ambition to track down the causes of dysfunction in the abuse of reason in order to hold open the prospect that reason may finally fulfil its destiny. The very diversity of Kant's writing is an aspect of the profound unity of his intellectual ambition. Under the gaze of reason, everything belongs to the same system. True knowledge cannot be gained by any faculty in isolation, no faculty can arrogate the powers of any other and none can achieve anything without the others.

The systematic unity and interconnectedness to which Kant aspires is at a far remove from the postmodern world of flux, slippage and radical incommensurability. In Lyotard's version of postmodernism the coalition of faculties is dissolved into a series of language games with no prospect of unity or final reconciliation. This is not tantamount to saying that we can know nothing for certain; on the contrary, if anything the postmodern condition is characterized by *too much* knowledge, and it is too readily available. Postmodernity realizes precisely what Kant strove to combat: a situation in which there is no regulative principle to ensure the unity of the knowable. And although he rejects the transcendental foundations of the Kantian system, Lyotard is no less aware than Kant would have been that this condition can rapidly become a nightmare.

## Postmodern theory-fictions

In the late eighteenth century Kant had given to philosophy the task of establishing the transcendental conditions of knowledge. Two hundred years later, in an article entitled 'Apathie dans la théorie' first published in 1975, Jean-François Lyotard set himself and his contemporaries an apparently more simple task, one which would involve renouncing the philosopher's epistemological ambitions: 'The big issue for us now is to destroy theory, and it's not by taking a vow of silence that we will succeed.'[12] Only five years earlier, in an interview entitled 'Sur la théorie' Lyotard's attitude to theory seemed altogether more anxious; asked what it meant to be engaged in theoretical research, he admitted that 'it's a question which troubles me enormously', and he expressed regret at the lack of a unified political theory.[13]

The five years that separate 'Sur la théorie' from 'Apathie dans la théorie' had seen Lyotard move further from the search for a socialist alternative to Soviet Communism, which had been a political objective of his *Socialisme ou barbarie* days, towards what he called paganism.[14] This entailed a political and intellectual commitment which was no less intense than before, but which jettisoned the ambition of justifying such commitment within a fixed theoretical system. So the whole theoretical project was judged to be misguided if it purported to establish a stable framework to resolve the thorny questions of truth and justice, beauty and desire. However, just as Kant's annulment of knowledge did not entail its simple abandonment, Lyotard's destruction of theory does not mean simply giving it up. In fact the final quarter-century of Lyotard's life which begins with 'Apathie dans la théorie' would be far more productive in terms of published work than the previous twenty-five years. Theory is to be destroyed from within itself, rather than from the outside. Chapter 7 returns to the significance of this for Lyotard and the poststructuralist understanding of theory more generally. For the moment, it is important to note that the means which Lyotard embraces for destroying theory is parody rather than derision or criticism:

> The destruction of theory can only take place through parody: it doesn't consist at all in *critiquing* theory, since critique is itself a theoretical *Moment* from which we shouldn't expect the destruction of theory. To destroy theory is to make pseudo-theories; the theoretical crime is to fabricate theory-fictions [*théorie-fictions*].[15]

This willingness to undermine the authority of theory through parody evidently marks a major departure from Kant's view of philosophy as occupying a legislative role in relation to other disciplines. Moreover, the linking of theory and fiction in Lyotard's 'theory-fictions' brings together forms of writing kept rigorously separate by Kant, who expressed misgivings about novels on the grounds that they 'weaken the memory and destroy character'.[16] However, in his later book *Le Différend* Lyotard places his work back within a Kantian framework as he distinguishes between *philosophy* and *theory*:

> The mode of this book is philosophical, reflective . . . Unlike a theoretician, [the author] does not presuppose the rules of his discourse, but only the fact that it must obey rules. The mode of the book is philosophical, and not theoretical (or other), insofar as the discovery of its rules is what is at stake, rather than knowledge of them being its starting point.[17]

The difference between theory and philosophy is that the theorist seeks to operate by rules which are known in advance, whereas philosophy only discovers the rules of its discourse as it progresses. Lyotard's distinction between *philosophy* and *theory* rests upon Kant's discussion of the differences between reflective and determinant judgement: the latter, like theory, subsumes the particular under the already-known universal; reflective judgement, on the other hand, occurs when the principle which might justify a judgement is not known in advance, so that there is no established rule for judging the particular. Lyotard's position is not that there are no rules, nor even that the rules are in principle unknowable, but rather that the rules are only *anticipated* at the time of writing. This is not, then, a refusal of order, but only the claim that it is not yet known, and that to take it as already known condemns thought merely to rediscover its own founding limitations.

Postmodern thought is reflective rather than determinant, it does not know where it is heading nor does it claim authority over its subject. Crucially, it understands itself as bound up with, rather than rigorously separate from, parody and fiction. The following sections examine the consequences of this for what is perhaps Lyotard's best-known and most influential book, *La Condition postmoderne*.

## Writing the postmodern

*La Condition postmoderne* may be, as I have just said, Lyotard's best-known and most influential book, and it established his reputation internationally as perhaps the most prominent theorist of postmodernism. The account which the book offers of the decline of 'Grand Narratives' has pretty much passed into the intellectual *doxa*, and it is often tacitly accepted even by scholars and critics who have little time for postmodernism in general. Yet *La Condition postmoderne* is also a work which few commentators seem to like very much. In his 430-page book on postmodernism Fredric Jameson barely mentions Lyotard at all, commenting only that his story about 'master narratives' is less interesting and plausible than others, and making of his version of postmodernism little more than a logically necessary variant within the range of possible positions.[18] The lynchpins of the book – its theory of narrative and its account of modern science – have both been discredited by influential critics.[19] Eagleton's book on postmodernism does not even list Lyotard in the index, and he appears in the text only as the occasion for a fairly obvious play on words.[20] Even relatively sympathetic commentators prefer other works by Lyotard. James Williams describes the profusion of responses to *La Condition postmoderne* as 'somewhat unfortunate because it tended to eclipse Lyotard's better work on similar topics, in [*Le Différend*]';[21] Perry Anderson describes the book as 'a misleading guide to Lyotard's distinctive intellectual position';[22] and whilst acknowledging that 'Lyotard is without question best known in the English-speaking world as the author of [*La Condition postmoderne*]', Geoffrey Bennington describes it as 'one of [Lyotard's] least representative books'.[23]

Lyotard apparently concurred in the rejection of the book: 'It's simply the worst of my books, they're almost all bad, but that one's the worst.'[24] With 231 footnotes, many of them substantial, in 100 pages of text, *La Condition postmoderne* has a scholarly apparatus which is untypical of Lyotard's work, and indeed of books of French philosophy in general; Lyotard's *Le Différend*, for example, contains 250 pages of text but not a single footnote. Yet the appearance of scholarship is deceptive. At the time of writing *La Condition postmoderne* Lyotard was entirely unaware of the architectural use of the term *postmodern* which had been central to its development and popularization;[25] and he conceded that the overall scholarly rigour of the work was not all it might have seemed: 'I made up stories, I referred to a quantity of books I'd never read, apparently it impressed people, it's all a bit of a parody.'[26]

This reference to parody may give pause for thought. Lyotard looks as if he is agreeing with his critics that his book should not be taken too seriously; however, only four years before the publication of *La Condition postmoderne*, in 'Apathie dans la théorie' Lyotard had proposed *parody* as the means of undermining the seriousness of theory which arrogated a position of mastery in respect of its objects of analysis. Moreover, the scholarly references – whether or not Lyotard himself had actually read the works concerned – put the reader of the book in precisely the position which Lyotard describes as that of the postmodern subject of knowledge: in the postmodern condition information is available to everyone to a bewildering degree (even more so now than in 1979 with the expansion of the internet), so that it is not so much a question of *what* you know as of knowing *how* to find something out, how to manipulate the available resources and what to make of the information which can be accessed.[27] The problem is one of legitimation not acquisition: information is easy enough to acquire, but knowing how to process and to assess it is another matter altogether. The footnotes tell us where to look, they do not tell us what to make of what we might find. So here we have an instance of how the book is bound up in the topic it analyses in a manner which is, in Lyotard's use of the terms, philosophical rather than theoretical. It does not claim for itself an authoritative foreknowledge of the rules which govern its own discourse. The subtitle of the book describes it as a 'Rapport sur le savoir', that is, a report *on* knowledge, which has knowledge as its subject, rather than a report that purports *to be* knowledge (it is not *un rapport savant*) or to be written *from a position* of knowledge (it is not *le rapport d'un savant*).

So Lyotard's comments on *La Condition postmoderne* may not after all constitute a clear-cut repudiation of his book. He did not abandon some of its guiding ideas, and he returned to it in later texts in order to clarify or refine his views. Of all the major thinkers commonly described as postmodern Lyotard is the only one who readily and repeatedly uses the term himself, and the word *postmodern* recurs in the titles of a series of his books and articles.[28] A substantial part of Lyotard's work is devoted to explaining and justifying what is meant by the postmodern. On the first page of *La Condition postmoderne* Lyotard offers what looks like an admirably succinct definition: 'Simplifying to the extreme, "postmodern" is held to be the incredulity toward metanarratives [*l'incrédulité à l'égard des métarécits*]' (7). As his text goes on to explain, this refers to the breakdown of belief in the 'Grand Narratives', such as Christianity and Marxism, which confer sense on history and experience by giving them direction and goals. But the tangles immediately start to appear. Commentators have been happy to point out that Lyotard himself is surely producing a metanarrative of his own in his account of the breakdown of metanarratives.[29] Certainly, in the opening lines of chapter 1, Lyotard's account of the advent of postmodernity looks like a grand narrative of historical change:

> Our working hypothesis is that knowledge changes status at the same time as societies enter into the so-called post-industrial age and cultures enter into the so-called postmodern age. This passage has been under way since at least the end of the 1950s, which mark the end of Europe's reconstruction.
>
> (11)

Elsewhere also, Lyotard places his own version of postmodernity, which insists upon the incommensurability of different discourses, at the culmination of a historically situated process: 'All the work of scientific, literary and artistic avant-gardes for a century have been leading in this direction, towards discovering the incommensurability of regimes of phrases amongst themselves.'[30]

It is not difficult to find fault with such comments, even within Lyotard's own terms. The sweeping conflation of *all* research in science, literature and art effectively appropriates a range of singularities to a single, totalizing perspective. And anyway the argument falls into a circular self-justification: all branches of the avant-garde are involved in this research because that is what makes them avant-garde; if they are not engaged in it, they are by definition not avant-garde. Lyotard's generalization is tautologically unimpeachable, but has little prospect of persuading dissenters. In other contexts he will respond to the difficulty of producing historical narratives about the end of historical narratives by denying or modifying the claim that postmodernity has anything to do with periodization. Thus, in a footnote to *Au juste* – indeed in one of only two footnotes to that book – Lyotard attempts to dispel confusion about the term *postmodern* by explaining that postmodern or pagan works are produced 'without assigned addressee and without regulative ideal' (*sans destinataire assigné et sans idéal régulateur*): 'Postmodern is not to be taken in the sense of periodization'.[31] In 'Réponse à la question: Qu'est-ce que le postmoderne?', on the other hand, Lyotard outraged some of his critics by claiming that, rather than being simply *different* from the modern, the postmodern was part of it and in some senses *prior* to it.[32] So the postmodern appears to be after, before, and simultaneous with the modern. Or perhaps the grand narrative about grand narratives was never so grand in the first place: introducing his 'postmodern fable' in *Moralités postmodernes* Lyotard describes it as perhaps 'the grand narrative which the world insists on recounting about itself after grand narratives have of course gone bust'.[33] Later he insists that what preserves his story from the fallacies of the grand narrative is that it is not centred on human consciousness, nor is it teleologically based on emancipation or hope;[34] but, as Perry Anderson points out, these were not defining criteria of Grand Narratives as discussed in *La Condition postmoderne*.[35]

## Problems of definition

Successive definitions of the postmodern, then, serve to add to the confusion rather than to clarify the situation. Rather than a single coherent account of postmodernism, Lyotard offers a series of approaches which do not always fit readily together. It would be easy to take his shifts and equivocations as evidence of a lack of rigour and therefore as grounds for dismissing him out of hand. However Lyotard is by no means alone in failing to give a self-consistent definition of postmodernism. Offering, but then fatally impugning, deceptively simple definitions is common to both opponents and proponents. At the beginning of *The Illusions of Postmodernism* Terry Eagleton gives a delightfully persuasive account of postmodernity (the period) and postmodernism (the movement):

Postmodernity is a style of thought which is suspicious of classical notions of truth, reason, identity and objectivity, of the idea of universal progress or emancipation, of single frameworks, grand narratives or ultimate grounds of explanation. Against these Enlightenment norms, it sees the world as contingent, ungrounded, diverse, unstable, indeterminate, a set of disunified cultures or interpretations which breed a degree of scepticism about the objectivity of truth, history and norms, the givenness of natures and the coherence of identities . . . Postmodernism is a style of culture which reflects something of this epochal change, in a depthless, decentred, ungrounded, self-reflexive, playful, derivative, eclectic, pluralistic art which blurs the boundaries between 'high' and 'popular' culture, as well as between art and everyday experience.[36]

Almost immediately, however, Eagleton stands back, as if things were going altogether too smoothly. His concern is, he says, 'less with the more *recherché* formulations of postmodern philosophy than with the culture or milieu or even sensibility of postmodernism as a whole'.[37] The terms *culture*, *milieu* and *sensibility* are already problematic, as is the bold claim to take these 'as a whole'; but now it turns out that the view of postmodernism which he has just presented, and which he will be arguing against, is no more than 'what a particular kind of student today is likely to believe'.[38] Eagleton concedes, and only weakly defends himself against, the charge that he is combating something that never existed in the form he depicts it:

In the process, I accuse postmodernism from time to time of 'straw-targeting' or caricaturing its opponents' positions, a charge which might well be turned back upon my own account. But this is partly because I have in my sights precisely such 'popular' brands of postmodern thought, and partly because postmodernism is such a portmanteau phenomenon that anything you assert of one piece of it is almost bound to be untrue of another. Thus some of the views I attribute to postmodernism in general might well be qualified or even rejected in the work of a particular theorist; but they constitute even so a kind of received wisdom, and to this extent I do not consider myself guilty of excessive travesty.[39]

So Eagleton is attacking not a particular view of postmodernism, but a *doxa* of which he is himself the author. Here we see another example of Picard's approach to Barthes discussed in chapter 1, whereby a critic puts words into his opponent's mouth in order to discredit him. Eagleton concedes that the charge of misrepresentation may be levelled against him, but since he is the only judge and jury in the suit, he has little difficulty in finding the charge unproven ('I do not consider myself guilty'). I wonder what Eagleton would think of an attack on Marxism which, rather than refuting what any particular informed Marxist might believe or argue, took as its target 'what a particular kind of student today' might think about Marxism.

The need to account for postmodernism, coupled with an awareness that any definition fails to dominate the field it surveys, recurs in more favourable accounts of the subject. Fredric Jameson's article 'Theories of the Postmodern' (reprinted in slightly different forms in *Postmodernism* and *The Cultural Turn*) adopts what I take to be a modernist response to the postmodern by attempting a classificatory scheme to explain the range of possible positions: thus an account of postmodernism may be anti-modernist or pro-modernist, and within each of those positions either anti-postmodernist or pro-postmodernist, giving four different positions (anti-modernist and anti-postmodernist, anti-modernist and pro-postmodernist, pro-modernist and anti-postmodernist, pro-modernist and pro-postmodernist); these four positions are then doubled to eight by the possibility that each of them is susceptible to a politically reactionary or a politically progressive expression. However, despite this attempt to classify different positions within postmodernism, in the Introduction to *Postmodernism* Jameson suggests that the topic is at least for the time being resistant to categorization and synthesis for necessary reasons; and despite his lack of interest in Lyotard's version of postmodernism, his position is surprisingly close to Lyotard's practice:

> As for *postmodernism* itself, I have not tried to systematize a usage or to impose any conveniently coherent thumbnail meaning, for the concept is not merely contested, it is also internally conflicted and contradictory. I will argue that, for good or ill, we cannot *not* use it. But my argument should also be taken to imply that every time it is used, we are under the obligation to rehearse those inner contradictions and to stage those representational inconsistencies and dilemmas; we have to work all that through every time around. *Postmodernism* is not something we can settle once and for all and then use with a clear conscience. The concept, if there is one, has to come at the end, and not at the beginning, of our discussions of it. Those are the conditions – the *only* ones, I think,

that prevent the mischief of premature clarification – under which this term can productively continue to be used.[40]

The Marxian ring of 'internally conflicted and contradictory' may have different lexical and philosophical roots from Lyotard's Kantian 'paralogisms',[41] but there is at the very least a convergence here in the suggestion that postmodernism is a difficult and elusive concept for internal and necessary reasons. It is inevitably problematic to give a global account of something which is supposed to be characterized by diversity, fragmentation and singularity, and which at the same time is said to be influential in fields as diverse as science, philosophy, architecture, art, literature, fashion and cookery. So the jury is still out, and not just for contingent reasons, on a series of crucial issues surrounding the question of postmodernism: is it a periodic or a non-periodic term, is it reactionary or progressive, descriptive or normative, the answer (to the problem of understanding what it means to live today) or part of the problem (the malaise of the modern world)? Bennington suggests that, rather than resolving such issues to find the true nature of postmodernism, we might see in the very disagreements to which they give rise an indication of the postmodern condition: 'In this sense, disagreement about the meaning or existence of the postmodern would itself be the postmodern, and we should have enforced at least the consensus that there is a dissensus.'[42]

## Introductions

Given these problems, how does one write about the postmodern condition? From the beginning, Lyotard's *La Condition postmoderne* presents itself as a book which is deeply implicated in the problems it sets out to diagnose. The three-page Introduction to Lyotard's book opens in self-reflexive mode: 'This study has for its object the condition of knowledge in the most developed societies' (7). There follows over the next two pages a very useful summary of the argument of the rest of the book: modern science legitimates itself by reference to a Grand Narrative; the postmodern, on the other hand, entails disbelief in such narratives and proposes instead the incommensurability of different language games, so that none can be reduced or explained in terms of any other; the criterion of the efficiency or 'performativity' in science and society has led to a situation of terror in which what does not serve the system is excluded, but postmodernism offers a way forward by fostering dissent, invention and heterogeneity.

Concluding this summary with a reference to questions which the study leaves open (9), Lyotard lays out in advance the direction that the rest of the book will take. But there are already odd elements here, particularly for any reader familiar with Lyotard's earlier work. The style is curiously dry, clipped and matter-of-fact, perhaps disorientating because it is so informative. Compare, for example, the first sentence of *La Condition postmoderne*, 'This study has for its object the condition of knowledge in the most developed societies', with the opening of *Dérive à partir de Marx et Freud*, which signals a reluctance to present what follows and thereby make it redundant:

> And is it necessary to present these essays? Don't they present themselves? To present them will be to re-present them, to put them in representation. I will place myself behind them, beneath them, I will say: this is what they mean. So my representation will say what they mean, and at the same time what they say will be made pointless, absent, with the value of illusion.[43]

In comparison with this intense focus on the problems inherent in writing an Introduction, things seem to be going much more smoothly in the opening pages of *La Condition postmoderne*. The book begins by giving a clear and helpful summary of its arguments. However, after two pages there is a break in the text, and when it resumes it returns to the self-reflexive mode with which it had begun: 'This text is a circumstantial piece [*un écrit de circonstance*]' (9). It also characterizes the status of its author in disarming fashion:

> It remains that the reporter is a philosopher, not an expert. The latter knows what he knows and what he does not know, the former does not. One concludes, the other questions, those are two different language games. Here they are mixed, with the result that neither one nor the other will work out properly [*ni l'un ni l'autre n'est mené à bien*].
>
> (9)

These three sentences throw a disorienting light on the Introduction we have just read and the text we are about to read. The summary we have been offered was written by a *philosopher*, that is, by someone who is not characterized in terms of his knowledge and authority over his subject; indeed, he does not even know what he does and doesn't know. So the book which is described in its subtitle as a report on knowledge is written by someone who denies having knowledge of the knowledge on which he is reporting. Moreover, Lyotard also warns us that he will break the rules of his own language game. On his own account as a philosopher, he should question rather than conclude; but he will mix these language games 'with the result that neither one nor the other will work out properly'.

This Introduction, then, is a very strange sort of text. It tells us that the author is not an expert, that he does not know about the knowledge he is to report upon, but that he will write as if he had the expertise he has just told us he lacks. It summarizes, and suggests it has no right to summarize. Here again, we might ask whether these confusions are attributable simply to intellectual confusion on Lyotard's part (what a mess this text is), or whether they indicate that the text itself, in its production and reception, is entangled with the issues it thematizes (this mess *is* the postmodern condition, the equivocations about knowledge and authority are inevitable as soon as anyone takes the risk of speaking at all from such a position). *La Condition postmoderne* is not and cannot be just *about* the postmodern condition; it is also written *from* the postmodern condition. It is part of its own topic, as both symptom and diagnosis. And this inevitably affects the text at every level. The strangeness of this Introduction, the disorientating moves with which it confronts the reader, are intimately bound up with the text's subject matter: the crisis of legitimation in postmodernity. And the inseparability of the text's theme from the manner in which it is written also explains why the question of performatives and performativity occupy an important and ambivalent position in the work.

## Performances

At the beginning of chapter 3 of *La Condition postmoderne* Lyotard introduces the notion of language games, taken from Wittgenstein's *Philosophical Investigations*, which will form the cornerstone of his argument in this work and *Le Différend*. He wants to show that speech as well as society more generally are constituted by a potentially limitless range of language games which no single discourse can dominate. To do this he analyses what he calls a denotative utterance, 'The university is sick', in which the addressee is implicitly asked to verify the correctness or falsehood of the statement. This is contrasted with 'The university is open', as spoken by a university rector at the beginning of the academic year:

> The second statement, called a performative, has the particularity that its effect on the referent coincides with its utterance: the University is opened by the fact that it is declared to be so in these

conditions. So it is not subject to discussion or verification by the addressee, who is immediately placed in the new context that has been created.

(21–2)

A footnote to the word *performative* makes explicit that Lyotard is alluding to J. L. Austin's use of the term in *How to Do Things with Words*: 'In the theory of language, since Austin *performative* has assumed a precise meaning' (21).

In the ensuing discussion it becomes clear that Lyotard is only loosely interested in Austin's original sense of the term *performative*, or in the difficulties Austin encounters in his attempts to distinguish performatives from constative utterances. Rather, for Lyotard (as for Derrida in *Limited Inc*.)[44] the performative occasions a sort of philosophical self-recognition. Austin provides a term which, with only a little adjustment, can become a theoretical fulcrum of Lyotard's quite different intellectual project. At the same time, the term *performative* occupies a privileged place because it divulges something crucial about the text's own activity. As Lyotard names the performative and cites Austin, his text is also itself performing something, changing the sense of the term by giving it a new context. So the reference to the performative discloses the text's own status as performance.

In this light it is particularly important that the initial reference is far from unambiguously positive. The footnote which attributes the performative to Austin goes on to anticipate the more negative connotations that the word will acquire in later parts of *La Condition postmoderne*, as it is linked with the attitude which values only what guarantees an efficient result: 'Later on it will be associated with the terms *performance* and *performativity* (especially of a system) in the now-current meaning of efficiency measurable by the relation input/output. The two meanings are not unrelated. Austin's *performative* realizes the optimal *performance*' (21). In this note Lyotard establishes a chain of related words (*performative, performance, performativity*) which will be discussed and used in the rest of the text. *Performativity* is defined by Lyotard as the optimization of the relationship between input and output; a system which runs well is one in which the least input produces the greatest output (25). In chapters 11 and 12 Lyotard shows how the criterion of optimal performance cuts across science, technology, social theory and education. In each case, what is best is what produces the best result, what serves the system best.

In Lyotard's account information technology creates new possibilities which maximize performativity in the field of knowledge. Postmodernity entails the massive availability of knowledge: 'From this point of view, it is not the end of knowledge that can be foreseen, quite the contrary. The Encyclopedia of tomorrow will be the information banks. They exceed the capacity of every user. They are "nature" for postmodern man' (84–5). In this context, the question which faces the scientist or educator is no longer the discovery or transmission of knowledge, but its optimal exploitation:

> The question, explicit or not, posed by the student who is seeking a profession, by the State or by the institution of higher education, is no longer: is it true? but what is its use? In the context of the mercantilization of knowledge, this latter question most frequently means: is it saleable? And in the context of the increase of power: is it effective? The disposition of the competence to perform seems to have to be saleable in the conditions described so far, and it is effective by definition. What ceases is to be effective is competence according to other criteria, such as true/false, just/unjust, etc., and of course weak performativity in general.
>
> (84)

The principle of performativity may not be entirely bad in itself. There may be nothing wrong, for example, in trying to get a car to burn less fuel and thus to produce a better performance for less input. But Lyotard is less sanguine about the extension of this principle across the whole social field. In effect, one language game, with its own set of rules and legitimating criteria, overwhelms all others, so that knowledge (is it true or false?) or justice (is it just or unjust?) are subordinated to a single question: is it efficient? Here, Lyotard is by no means unequivocally celebrating postmodernity, as is largely assumed.[45] The postmodern condition is characterized as the nightmare of performativity; however, Lyotard shows that postmodernity also provides the resources to transform the situation. The idea of performance requires a stable system in which input and output can be calculated (90); however quantum mechanics and subatomic physics disrupt the stability of the system and discover instead undecidability and indeterminacy:

> By concerning itself with undecidables, the limits of precise control, quanta, conflicts caused by incomplete information, 'fracta', catastrophes, pragmatic paradoxes, postmodern science theorizes its own evolution as discontinuous, catastrophic, non-rectifiable,

paradoxical. It changes the meaning of the word knowledge, and it explains how this change can take place. It produces not the known, but the unknown. And it suggests a model of legitimation which is absolutely not that of the best performance, but that of difference understood as paralogy.

(97)

This passage has been severely criticized for revealing Lyotard's limited knowledge and understanding of modern science.[46] The issue here, though, is what sort of language game Lyotard is adopting in his account of modern science. In his Introduction he admitted that he was not speaking as an expert who knows what he is talking about. Rather than *describing* a state of knowledge, Lyotard is attempting to discover or to create an alternative, as yet unformulated, paradigm for the legitimation of knowledge. His text is engaged in the endeavour to conceive of something which does not yet exist, though its possibility is anticipated in some aspects of modern science. Lyotard knows that he cannot simply cast off the principle of performativity: 'But there is no question, in any case, of proposing a "pure" alternative to the system: we all know, as the 1970s draw to an end, that it will be like the old one' (107). Even so, it may be possible to unhitch performativity from its subordination to the stultifying criterion of maximum efficiency. Again, *La Condition postmoderne* is entangled in the problems it analyses. Lyotard gestures towards, and attempts to anticipate in his own writing, an intellectual performance which defies any calculation which can predict its results in advance. In the process he doesn't offer knowledge, or the transcendental conditions which make knowledge possible, but a glimpse of what it might mean to think without knowing in advance where thought might lead.

The book which reports on the postmodern condition is also an instance of that condition; and the aporia that it thereby occupies consists in its offering itself as performance, subject to the laws of performativity, even when those laws are diagnosed as what is most terroristic in postmodernity. In *Le Différend* Lyotard indicates that the performative is not, after all, one type of phrase amongst others, but a possibility inherent in all speech acts:

So the normative: *We decree that it is obligatory to perform such and such an action* would immediately place the speaker in a position of sovereignty. – But what are vaguely called these 'effects' may be observed in all phrases, whatever regime they belong to, because they are simply the unfurling of the instances of the universes which they present and of their respective positions. So the term *performance* is so extended that it loses its ability to designate a specific regime of phrases.[47]

So performance is everywhere, including – and perhaps especially – in the text which denounces, celebrates and loathes performativity. It seeps into the pursuit and production of knowledge as well as into its use, dissemination and reception. And it displaces the Kantian question 'What can I know?' by inserting the question of knowledge into the postmodern cacophony of language games and competing performances.

## Postmodern Kant

In the *Critique of Pure Reason*, following Aristotle, Kant defines the logical paralogism as 'a syllogism's wrongness [*Falschheit*] as regards form, whatever its content may be' (382). In the *Logik*, again he insists on the *wrongness* of the paralogism: it is a false conclusion or fallacy (*fallacia, Trugschluß*) through which the thinker is misled, albeit with no intention to deceive.[48] Kant does allow for what he calls a 'transcendental paralogism' in which false inferences have a transcendental basis: 'Such a fallacious inference will thus have its basis in the nature of human reason, and will carry with it an illusion that is unavoidable although not unresolvable' (382). Kant here accepts that some mistakes are inevitable; his example is that the concept or judgement *I think* leads to inferences concerning the substantiality, simplicity, identity and relations of the soul. We may be bound to make such inferences, but they are still wrong and can be demonstrated to be wrong because they make the impossible leap from sensible intuitions to transcendental conditions; the experience of thought cannot tell me anything about the nature of the thinking substance. So even Kant's concession that such errors are unavoidable does not make them any less erroneous. The paralogism is a mistake, moreover it is a mistake that can be rectified if we address it correctly; it is certainly not, as it is for Lyotard, a summons to dissent or the revelation of an emergent knowledge which disrupts the established rules of thought.

It may look as if there is a gulf separating Kant's systematic unity of knowledge from Lyotard's catastrophic, paradoxical, paralogistic postmodern epistemology. The differences between them are in part what has led some to describe the project of Enlightenment as fundamentally incompatible with (or betrayed by) postmodern thought; the rationalist universalism of the Enlightenment could never recognize itself in the allegedly irrationalist, relativistic dystopia of postmodernity. Yet it is at the very least striking that, whatever separates the two thinkers, Lyotard's engagement with Kant is consistent and ongoing.[49] In numerous detailed discussions, Kant is never simply put in the role of the big bad Enlightenment ogre to be vanquished by our postmodern hero. In the discussions of *Au juste*, which constantly revolve around Kant, Lyotard insists that he is adopting 'a Kantian position', even if Kant might have difficulty recognizing it as such.[50] And at the beginning of *Le Différend*, Kant's *Critique of Judgement* and his historico-political writings are cited along with Wittgenstein's *Philosophical Investigations* and posthumous writings as 'epilogues of modernity and prologues to an honourable postmodernity'.[51]

The importance of Kant for Lyotard is illustrated in *Le Différend*. In this work Lyotard intercalates a number of lengthy Notes dedicated to major thinkers such as Plato, Aristotle, Hegel and Levinas; whereas each of these thinkers gets only one note each, Kant is the subject of no fewer than four. Of these, the first is most relevant to the question of epistemology.[52] Lyotard describes how in the *Critique of Pure Reason* there is no simple immediacy of the given; for Kant, the world is given *to a subject* capable of receiving it, and whose capacity to receive it crucially determines how it is received. Kantian presentation (*Darstellung*) is not an immediate presentation of the world in its simple there-ness, rather it is a representation of the world by the subject to itself. The world 'in itself' is not available to experience. So Kant focuses on the world in as far as it can be known, that is, in as far as it conforms to the epistemological capabilities of the subject of knowledge. Kant may not have taken the step of abandoning the noumenal altogether, but he argues that it lies completely outside the realm of the knowable. Despite an edge of antagonism is his language (he speaks of Kant in terms of censorship and repression, for example),[53] Lyotard describes Kant's thought in terms which suggest that, with relatively little adjustment, it is compatible with postmodernist epistemology.

This postmodern Kant is admittedly a very partial creature. Lyotard's Kant is the Kant of (a certain reading of) the *Critique of Judgement* rather than the *Critique of Pure Reason*, or reflective judgement rather than determinant judgement, the sublime (which exceeds rules and boundaries) rather than the beautiful (which conforms to them), the Idea beyond cognition rather than regulative principles. How far it is possible to separate all these whilst remaining faithful to Kant's texts and thought is a moot point. Lyotard's arrogations of Kantian positions thus entails a strategic and crucial shift of emphasis, from harmony and systematic unity to excess and incommensurability. The Kantian 'conflict of the faculties' could be settled, however unlikely in practice such a settlement might be, if the freedom and autonomy of the philosophy faculty were accepted in a just and rational society; the Lyotardian *différend*, on the other hand, is not susceptible to final resolution, even in theory, because all language games and regimes of discourse intransigently obey different rules. For Kant, philosophy is the discipline with intellectual authority over other disciplines; for Lyotard it can only ever be one discourse amongst others.

On the other hand, perhaps postmodernism gives voice to a strife or violence which is the founding condition of Kantian harmony, the condition which Kant both enunciates and dissembles.[54] The tension of Kant's successful dinner party, discussed earlier in this chapter, lies in the knowledge that guidelines are needed because strife may break out at any moment. In other texts Kant indicates that harmony and resolution are less probable than their opposites. The preliminary comments to his sketch for an end to war are prefaced by a reference to 'philosophers who blissfully dream of perpetual peace'.[55] Perpetual peace is ironized as a fantasy solution to real conflict. The *coalition* of faculties, to which I referred earlier, gives too serene a picture of the vying for authority in which different powers are engaged; an abyss separates the noumenal from the phenomenal, the Moral from the True. In Lyotard's terms, incommensurability reigns, even where the possibility of resolution is affirmed.[56] By the end of the first and most important essay of *The Conflict of the Faculties* Kant has demonstrated that conflict is not necessary in a properly ordered university; but then, disconcertingly, he steps back from what had seemed the conclusion to which his argument had been leading all along. In certain circumstances (in this instance, when the theology faculty presents its teaching as rational rather than revealed) conflict turns out after all to be inevitable, permanent and unresolveable:

> This conflict cannot and should not be settled by an amicable accommodation . . . This conflict can never end, and it is the philosophy faculty that must always be prepared to keep it going . . . Consequently, the philosophy faculty can never lay aside its arms in the face of the danger that threatens the truth entrusted to its protection, because the higher faculties [theology, medicine and law] will never give up their desire to rule.[57]

Here, then, it is the duty of the philosophy faculty – and the philosopher – to maintain conflict even if an amicable accommodation seems possible. Perpetual peace is the fantasy solution which is only half desired and never fully embraced. Postmodernism, with its relativities, heterogeneities and *différends*, may be the Other of Enlightenment rationality, but it is an Other which already haunts the discourse of universal reason, always liable to emerge like the repressed unconscious where it is least expected and most disruptive.

Kant's treatment of knowledge is certainly very different from Lyotard's, but there are nevertheless important lines of affiliation. Even in the epistemology of the *Critique of Pure Reason*, performance plays a decisive role: what the subject of knowledge knows is not the world 'in itself', but the world as he is capable of knowing it, the world as premade by the ways in which he looks at it. Knowledge is produced as much as it is received, and the subject of knowledge is in turn produced as subject as he produces the world he comes to know.[58] Perhaps Kantian knowledge is therefore not so very unlike Lyotard's postmodern version, a relationship with a world incommensurate with the languages or faculties which purport to apprehend it, in which what is at stake is what we make of knowledge and what it makes of us.

# Chapter 4

# After ethics
## Levinas without stories

> Without storytelling there is no theory of ethics. Narratives, examples, stories . . . are indispensable to thinking about ethics.[1]

One of the most persistent and damaging allegations made against post-structuralism is that it effectively destroys the grounds of any ethical enquiry or action. Christopher Norris speaks for many in describing the 'decentring of the subject' as having disastrous ethical consequences: 'By "decentring" the subject to the point of non-existence – reducing it to a mere position within discourse or a figment of the humanist Imaginary – post-structuralism has removed the very possibility of reasoned, reflective, and principled ethical choice.'[2] On the other hand, it has been argued that ethics has been one of the abiding concerns of post-structuralist thinkers. Lacan's seminar on 'L'Ethique de la psychanalyse' was held in 1959–60, though not published until 1986. Derrida's engagement with the ethics of Emmanuel Levinas extends from one of his earliest essays, 'Violence et métaphysique' (1964), through a second long article published in 1980 ('En ce moment même dans cet ouvrage me voici') and to *Adieu à Emmanuel Levinas* (1997), which contains a funeral oration delivered after Levinas's death in 1995 and a conference paper given a year later.[3] Other thinkers' concern for ethics is confirmed by titles such as Nancy's *Impératif catégorique* (1983), Irigaray's *Ethique de la différence sexuelle* (1984), or Lyotard's *Moralités postmodernes* (1993). With some exasperation Alain Badiou described ethics in 1993 as 'the principal philosophical "tendency" of the moment' (*la 'tendance' philosophique principale du moment*).[4] Ethics, it seems, was the word on everyone's lips, and increasingly, poststructuralism has been depicted by critics sympathetic to it as centrally and urgently concerned with ethics;

for example, Simon Critchley argued in his important study *The Ethics of Deconstruction: Derrida and Levinas* (1992) that 'Derridian deconstruction can, and indeed should, be understood as an ethical demand, provided that ethics is understood in the particular sense given to it in the work of Emmanuel Levinas'.[5]

In Critchley's comment, the final clause is important: *provided that ethics is understood in the particular sense given to it in the work of Emmanuel Levinas*. Levinas's thought has been discussed at length not only by Derrida, but also by other major thinkers such as Irigaray, Lyotard and Ricoeur, and he has become the almost obligatory reference point for any consideration of poststructuralist ethics. The claims made by his admirers border on the exorbitant. Jill Robbins asserts that 'within recent Continental philosophy, Emmanuel Levinas has decisively renewed the question of the ethical',[6] John Llewelyn adds that 'his works demand not to be left unread',[7] and Derrida claims that 'the repercussions of his thought will have changed the course of philosophical reflection in our time'.[8] In recent years Levinas has acquired a stature and authority that are almost unchallengeable.[9] Of an older generation than most of the poststructuralists, Levinas played an important role in introducing the thought of Husserl and Heidegger in France in the 1930s, and most of his work for the first three decades of his publishing career was in the field of phenomenology. He was already in his mid-fifties when, in 1961, he published *Totalité et infini*, which gave an ethical inflection to phenomenology and would become the cornerstone of his huge philosophical influence. By the time he published his second philosophical masterwork, *Autrement qu'être ou au-delà de l'essence* (1974), his place in contemporary thought was established. Yet Levinas's ethics is nothing like what a student of Aristotle, Hobbes or Kant might have expected it to be, as it has precious little to tell us about virtues, rights, duties or the public good. Levinas does not aim to contribute new insights to the existing problems of ethics, but rather to alter the sense in which ethics is understood.

In part, and crucially, this entails a rehabilitation of subjectivity against the claim that the subject is dead. In the preface of *Totalité et infini* Levinas describes his book as 'a defence of subjectivity'.[10] This puts him at odds with the prevailing anti-humanism of French thought at the time, which has been attributed to its radical questioning of subjectivity from the diverse standpoints of psychoanalysis, Marxism, semiotics, anthropology or deconstruction. As reflected in the passage from Norris quoted above, or in a more sustained way in Ferry and Renaut's *La Pensée 68*, the ethical and political objection to poststructuralism depends upon the argument that it dislocates or 'decentres' the human subject, leaving it incapable of choice or agency, and there-fore undermining the grounds of ethical action; without subjectivity there can be no ethics. Levinas provides a resource for poststructuralist ethics not because he provides a decisive counter-argument to this line of reasoning, but precisely because he endorses it. Levinas's satire of Parisian intellectual fads of the 1970s could readily be approved by the opponents of poststructuralism:

> End of humanism, of metaphysics – death of man, death of God (or death to God!) – apocalyptic ideas or slogans of intellectual high society. Like all demonstrations of Parisian taste – or distaste – these words are imposed with the tyranny of the latest fashion, but they are made affordable to all and degraded.[11]

Levinas's objection to humanism is that it has not been sufficiently humanist, that it has not gone far enough in preserving the human and promoting the humane. And he entirely accepts that ethics requires a subject which survives in some form. But the Levinasian subject is not autonomous and transparent to itself; it is destitute, radically fractured, exposed to alterity and defined by that exposure: 'Subjectivity realizes these impossible demands: the astonishing fact of containing more than it is possible to contain. This book will present subjectivity as welcom-ing the Other, as hospitality.'[12] Ethics, in Levinas's sense, is this origi-nary exposure to the Other through which the subject discovers itself at the same moment as it discovers that it is not alone in the world, that it is not the master of all it surveys. Subjectivity is hospitality because, before all choice or conscious engagement, it is open to the Other and responsible for its wellbeing; the subject is *hôte* (host), both host and guest, and also *autre* (other), not self-sufficient and self-contained, and (in the vocabulary of *Autrement qu'être*) *otage* (hostage), held by and prey to the Other.[13] This ethics does not teach us how to be good; it teaches us that goodness, peace, generosity and responsibility are the original terms of our relation with the Other, though we can of course reject them if we choose; war, violence and murder are always possible, commonplace even.[14]

Levinas makes two moves which are decisive for his subsequent influence. First, he takes ethics from its position as one branch of phil-osophy amongst others and makes of it instead the key discourse for understanding fundamental human relations; and second, he develops or inflects a vocabulary which will become virtually indispensable to many of his readers and successors: the Other, responsibility, proximity, face (*le visage*), vulnerability, the face to face, justice, the third (*le tiers*), and so on. However, the relative familiarity of the words used by Levinas can be misleading. The face, for example, reveals to me the vulnerability and otherness of the Other; but Levinas warns that the face in this sense should not be understood in phenomenological terms and confused with a part of the physical human body.[15] So, Levinas's vocabulary proves to be difficult to grasp and open to misunderstanding. This provokes a minor industry in introductory guides (to which I have also contributed); at the same time, commentators have an unnerving tendency to replicate or even to compound the extraordinary difficulty of Levinas's writing rather than to elucidate it.[16] The difficulty of understanding Levinas's thought at a very basic level also has consequences for the comprehension of its broader significance. In the original ethical encounter described by Levinas, the face of the Other reveals to me my infinite responsibility and issues the command, 'Thou shalt not kill' (*Tu ne tueras pas*); yet we all know that murder does take place, and Levinas offers little by way of explanation of why we *should*, and why we *don't* obey this command. This raises an important question: how does 'ethics' in Levinas's sense help us to make decisions about real moral, political or legal dilemmas? Repeatedly in the second long essay in *Adieu à Emmanuel Levinas*, Derrida touches on the problem of relating Levinas's ethics of hospitality to politics and justice.[17] Finally Derrida acknowledges Levinas's total silence over the 'rules' or 'schemes' that would mediate between these domains.[18] This leads to a conclusion which risks encouraging those who accuse poststructuralism of being ethically and politically ineffective: there are no general principles that can be 'applied' in particular contexts, so every situation has to be assessed on its own terms, through the lens of Levinas's ethical notions.[19]

Ethics, for Levinas, is an unconditional demand; yet it is never entirely clear in detail what is being demanded of us. As Derrida suggests, even the command 'Thou shalt not kill' (*Tu ne tueras pas*) does not necessarily mean that killing is always wrong, so the one absolute rule that Levinas offers us turns out not to be absolute at all.[20] Levinas puts the Other at the centre of ethical reflection, though he does not tell us in detail how we should treat the Other, or even others. What has been called Levinas's 'postmodern ethics'[21] is an ethics without foundation, rules or universal principles. In this respect, it is at a far remove from the ethics of Kant, whose categorical imperative is characterized precisely by its validity for all people in all situations; for Kant, if it is wrong to lie, for example, it is wrong always and absolutely. In Levinas's thought the hiatus between ethical responsibility and actual decisions that have to be made is not simply a flaw or a blind spot. The reluctance to provide moral guidelines is consistent with his belief that our debt to the Other far exceeds our ability ever to pay it, to be finally and definitively 'moral' by 'acting in the right way'. We can't get ourselves off the ethical hook that easily. The rest of the current chapter explores this hiatus further from the particular angle of Levinas's refusal to give examples, to tell stories which might illustrate, test or strain his ethics. Examples might have helped to provide the missing link between ethical relations and real situations, as well as making the texture of his writing more hospitable; Levinas's avoidance of them is both a refusal to provide such links and an unease in face of the semantic excess which the story might bring with it. First, though, the chapter makes a detour via Kant. A brief examination of Kant's use of examples will suggest how, curiously, narrative invites an element of dissidence into an ethical discussion designed to exclude it. This will contrast sharply with Levinas's avoidance of possible dissidence in an ethics which precisely would seem to invite it.

## Kant's examples

Kant, it is true, uses examples only sparingly.[22] Moreover, Kant's reluctance to tell stories is entirely in accord with his ethical theory. He makes no allowance for individual situations or circumstances; he excludes all pathological factors from moral decision-making and appeals instead to universal rational principles applicable in all cases. There are to be no exceptions or attenuating circumstances. If Kantian moral subjects live in a perpetual state of tension, it is not because they do not know the right thing to do; it is rather because they can never be certain that they have done the right thing for the right reason (i.e. not just in accordance with duty, but more importantly for the sake of duty).[23] Kant does not need to offer examples which would support or probe his ethical theory because no particular situation, nor any number of particular situations, would ever give rise to an ethical maxim which could not be discovered by reason alone. Conversely, the fact that in any particular case something might or did take place can have no bearing whatever on the principles of duty which should command the actions of an ethical subject.[24]

So Kantian ethics barely needs examples; its commanding force is independent of any actual circumstance or any individual subject's ability to obey it. Even so, Kant is keen to show that his categorical imperative does resolve real moral questions. In the *Grundlegung zur Metaphysik der Sitten* he offers two formulations of the categorical imperative: 'act only according to the maxim which you can also wish to become a general law . . . act as if the maxim of your action should become a general law of nature through your will' (42, 43).

Kant then offers four cases where this imperative might be invoked. Is it permissible for someone to take his own life? Should someone in great need borrow money which he knows he cannot repay? Should someone develop his natural talents to the best of his ability? Should someone help others when he has no need to? In Kant's treatment of these cases, it is hard to escape the suspicion that the categorical imperative serves largely to reinforce already-established values and convictions rather than genuinely to discover the solutions to moral quandaries. Kant's aim is to give morality a firmer foundation rather than to change it radically. Thus, it turns out to be wrong to take one's life and make false promises to repay money, and right to develop one's talents and to help others. From a Levinasian perspective, it is striking also that the first three of these examples are largely concerned with the self's relation to itself and its own duties, rather than the relation of self to Other. Even the false promise is forbidden not because it is wrong to lie to others, but because it would make all promises worthless if they could be broken when it suited us. Kantian ethics is essentially an ethics of sameness: the same commands are binding on all rational subjects in all situations and are founded on the unbreachable unity of reason. Levinas describes how Kant's position depends upon 'a plurality of free wills, united by reason' (*une pluralité de volontés libres, unies par la raison*);[25] but, Levinas suggests, this does not account for the possibility that the freedom of others may be limited or even negated by my own, rather than being reconciled with it through the universality of reason. Rather than the rights of man based upon the unity of reason, Levinas recommends 'the rights of the other man' (*les droits de l'autre homme*) which begin with a recognition of alterity.

However, Kant's fourth example does explicitly deal with the relation of self to others, and the difficulties which arise with this example highlight tensions within the categorical imperative. Should I help others? Kant concedes that there could be a general law that everyone should be concerned only with themselves; but he is clearly dissatisfied with this, and he goes on to add that I could not *wish* this to be a general law, because I would thereby forfeit any chance of being helped by others if the need were to arise. But in Kantian terminology, this comes dangerously close to making the imperative *hypothetical* (i.e. undertaken with some other end in mind) rather than *categorical* (undertaken only for the sake of duty): I help others *because I might one day require their help*, rather than because it is my unconditional duty to help them. That Kant is uneasy with this suggestion is suggested by the way he subsequently returns to the example. A few pages later, he offers a new formulation of the categorical imperative based on the precept that all rational beings are ends in themselves: '*Act as if you are always treating humanity, in your person and that of all others, as an end and not just as a means*' (52). This new formulation allows Kant to deal with his four examples once again. The solutions are identical, though the routes by which they are reached are different. In discussion of the fourth example, Kant now explains that happiness is the goal which all humans share; humanity could continue to exist if no one contributed to the happiness of others, but if humanity is an end in itself, then the goals of all members of humanity should also be as far as possible my own goals; therefore it is my duty to contribute to the happiness of others (53). From a Levinasian perspective again, it is striking that this example, which seemed to raise the question of others and otherness in ethical enquiry, is now given a twist which calls it back to the ethics of sameness: I help others because humanity is united through reason, and thus the ends of others turn out to be my own ends.[26]

All of this is coherent in terms of Kant's overall philosophical position. But we might also have the impression that something has happened here through the mediation of the example which disrupts the placid self-assurance of the text. In its initial appearance the example occasions a certain embarrassment because it does not serve to illustrate its point as neatly as it might. It is unruly,[27] it is not comfortably explained or contained by the intellectual framework which it was supposed to serve, it perhaps discloses a weakness which in turn provokes more thought and fresh elaborations of the imperative. Indeed, although the categorical imperative is supposed to be single and immutable, it is susceptible to a range of different formulations which give it a flexibility it might not otherwise have.[28] Its ability to deal with different examples is in part made possible by this perhaps unexpected malleability. The example, as it were, keeps the imperative on its toes, tests it and may find it wanting. And it risks provoking the reader's dissent even when it seems designed to assure assent.

Kant's discussion of the 'benevolent lie' is an excellent case in point here. Kant wrote the article 'On a supposed right to tell lies from benevolent motives' in response to objections made by the French thinker and writer Benjamin Constant to his categorical imperative. According to the categorical imperative, lying must always and unconditionally be wrong, since a rational subject could not possibly want lying to become a universal principle. Rejecting this position, Constant suggests that the duty to tell the truth only holds when the person to whom one is speaking has a right to the truth; that right is forfeited by anyone who intends to do injury to others. There might, therefore, be cases where it was right to lie, for example if we were asked by a murderer if his intended victim were hiding in our house. Kant's response to this is robust and uncompromising.[29] Where an answer cannot be avoided, it is the formal duty of everyone to tell the truth, even if this causes harm to others. If you tell the truth, you are faultless; if you tell a lie, however good your intentions might be, you make yourself responsible for whatever unforeseen consequences might ensue. Kant demonstrates this by imagining an unexpected outcome to the benevolent lie:

> It is possible that whilst you have honestly answered Yes to the murderer's question, whether his intended victim is in the house, the latter may have gone out unobserved, and so not have come in the way of the murderer, and the deed therefore have not been done; whereas, if you lied and said he was not in the house, and he had really gone out (though unknown to you) so that the murderer met him as he went, and executed his purpose on him, then you might with justice be accused as the cause of his death. For, if you had spoken the truth as well as you knew it, perhaps the murderer while seeking for his enemy in the house might have been caught by neighbours coming up and the deed been prevented.[30]

Kant argues that if you lie to avoid a murder being committed, but unwittingly bring it about, you are responsible for it. Kant therefore rejects the benevolent lie and concludes that to be truthful is 'a sacred unconditional command of reason, and not to be limited by any expediency'.[31] Moreover, the lie always does harm; if it does not injure another individual, then it still damages mankind generally, 'since it vitiates the source of justice'.[32]

In this exchange with Constant, Kant's position is apparently clear and argued uncompromisingly through his appropriation of the example imagined by his opponent. But the nature of exemplarity is such that it tests a theoretical position as much as it reinforces it; the example introduces an element of risk into the fabric of assertive discourse. Kant attempts to parry that risk by asserting control over the significance of his example but, quite simply, the reader may be unconvinced. Informed commentators have described Kant's views on lying as 'inhuman' or even 'frankly lunatic'.[33] The narrative whereby our friend escapes but is then discovered by the murderer because of our 'benevolent lie' may seem so strained and contrived that we would not accept that in such circumstances we should be held responsible for the crime. And the abstract ideas of 'injuring humanity' or 'vitiating the sources of justice' may carry little weight if our lie were to succeed in preventing a murder. These suspicions might in turn lead to doubts about the very coherence of the categorical imperative. If it cannot provide a persuasive response to a fairly simple moral dilemma, then perhaps it is fatally flawed.

According to Kant's ethics, the same rules founded in the unity of reason should be valid for all subjects in all circumstances. Yet it is striking that his examples concerning the treatment of others cause a momentary faltering in the authority of the categorical imperative. The story signals a potential blind spot inviting an elucidation which may not be convincingly achieved. Another way of putting this is to say that the story is a site of disruption or resistance through which the text is fractured, brought up against its own otherness to itself. Through the example, the Other slips into the discourse of the same and insinuates a breach within it. The smooth surface of the text is broken, disclosing a moment of indecision, suggesting that the argument is not yet closed, that further revisions to the theory are still possible or necessary, that the Other's voice may still be heard.

Presented in this way, exemplarity might seem to be the ideal vehicle for Levinas, as he endeavours not merely to theorize alterity and openness to the Other, but positively to make his text a place where the encounter with the Other may be staged and experienced. But this is in fact far from the case. Whereas Kant's discourse of sameness fairly readily and generously entertains its narrative Other, Levinas's ethics of alterity is characterized by its aversion to storytelling and to the waywardness of meaning that even minimal narratives introduce into the text. The rest of this chapter will explore Levinas's hostility to literature and his attempt, particularly in *Autrement qu'être ou au-delà de l'essence*, to elaborate an ethics without stories; my guiding suspicion is that the absence of stories in Levinas may disclose a significant blind spot in his thinking just as their presence does in Kant.

## Levinas and literature

I once wrote that it would be hard to think of a philosopher who was less of a storyteller than Kant.[34] In retrospect, that view seems misguided since, in comparison to Levinas, Kant looks like an enthusiastic raconteur. Jill Robbins has observed the rarity of examples of ethical language in Levinas's writing: '*Bonjour*', '*Après vous, monsieur*', 'Thou shalt not kill', 'Here I am'. Few examples of ethical action are offered either: taking the bread from one's own mouth and giving it to the other, assuaging thirst or giving to drink, giving the coat from one's shoulders, clothing the naked and feeding the hungry, sheltering the shelterless, turning one's cheek to the smiter.[35] Levinas does not follow the Kantian move of attempting to show how his ethics might resolve tricky ethical dilemmas. There is no equivalent in Levinas of Kant's example of lying to the murderer, and it is difficult to say how he would deal with a case such as this. When Robbins attempts a Levinasian reading of the story of Cain and Abel, she is careful to underline that Levinas might not endorse what she has said, and indeed she gives some evidence that he would not.[36] In fact, what is un-Levinasian is not so much any particular analysis of an example as the extended discussion of examples at all, at least (as shall be discussed in a moment) in a secular context. There are plenty of allusions to a restricted range of literary authors – Dostoyevsky, Rimbaud, Shakespeare – but these are rarely more than passing references. More characteristic of Levinas's philosophical writing is a reluctance to engage in discussion of specific situations, real or imagined. As Herman Rapaport observes, Levinas 'has never mounted an extensive or systematic meditation that considers historical particulars or examples'.[37]

Levinas's aversion to examples can be related to a broader aversion to art and literature which surfaces most explicitly in his article 'La Réalité et son ombre', first published in *Les Temps modernes* in 1948. Here, writing in a journal founded and edited by Sartre, Levinas provocatively argues against Sartre's enthusiasm for committed literature. Levinas attacks art because it is irresponsible and inhuman, it is a form of idolatry which puts the mind to sleep and shrouds it in darkness; in Seán Hand's words, it 'actively promotes a pact with obscurity'.[38] Literature does not escape this assault. Narrative fiction falsifies the nature of the self and the experience of time and freedom:

> The fact that characters in a book are doomed to the infinite repetition of the same acts and the same thoughts is not simply due to contingencies of the narrative, exterior to those characters. They can be narrated because their being *resembles* itself, is doubled and immobilized . . . Through its reflection in narrative, being has a non-dialectical fixity, it halts dialectics and time.

> The characters in novels – enclosed beings, prisoners. Their
> story is never finished, it is still going on, but it does not advance.
> The novel encloses beings in a destiny despite their freedom.[39]

The point here is that falsification takes place *through the very act of narration*. What is at fault is not any particular novel or any particular novelist; better writers would never be able to be more truthful. Once something is narrated it becomes subject to an inescapable process of distortion and mystification. Even the most capable writer is condemned to sink down into the quagmire of fiction:

> The most lucid writer finds himself in the bewitched world of
> images. He speaks as if he was moving in a world of shadows –
> through enigmas, allusions, suggestion, in the equivocal – as if he
> lacked the strength to deal with realities, as if he couldn't advance
> towards them without vacillating, as if, bloodless and clumsy, he
> always committed himself beyond what he intended, as if he spilt
> half the water he brings us.[40]

Levinas offers the writer no alternative. Literature *qua* literature is obscure, absurd, selfish, cut off from lucidity; and crucially, in moral terms it is pernicious because it fails to acknowledge the priority of the relation with the Other. Fiction's 'pact with obscurity' is inherent in its dependence upon narrative; and this in turn strengthens the suspicion that Levinas's hostility to examples is largely bound up with their narrative nature, and the possibilities of ambiguity, misreading and aberrant interpretation which recourse to narrative might introduce into the text.

'La Réalité et son ombre' is by no means Levinas's final word on the subject of art, and commentators have noted a 'softening' of his attitude in later texts.[41] Some shift in his attitude needs to be discovered if art is in any way to be rehabilitated from a Levinasian perspective, and if the 'unbridgeable chasm between art and ethics'[42] is after all to be bridged. It is certainly the case that Levinas is not always as uncompromising as in 'La Réalité et son ombre'. Indeed, the year before that article was published Levinas had written an essay on Proust, 'L'Autre dans Proust', later reprinted in *Noms propres*, which seemed much more positive about the potential of art. Having dismissed various superficial readings, Levinas promises to tell us what is 'essential' about Proust;[43] this is summarized in the final sentence of the article:

But the most profound teaching of Proust – if however poetry involves any teaching – consists in situating the real in relation with what for ever remains other, with the other as absence and mystery, in finding it in the very intimacy of the 'I', in inaugurating a dialectic which breaks definitively with Parmenides.[44]

If Levinas's aside 'if however poetry involves any teaching' seems a little grudging, the use of the word teaching (*enseignement*) is nevertheless significant, since this is a word he uses, for example in *Totalité et infini*, to describe a productive collaboration between self and Other. Contrary to what 'La Réalité et son ombre' suggests, the literary work may be open to the Other, and indeed its essential lesson may be openness to the Other. But other aspects of this conclusion also give pause for thought. The literature which might (and only *might*) have something to teach us is described as *poetry*, not narrative fiction. Proust has something to teach us – if he has something to teach us – *as a poet*, not as a novelist. Moreover, it is to say the least striking that Proust's most profound lesson turns out to be uncannily close to views that Levinas would spend the last fifty years of his career promoting. The suspicion arises, at least in my mind, that Levinas is not so much describing Proust's teaching as reiterating his own. The most profound thing that Proust teaches him is what he already knew.

Commentators are undoubtedly right to insist that Levinas's hostility to art and literature undergoes shifts, and it would be wrong to identify his final view simply with what he says in 'La Réalité et son ombre'. But if Levinas does express more receptive attitudes to art and literature in general, he does not, to my knowledge, soften his position on *narrative*. This is perhaps why, in so far as he teaches anything, Proust teaches *as a poet*. Levinas's 1973 article on the Hebrew writer Agnon, 'Poésie et résurrection: Notes sur Agnon', also reprinted in *Noms propres*, is another piece cited as evidence of his more positive assessment of literature. Here again, as in the discussion of Proust, finding ethical meaning in a narrative text depends upon discarding the narrative aspects as inessential and redescribing the work as poetry: 'From this point one can read Agnon as pure poetry . . . The poetic meaning of his work exceeds anecdotal or social curiosities, the tale or the "fable" in which they are sought.'[45] On the basis of this move, Agnon's writing can now be appropriated. It turns out to be, as Robbins puts it, 'ethical in precisely Levinas's sense'.[46] I suspect, though, that this neat match between Levinas and Agnon is in large measure generated by Levinas's inability to find anything other than his own teaching in the texts he reads. If Paul Celan, to cite a further example, reveals poetry as 'a new modality of the *otherwise than being* [*l'autrement qu'être*]',[47] Levinas's recourse to his own terminology is again no coincidence. Like Proust and Agnon, Celan can teach only those lessons that Levinas is willing to hear.[48]

So, even in his more sympathetic accounts of literary works, Levinas typically endorses them only in as far as they echo his own ethics of alterity. In part, I am simply suggesting that Levinas is a bad reader of literary works, in that there is a degree of monotony and predictability in his responses to them. But this in itself is significant. Reading the texts of others never quite becomes the encounter with the Other which occupies such a decisive role in Levinas's thought. This failure to read also suggests that his hostility and suspicion to literature in general and narrative in particular are never entirely overcome. Levinas remains uncomfortable with the idea that a text may be a site of otherness, and in consequence his readings never achieve the questioning and fracturing of sameness that the encounter with the Other is supposed to occasion. He remains locked within his own perspective rather than having that perspective challenged and modified. If there is otherness to be encountered in the text, the encounter is missed because Levinas finds only the reflection and confirmation of himself.

## Sacred examples

This failure of reading is surprising, and all the more significant, because in different contexts Levinas has proved himself to be a very brilliant and resourceful reader of texts, including narrative texts. From 1960 onwards, Levinas's commentaries on passages from the Talmud became a regular feature at the annual Colloque des Intellectuels Juifs de Langue Française, and these in turn produced a stream of publications which form an important part of his work.[49] In these commentaries, Levinas typically takes a passage from the Talmud and explores aspects of its religious, philosophical, political and contemporary relevance in a much more free, interrogative, open and humorous manner than can be found in any of his encounters with secular authors.[50] The Talmud, in Levinas's understanding, is an inexhaustible text, full of apparent contradictions but held together by a powerful, albeit invisible, coherence. It calls for commentary, discussion and argument. No interpretation will ever be definitive because there is always more to be said, new connections and resonance to be found. The pages of the Talmud, according to Levinas, 'seek contradiction and hope to find in the reader freedom, invention and audacity'.[51] Boldness of interpretation is *permitted*, even *required* as the only adequate response to a text blistering with meaning.

In this conception, interpretation is a project which can never be completed: 'seeking new teachings, hermeneutics incessantly returns towards verses which have already been interpreted, but which are inexhaustible.'[52] The productive inexhaustibility and the interpretative boldness which it authorizes are founded on Levinas's view of language as pre-eminently exposure to the Other rather than a pointer towards unequivocal meanings. In the Talmud, then, Levinas finds something much more like an encounter with the text as Other than he was prepared to envisage for secular works. Hermeneutic audacity is a response to an ethical summons issued by the written text despite Levinas's guarded response to literature: 'writing is always prescription and ethics, the word of God which commands me and dedicates me to the other'.[53] But here, a problem arises: does *writing* (*écriture*) in this quotation refer only to Holy Scripture (*écriture sainte*), or to writing in general? Why is it that the Talmud may challenge and extend my understanding as if it were a textual manifestation of the Other, but other texts may not?

Exceptionally, in *L'Au-delà du verset* Levinas envisages the possibility that some secular texts might approach the pre-eminent status of the Talmud. All literature, Levinas concedes, commemorates or awaits the religious essence of language, 'whether it celebrates it or whether it profanes it'.[54] This explains the importance granted to 'so-called national literatures, Shakespeare and Molière, Dante and Cervantes, Goethe and Pushkin': 'Signifying beyond their surface meaning, they invite exegesis, whether direct or tortuous – but in no way frivolous – which is a spiritual life.'[55] Later in the same book, Levinas again suggests that 'national literatures' may approach the dignity of sacred texts; they may also be inspired, in the sense of embodying an ethical exposure to the Other which ensures that they are always available to fresh exegesis because they mean more than they say.[56] This prompts a series of questions concerning the special status of sacred texts: 'But what is it that establishes a book as the Book of books? What makes a book the Bible? How is the divine origin of the Word signalled, how is it signed in Scripture?'[57] In other words, why is the Bible or the Talmud different from any other text? Levinas leaves his questions unanswered.

In these comments Levinas suggests a hierarchy of texts based upon their capacity to articulate the call of the Other, underpinning the degree of respect that should be accorded them. Sacred writings are at the summit, approached by 'national literatures', which – judging from the examples of Shakespeare, Molière and so on – presumably refers to the great literature of national canons, and at the bottom of the scale are other secular texts not worthy of canonical greatness. But Levinas offers no justification for the belief that some texts articulate the ethical command of language better than others. The hierarchy looks eminently fragile, resting only on an act of faith and a respect for tradition. The assertion that 'writing is always prescription and ethics, the word of God which commands me and dedicates me to the other'[58] potentially opens up the possibility of an ethics of reading applicable to secular texts, sought by literary-minded commentators such as Eaglestone and Robbins. But Levinas himself does not go down this route; the forms of bold yet respectful attention accorded to the Talmud are not replicated in his response to other texts. Levinas offers the possibility of a different approach to literature, but remains guarded.

This also results in a split response to narrative examples. In the Talmud and in his readings of it, examples play an important role. They are never mere illustrations, since they are dynamically involved in the unending process of meaning:

> Things which are designated in a concrete way, without fading away in front of their concepts, will on the contrary be enriched with meanings through the multiplicity of their concrete aspects. This is what we call the paradigmatic modality of Talmudic reflection: notions remain constantly in communication with examples, or they return to them, even though they ought to have been happy to serve as springboards to reach generality, or else they illuminate thought which probes by the secret light from hidden or isolated worlds in which it irrupts.[59]

Here, Levinas comes close to describing the example as functioning in something like the manner we saw in relation to Kant, as a textual instance which keeps meaning in circulation rather than tying it down. In the Talmud, notions are 'as if welded to examples', discussion 'ceaselessly returns to examples, lets new concepts sprout in them and sets off again in new directions'.[60] Levinas suggests that there is a constant, unstoppable exchange between notion and example, in which neither occupies a stable position as illustration or truth of the other. The example is insolent and disruptive in regard to the authority of the notion. In this respect, the relation between notion and example might be comparable to that between self and Other, when the latter is an unanticipated, unassimilable putting-into-question of the former. And yet, outside the context of his Talmudic readings, the example is most conspicuous for its absence from Levinas's writing. Its dissident voice is unheard and unwanted.

## Without stories

So far I have suggested that Levinas's aversion to examples is related to their narrative format, and so to the unpredictable disruptions brought about by stories and their potential to generate interpretation. I want now to follow some of the traces of this aversion to narrative in what is perhaps Levinas's most difficult work, *Autrement qu'être ou au-delà de l'essence*. In the Preface to his earlier work *Totalité et infini* Levinas announces the aims of his book and implicitly acknowledges its narrative component: '[This book] will recount how the infinite is produced in the relation between the Same and the Other and how, being unsurpassable, the particular and the personal magnetize in some way the very field in which this production of the infinite is played out.'[61] The use of the word *recount* (*raconter*) here is interesting. Levinas informs us that he is going to tell a story; and indeed parts of *Totalité et infini* can be taken as a sort of narrative, in which the self-possession and self-satisfaction of the Same are fractured through the encounter with the Other. When the face of the Other appears to the self and announces the prohibition of murder, a fundamental ethical relation is discovered. But to put things in these narrative terms is already a falsification: there is no self before the discovery of the Other, no event through which the Same is fractured, and the encounter does not take place in empirical, recountable time. Part of Levinas's dissatisfaction with *Totalité et infini*, then, is precisely its over-hasty succumbing to narrative. *Autrement qu'être*, published over a decade later, can be read as an attempt to wrest philosophical discourse and Levinas's own writing away from its contamination by narrative. Philosophy has been turned into a story with which Levinas's practice strains to break, though he knows that the endeavour will inevitably fail:

> But the philosophical discourse of the West can find, in the debris or in the hieroglyphs, the interrupted discourses of every civilization and of the pre-history of civilizations, even if these discourses might seem to be separate. This discourse will affirm itself to be coherent and unified. By relating the interruption of discourse or my removal from discourse, I re-tie the thread. If the philosophical discourse is broken, withdraws from speech and murmurs, is spoken,

it nonetheless speaks of that, and speaks of the discourse which a moment ago it was speaking and to which it returns to say its provisional retreat. Are we not at this very moment in the process of barring the way out that our whole essay attempts, and of encircling our position from all sides? The exceptional words by which is said the trace of the past and the extravagance of the approach – One, God – become terms, re-enter the vocabulary and are put at the disposition of philologists, instead of confounding philosophical language. Their very explosions are recounted [*Leurs explosions mêmes se racontent*].[62]

The tyranny of Western thought is tied to its capacity to maintain its own *plot*. Anything which questions or endeavours to disrupt it turns out to be part of the grand narrative. Even what seeks to destroy the narrative is recuperated to the story, including Levinas's text at the moment of writing. The difficulty of Levinas's project is suggested in the final sentence here, 'Their very explosions are recounted'. Even the reflexive form of the verb (*se racontent*) implies a process beyond the influence of the author, as the endeavour to dynamite the philosophical tradition can be incorporated within the story of that tradition. *Autrement qu'être* refuses narrative, but also knows that recuperation awaits it at every stage. If the text often appears sibylline to the point of obscurity, it is in order to delay as far as possible its reinsertion in the history and the story of philosophy.

Levinas's reluctance to use examples and his guarded response to narrative literature are reflected here in his rejection of emplotment and the particular distortions and violence which it involves. Emplotment is the characteristic activity of a unifying logos which holds 'the last word which dominates all meaning, the word of the end' (262). Narrative takes the disparate, the unique, the singular, and weaves them into a coherent, meaningful web. The resistance to emplotment is then part of the subversion of thematization undertaken in *Autrement qu'être*. Following the distinction between the Said and Saying (*le Dit* and *le Dire*) which is pivotal in Levinas's later thought, the specific content of an utterance is less fundamental than Saying itself, understood as the pre-original exposure to the Other. This Saying is concretized in the Said, which is the domain of meanings, propositions and themes, but the Said always betrays Saying: 'Betrayal which is the price of everything being shown, even the unsayable, and by which is possible the indiscretion regarding the unsayable which is probably the very task of philosophy' (19). Thematization is both violent and inevitable; without it there would be no text and no philosophy, it wrenches the unsayable into the Said and forces on it a meaning alien to it. This explains the rebarbative quality of Levinas's prose, or what Ricoeur has called the 'verbal terrorism' of *Autrement qu'être*.[63] Levinas knows that thematization is the domain of philosophy, but also that it betrays what he really wants to approach: the ethical relation with the Other. So he adopts a textual practice which makes assertions but which obstructs easy comprehension, 'a saying which must also unsay itself' (*un dire qui doit aussi se dédire*) (19).

So emplotment is rejected because of its complicity with thematization and meaning; it is the violence of the Said on Saying which will inevitably occur but can be resisted through the text's vigilant self-subversion. This does not mean that emplotment, the process of making coherent explanatory narratives, is simply excluded from the text. Perhaps surprisingly, it repeatedly emerges at the heart of Levinas's discussion of Saying. Saying turns out, after all, to have a story, as is suggested in the repeated use of the word *intrigue*, one of the principal meanings of which is *plot*: 'The original or pre-original saying – the word of the fore-word [*le propos de l'avant-propos*] – forms a plot [*intrigue*] of responsibility' (17); 'The plot of Saying which is absorbed in the Said is not exhausted by this absorption' (79); 'The plot of proximity and communication is not a modality of knowledge' (82). Saying has its own plot, yet the very possibility of telling the story is put into doubt even at the moment when it is revealed to be a story: 'Can one attempt to show the crux of a plot which is not reduced to phenomenology – that is, to the thematization of the Said . . .?' (78). How do you tell an untellable story? *Autrement qu'être* may be read as the attempt to answer this question as it incessantly gestures towards the plot of Saying, generating a discourse which is intensely focused on its own impossibility.

In chapter 4 of *Autrement qu'être*, as Levinas elaborates some of the key terms of his book, the distraught, traumatized quality of the prose escalates. The subject is described as accused, persecuted, obsessed by the Other, as a sacrifice or hostage who must substitute for the Other and expiate for his crimes. So the text appears as if it gathers together the shards of an untold story involving violence and distress, and which it insists cannot be reconstructed. The whole chapter has the quality of a commentary on a novel we haven't read, and we can only try to work out its plot on the basis of the clues in front of us. The story is untellable, as it falls 'short of all memory, all recall', it cannot be 'converted to memory', it occurs outside 'any memorable past' (165), it is located only in an '*Anteriority anterior to any representable anteriority*'

(195). Whilst the repeated use of the word *plot* suggests the possibility of telling the story, Levinas ensures that it is also untellable. No memory or narrative could reconstruct this story, and even the words which might evoke it evaporate or collapse into one another as we look at them. In Eaglestone's account, 'dazzlingly, "substitution" becomes "one-for-the-other" becomes "hostage" becomes "sacrifice" becomes "exposure" becomes "passivity beyond passivity" becomes "proximity" becomes "trauma" becomes "here I am"'.[64] In the simultaneous refusal of storytelling and the shattered legibility of an untold story, it is possible to see one of the key stakes of Levinas's ethics: the problem of how to translate the unconditional responsibility for the Other into our own lives. The examples which might link my responsibility to my actions, my Saying to my Said, are precisely missing or unrecognizable. Stories are withheld or dispersed and fragmented precisely because to answer the question 'What does this mean?' would betray or falsify the meaning it should have.

In order to come to terms with the astonishing difficulty of *Autrement qu'être*, commentators have suggested that there is 'an intricate relationship between the way in which Levinas's language works and what he wants to say';[65] the text 'maintains the interruption of the ethical Saying within the ontological Said';[66] it 'performs what the discourse discusses'[67] as it endeavours to preserve 'its openness, its function as address, exposure and risk'.[68] Such readings see the aversion to thematization, exemplification and emplotment as woven into the fabric of the text. They also suspend, or at the very least demote, the declarative function of the philosophical text. Levinas's work becomes 'the performative enactment of ethical writing',[69] and as performative it 'echoes literary writing' and becomes 'a part of literature', thus 'opening up literature to the possibility of the ethical saying'.[70] In these accounts, the text is opened out to the reader-Other and its complex verbal fabric is understood as an ethical performance in its own right. And as an instance of Saying, it is only appropriate that it should destabilize its own meanings, rejecting or shattering the themes, stories and examples that would too readily betray the text's exposure to the Other by subordinating it to ossified meanings. Levinas's 'ethics of hospitality' which Derrida has discussed at length would thus be exemplified in this text without examples.[71]

I wonder, though, how many readers actually find *Autrement qu'être* to be a hospitable text. The opening dedication to victims of the Holocaust is moving, but barely welcoming; and the following passage in Hebrew script will be totally opaque to those readers, I suspect most of us, who are literally incapable of reading it. The prose of the following work might be challenging, exciting, shocking, exhilarating, frightening or fascinating, but I am not sure that I would describe it as *generous* or positively hospitable. If the text is performative, as everyone seems to agree, it seems at least feasible to wonder whether what it performs is an ethical *exposure* to the reader-Other or the reader's *exclusion*. I take it that a text's openness to the Other would be the acceptance of its susceptibility to readings which were not anticipated, which come as a surprise or shock. But through the dizzying textuality of *Autrement qu'être* emerges an impulse to restrain meaning rather than to release it. Most importantly, this can be seen in Levinas's discussion of Saying. Levinas presents Saying as a mode of vulnerability and exposure, yet the opposition between the openness of Saying and the closed meanings of the Said is misleading. Saying also has a meaning, and Levinas stresses the importance of *fixing* that meaning: 'This Saying is to be attained as a precondition to the Said, or the Said is to be reduced to it. It is a matter of *fixing the meaning [Il s'agit de fixer le sens]* of this precondition. What does Saying signify before it signifies a Said?' (78; my emphasis). Here, it is the Said which looks unruly, ambiguous, needing to be 'reduced' to Saying in order to tame its betrayals. The meaning of Saying, on the other hand, is clear, fixed, and stated unequivocally: '[Saying] is the proximity of the one to the other, commitment of the approach, one for the other, the very significance of signification [*la signifiance même de la signification*]' (17). Saying doesn't just have meaning, it is the very source or process of meaning, 'the very significance of signification' (*la signifiance même de la signification*). In contrast, the Said is treacherously unstable. Its meanings are 'fables' (81), riven with ambiguity, prone to misunderstanding, whereas the ethical significance of Saying is fixed and absolutely unambiguous. Levinas's prose does not seem to permit for one instant that its assertions about Saying could be open to question and dispute.

Levinas resists narrative because it is the means by which the logos imposes a single, coherent meaning and recuperates deviance and aberrance. Yet this does not fully explain Levinas's hostility to stories. When, in Talmudic mode, he enthuses about the rich hermeneutic potential of examples, it is because they leave meaning radically open rather than because they close it down prematurely. His avoidance of exemplification in his philosophical works thus takes on a different aspect. In as far as the example belongs to the domain of the Said, its radical openness threatens the unequivocal truth of Saying, namely the knowledge that ethics resides in the exposure to the Other. To tell stories about what this means might inadvertently challenge the very meaning they were supposed to illustrate. The story embodies, as it were, the wrong sort of otherness; not the sort that the Levinasian ethical subject is supposed to welcome, but an otherness which may be too disruptive, too traumatic for even Levinas to contemplate. It might even bring us to question the truth of Saying and the primacy of ethics. The problem of stories is not that they immobilize meaning, but that they do not immobilize it enough. The Said is too equivocal for Saying's ethical demands. The vulnerability, the exposure to the Other's possibly dissident gaze which the narrative conveys, is the wrong sort of vulnerability; and for all its performance of ethical openness, Levinas's prose contrives to arm itself against the story-loving reader-Other who might ask the wrong questions.

## Conclusion

The presence of examples in Kant's texts exposes his thought to an element of risk in that the example may reveal a weakness within his ethics; in Levinas's writing, on the other hand, weakness is disclosed by the *absence* of examples, related to a more general suspicion of narrative literature except in the privileged context of the Talmud. Whilst writing about exposure and openness, he is reluctant to expose or open up his own thought. His writing remains curiously enclosed on itself and its own concerns; occasional forays into texts by others rarely add anything new, despite the theoretical desire for authentic encounter.[72]

Finally, this may tell us something about ethics and stories, and the ethics of stories. The Kantian question 'What ought I do?' offers a rich potential for generating narratives. But stories behave badly. Despite what the humanist strain of ethical criticism would like to think, stories are not nice, or not only nice; they are also demanding, deceitful, misleading, violent and disturbing. They echo the mess and confusion of our lives and contribute to it – and certainly not always in a positive way. Perhaps the role of philosophy is to help dispel the confusion. In the reading I have suggested here, Levinas's resistance to stories is a rejection of their resistance to what he wants them to mean. That is also legible in Kant's attempts to master his wayward examples, but I am also attracted by the thought that Kant knew full well that the story threw a theoretical spanner into his philosophical machine. Like the rest of us, Kant would have lied to the murderer if he thought it might help, even if he couldn't quite explain to himself why. Perhaps, then, philosophy and stories realize themselves most when they add to the confusion rather than dispelling it. Samuel Beckett described writing as the endeavour 'to find a form to accommodate the mess',[73] though in his texts the mess constantly seeps into the form. And perhaps, after all, it is the mess which redeems the form, which keeps us from its terrible clarities, and which represents the better part of philosophy, and stories, and our lives.

# Chapter 5

# After hope
## Althusser on reading and self-reading

> For nearly a century now we can read it [Marx's *Das Kapital*], every day, in all clarity, in the dramas and the dreams of our history, in its debates and its conflicts, in the defeats and the victories of the workers' movement, which is indeed our only hope and destiny.[1]

> If there is any hope, it is in mass movements.[2]

For a period during the 1960s and 1970s, Louis Althusser was probably France's and possibly the world's best-known Marxist philosopher. He could readily be associated with a range of concepts and terms: epistemological break, interpellation, overdetermination, process without subject, symptomatic reading, Repressive State Apparatus and Ideological State Apparatus. But the theoretical edifice was weakened by its inability to account for the events of May 1968 and it was brought into further question by Althusser's subsequent self-criticisms and partial recantations, his ambiguous rejection of his own theoreticism and his failure either to break with or remain comfortably within the French Communist Party. By the late 1970s Althusserianism could be dismissed as a spent force, and Althusser 'effectively ended' his career[3] by a frontal assault on his party. There only remained for him to play out a sad history. In 1980 he murdered his wife, spent the next few years in mental institutions and died in relative obscurity in 1990 after years of psychological and physical illness. The posthumous publication of his autobiography, *L'Avenir dure longtemps* (1992), showed up the severe mental disorders that had always been a dark presence in his life and thought, permitting his intellectual achievements to be discredited in the now-glaring light of his crime and madness. A bleak story, but perhaps also a morality tale of sorts, illustrating the demise of Marxism and the poverty of theory.

But the story can also be told differently. Althusser's pupil, friend and collaborator Etienne Balibar has described his sense of disorientation on reading, in 1979, a draft article on psychoanalysis in which Althusser repeated phrases and arguments already used in an article published fifteen years earlier. In the two pieces, however, the same arguments and formulations were being used to support diametrically opposed conclusions: Lacan is a faithful reader of Freud, Lacan replaces Freudian theory with his own; Freudian psychoanalysis is a science of the unconscious, those who deviate from Freudian pyschoanalysis do so in order to establish a science of the unconscious.[4] This brings to light a self-destructive, self-deconstructive impulse in Althusser's intellectual posture which may be more important than any particular concept or thesis. As Žižek puts it, in Balibar's account the last phase of Althusser's thought appears as 'a systematic pursuit of (or exercise in) self-destruction, as if Althusser was caught in the vortex of a systematic undermining and subverting of his own previous theoretical propositions'.[5] In this perspective, the demise of Althusserian Marxism is not so much the failure of an intellectual project as the realization of an endeavour to achieve self-erasure. Even the murder of Althusser's wife Hélène, his madness and final obscurity, can now be read (thanks to evidence provided by L'Avenir dure longtemps) as aspects of his desire to disappear from his own narrative.

A major problem in understanding Althusser and his significance, then, arises from the availability of competing narratives to account for his life, thought and career. However, whichever version one prefers, there is not much here which is self-evidently to do with hope. Even if Marxism in general can be regarded as a secularization of the eschatological aspirations of Christian thought, in which the classless society replaces the kingdom of heaven,[6] Althusserian Marxism holds out no such prospect. If history is a process without subject, it is also a process without aim or end; the historical dialectic is always overdetermined, the superstructure interferes with the infrastructure rather than being obligingly transformed by it, there is always too much going on and too many factors to be accounted for to ensure a smooth continuation of the process of the past and present into a foreseeable future. Althusser may dutifully pronounce his hope in the workers' movement (as the above epigraphs indicate), but such hope is without justification or foundation, wishful rather than proven. Even so, this chapter suggests that Althusser's texts do take up a position on hope, precisely in as far as they raise the problem of narrating and understanding the relationship between life and thought. The key issue here is the link between hope and meaning. Hope is precisely the hope that things are not random, that there is some sense and order behind the mess of our lives. But who or what provides that form? In the present context, the diffi-culty of 'making sense' of Althusser, of his life and work and the rela-tionship between them, is not just a problem for his friends, opponents and readers; the question of how sense is made and perceived, of how a text, or a life, or history, might hang together in a meaningful way are questions negotiated by Althusser throughout his writing. The chapter examines Kant's exploration of his third question, 'What may I hope?', and then returns to Althusser to discuss how his elaborations on sense and senselessness divest Kantian optimism of its transcendental ground-ing and resituate what hope there may be in the reign of chance that Kant sought to combat.

## Kant's hope

Although each of Kant's questions brings with it its own specific problems, those relating to the nature of hope are particularly acute. Whereas both the question of knowledge (What can I know?) and the question of duty (What ought I to do?) have their own proper domain and approach, the question of hope requires that there be some link between areas which initially seem necessarily separate. Kant warns, for example, that the moral law and the pragmatic law should not be con-fused. The former, in the version of it given in the *Critique of Pure Reason*, commands: '*Do that whereby you become worthy to be happy*';[7] the pragmatic law on the other hand advises us only to do what would actu-ally make us happy. Being happy and being worthy of happiness are evidently quite different; giving all my money to the poor may make me worthy of happiness, but it may also make me miserable. It is the nature of hope that it forecasts the possibility that the pragmatic law and the moral law may be one day reconcilable, that doing what makes us worthy of happiness will also result in our happiness.

How, then, can *being worthy of happiness* and *being happy* be brought together, when the differences between them are glaring? What Kant calls *the moral world*, the world in accordance with all moral laws, is 'a mere idea', but it is also practical in that it can and ought to have an influence on the world of sense (738). The aim of moral action is ulti-mately to bring the world of sense ever more in line with the intelligible world, in which the distribution of happiness is exactly commensurate with morality. Although we cannot achieve this individually, we can strive towards its achievement. The perfect coincidence of morality and happiness in the intelligible world requires there to be an underlying metaphysical order which must also have consequences for the world of sense; the intelligible world is held together by a guiding unity of purpose, or what Kant calls 'a wise originator and ruler':

> Reason finds itself compelled either to assume such a being, along with life in such a world, which we must regard as a future world; or to regard the moral laws as idle chimeras, because without this presupposition the necessary result that reason connects with these laws would have to vanish.
>
> (740)

Reason is faced with a stark choice: either the moral laws are held together by a purposive unity deriving from the will of a supreme being, or they are idle chimeras. The latter prospect is clearly intolerable to Kant, so the existence of a wise originator and ruler emerges as the only possible option. Without it, the intelligible world would fall into the same disorder as the world of sense, and that would be contrary to the demands of reason. But if a supreme being rules over the intelligible world, that being could not merely abandon the world of sense to purposelessness. It must be his will to bring the world of sense to ever greater harmony with the intelligible world; and this is achieved by obedience to the moral law. As more people become worthy of happiness, their chances of also being happy are correspondingly increased.

The *Sinn* (sense) of Kant's *Sinnenwelt* (world of sense) has the same polysemy as the French *sens*: sense, meaning and direction. In itself, however, the world of sense does not *make sense*, it cannot provide its own purpose and direction. It is only in the intelligible world that the unity of meaning lacking in the world of sense can be located; but that unity, whilst remaining absent from the world of sense, may nevertheless maintain an unperceived influence over it. Kant's discussion of hope turns out to be a theory of the relations between reason and history in which the world of sense does after all make a kind of sense. In the opening paragraph of Kant's 'Idea for a universal history with a cosmopolitan purpose', the connection between hope and the sense–direction–purpose of history is immediately established:

> History . . . allows us to hope that, if it examines the free exercise of the human will *on a large scale*, it will be able to discover a regular progression among freely willed actions. In the same way, we may hope that what strikes us in the actions of individuals as confused

and fortuitous may be recognized, in the history of the entire species, as a steadily advancing but slow development of man's original capacities.[8]

Individual subjects are 'unwittingly guided in advance along a course intended by nature', unconsciously promoting an end of which they may know nothing (41). The very first of Kant's propositions in his 'Idea for a universal history with a cosmopolitan purpose' insists that '*All the natural capacities of a creature are destined sooner or later to be developed completely and in conformity with their end*' (42). This principle comes first because without it all prospect of sense and purpose in history would collapse: 'For if we abandon this basic principle, we are faced not with a law-governed nature, but with an aimless, random process, and the dismal reign of chance replaces the guiding principle of reason' (42).

This has the consequence that the gulf separating the world of sense from the intelligible world is not after all unbridgeable, even if their final unification is no more than a distant prospect. One day, human-kind may yet be both worthy of happiness and happy, and the world of sense may yet be redeemed from its meaningless randomness. The topic of hope in Kant's thought cuts across all those distinctions which looked irredeemably opposed: the purposive unity of the intelligible world can after all be found in the sensible domain, morality may be rewarded with happiness, what *ought to be* the case *will be* the case, principles of reason operate in the realm of experience. The suspicion may arise that Kant feels obliged to argue for this position because the alternative is too appalling: without such hope, moral laws would be 'idle chimeras', and history becomes an 'aimless, random process' governed by 'the dismal reign of chance'. Kant insists on the powers of reason rather than simply abandoning the world of sense to its own unruliness. What he offers by way of response to his own question 'What may I hope?' is the slow unfurling of meaning in history: I may hope that what appears to be the dismal reign of chance has a purpose that I cannot yet perceive, that the supreme being rules over the sensible world as much as the intelligible world. Kantian hope depends upon the intimation of mean-ing even in a domain where such meaning may seem out of place (the world of sense), and even when the agents through which meaning comes about have no perception of the broader drama in which they are playing. In effect, I may hope that there is reason to hope. And not only *may* I hope, but I *must* hope if there is to be any prospect of trans-forming the mess of our lives into some meaningful whole.

## Reading/meaning

Apart from two articles published in the Stalag journal whilst a prisoner of war,[9] Althusser has little directly to say about hope. But, as a Catholic converted to Marxism – from religious to secular versions of hope – he writes throughout his career about the question of meaning: how it is to established and understood, how we are to make sense of history or lives or texts in face of the apparent senselessness of it all. Most of all, his posthumous autobiography, *L'Avenir dure longtemps*, reviews his past and especially the murder of his wife Hélène in the attempt to find coherence in his own life. The situation there is complicated by his own avowed madness, which adds a further twist to the problem of self-understanding: how should we, as readers, endeavour to make sense of the sense the madman makes of his own life? But the precarious tension between meaning and senselessness is not confined to Althusser's final texts; even his 'classic' Marxist writings of the 1960s revolve around the issue of how to make sense of experience and history. The rest of this chapter, then, discusses the question of meaning as posed in and by Althusser's writing, initially in the theory of reading elaborated in *Lire le Capital* and through the problem of transference in one of his essays on psychoanalysis, and then in his autobiographical texts; finally, we will see how Althusser's endeavour to make sense interrupts the Kantian relay between hope and meaning and finds the remnants of hope in the deferral of assured meaning rather than in the distant prospect of its realization in the phenomenal world.

As a reader of Marx, particularly in his two major texts of 1965, *Pour Marx* and *Lire le Capital*, Althusser's fundamental concern is much the same as Lacan's in his engagements with Freud. Each thinker attempts to isolate what is genuinely revolutionary in the Freudian or Marxist project. This entails close attention, but not slavish subservience, to the letter of the texts they are studying; and the possibility is always open that Marx or Freud, being still partially caught up in the intellectual traditions with which their works mark a decisive break, did not themselves fully understand the true significance of what they were doing. So Althusser poses the question: what is the Marxist philosophy which Marx himself never formulated, what is the theoretical revolution which Marx enables without fully enunciating? Part of the answer to this is afforded by the distinction between science and ideology. What is unique about Marxism is that it provides the means for a proper understanding of the ideology *of which it itself is a part*; it grows out of ideology and, like all other human activities, it belongs to ideology, but it is also a science which permits ideology to be seen for what it is. Marxism is thus both a view *from somewhere* (it is part of what it sees) and a view *from nowhere* (it sees everything). We shall see later that this problematic position is reproduced in a different form in Althusser's autobiography, where the ability of the speaking voice to understand its own genesis and situation is both vital and impossible. For the moment, it is important to note the privilege accorded to Marxist philosophy, or Theory (as Althusser sometimes calls it); it alone is capable of achieving understanding free from the distortions of ideology. This is what Žižek calls Althusser's 'theoreticist elitism . . . which allows theoreticians to "speak for" the masses, to know the truth about them'.[10]

Certainly this theoreticist elitism made Althusser a suspect figure within the Communist movement. In the present context, however, what is most pressing (and again, this will re-emerge in Althusser's autobiography) is the problem of how one person or agency can speak the truth of another. For not only does the Theorist put himself in a position of speaking for the masses, and speaking of ideology without what he says being vitiated by his own ideological situation, but Althusser also puts himself in the position of speaking for Marx, as the title of *Pour Marx* suggests. Because Marx never fully formulated a Marxist philosophy, his texts require the supplement of Althusser's interpretation in order to bring out what was always there, but in inchoate form, misrecognized by its own originator. In the first section of *Lire le Capital*, 'Du "Capital" à la philosophie de Marx', Althusser develops a theory of reading which explains his stance as interpreter of Marx. He argues that the three masters of suspicion, Marx, Nietzsche and Freud, have renewed our ability to understand the meaning of human actions; and significantly it is Freud who takes pride of place:

> It is since Freud that we have begun to suspect what listening, therefore what speaking (and keeping silent) *means*; that this '*meaning*' of speaking and listening discovers, under the innocence of speech and listening, the identifiable depth of a second, *quite different* discourse, the discourse of the unconscious. I would dare to suggest that it is since Marx that we should begin to suspect what, at least in theory, *reading* and therefore writing *means*.
>
> (6–7)

The fact that the tribute to Freud precedes the reference to Marx, who nevertheless came before Freud, suggests that it is through the Freudian revolution that the Marxist revolution is to be understood. A footnote to the first sentence quoted above pays particular homage to Lacan's reading of Freud. Perhaps surprisingly, then, psychoanalysis rather than Marxism appears as the key discourse for understanding the texts of Marx, since it is psychoanalysis which provides the insight that what is unsaid may provide the meaning of what is said. Althusser's account of Marx's development as a reader suggests that Marx perceives this without formulating it as explicitly as Freud and Lacan. According to Althusser, Marx initially subscribed to a religious myth of reading 'which makes a written discourse into the immediate transparency of the true and makes the real into the discourse of a voice'(7). According to this myth, a text – and even history itself – is expressive; it is as if a voice, the logos, were speaking through them, and the interpreter needs only to hear correctly what that voice is saying. Marx's true originality begins to emerge when he breaks decisively with this view of reading:

> It is for a necessary reason that Marx could become Marx only by founding a theory of history and a philosophy of the historical distinction between ideology and science, and that in the last analysis this foundation was brought about through the dissipation of the religious myth of *reading*. Whereas the young Marx of the Manuscripts of 44 read human essence in the transparency of its alienation, as it were an open book, immediately, *Capital* on the contrary takes precise account of a distance, of a gap inside the real, inscribed in its *structure*, such that their effects are themselves illegible, and they make the illusion that they can be read without mediation into the ultimate and supreme of their effects: *fetishism*.
> (8)

The belief that texts say what they mean and mean what they say is identified as a form of fetishism, and in context that term seems to be used at least as much in the psychoanalytic sense as the Marxist: the fetish hides what must not be spoken in an apparently more socialized form of behaviour or discourse, out of which the hidden meaning emerges only obliquely. Readers should look for what the text doesn't know that it is saying and be as attentive to what *isn't* said as they are to explicit statements. Crucially, Althusser also makes a connection between reading a text and grasping the meaning of history. In neither case is there a voice or a message which, once understood, will bring the work of reading to an end.

So, in order to tell the truth – of the masses, of history, of a text or of Marx – it is necessary to grasp that the truth is never what the subject reveals of itself. To illustrate this, Althusser draws on Marx's practice as a reader in *Capital*; and specifically (anticipating and perhaps influencing Derrida's 'double science' of reading), he refers to Marx's 'double reading [*lecture double*]' (10).[11] Initially, Marx reads the texts of his precursors (such as the political economist Adam Smith) in the light of his own opinions, correcting the errors of the earlier author by reference to what he believes he can see more clearly. This is a classic move of argumentative discourse, but it is accompanied in Marx by a second, radically different form of reading. Marx shows what his precursor has not seen, but also the structural interdependence of what is seen and what is not seen, how each implies and relies on the other; he finds a means of understanding the ideological conditions which determine both the visibility of what is seen and the invisibility of what is unperceived:

> So the blunder [*la bévue*] is not to see what one sees, the blunder is not about the object, but *sight* [*la vue*] itself. The blunder is a blunder which concerns *seeing*: so not seeing is internal to seeing, it is a form of seeing, so it is in a necessary relation to seeing.
>
> (14)

Marx's second reading is what Althusser calls a 'symptomatic reading' (*lecture symptomale*), a reading which 'detects the undetected in the very text that it reads', finding in the text a second text which 'is articulated in the lapses of the first' (23). The references to symptoms and lapses might again suggest that Althusser is thinking of psychoanalysis, as the reader tracks the text's meaning through its silences, blanks and repressions. And Marx's approach to Smith is replicated in the approach to Marx adopted in *Lire le Capital* by Althusser and his fellow authors:

> We have merely tried to apply to the reading of Marx the *'symptomatic' reading* through which Marx managed to read the unreadable in Smith, by measuring its initially visible problematics against the invisible problematics contained in the paradox *of a response corresponding to no question which had been asked.*
>
> (23)

The absolute novelty of Marxist theory is that it both understands ideology and its own position within ideology. Marx's advance on Adam Smith, for example, is his ability to see the blanks of Smith's discourse which betray its real significance. But Marx did not fully understand his

own theoretical revolution, which is why his texts are themselves susceptible to a symptomatic reading, a sort of conceptual make-over
practised by Althusser to bring out what was there all along, but insufficiently theorized. However, any prospect that the 'symptom' has finally
been traced back to its first cause recedes as Althusser acknowledges his
own imbrication in the search to make sense. The meaning of Smith is
to be found in Marx, the meaning of Marx is to be found in Althusser,
and the meaning of Althusser is also presumably to be found elsewhere.
Although part of the aim of the symptomatic reading seems to be to pin
down meaning in order to account for the unique ability of Marxism to
speak the truth of others, its effect is also to open up meaning to a
process of supplementation which need never end. The identification of
gaps or blanks within a text serves as a simple illustration of this.
Althusser draws attention to what is unthought in Smith by inserting
ellipses into his text: 'The value of (. . .) labour is equal to the value of
the means of support necessary for the maintenance and the reproduc-
tion of (. . .) labour' (15). Althusser makes the point that, rather than
giving a persuasive account of the value of work, Smith's formulation
distracts from it and fails to question the meaning of its own key terms.
But there is no way of determining once and for all where there is a
blank and where there isn't one. The sentence could be rewritten in any
number of different ways, each drawing attention to a different blank:
'The (. . .) value of labour is (. . .) equal to the value of the means of
support (. . .) necessary . . .' Until we know how many blanks a text contains, we can't even begin to be sure that we have tracked down its
possible meanings; and the interpreter's text may always be susceptible
to further symptomatic reading because of the innumerable gaps which
may be attributed to it.

Far from providing a means of fixing meaning, symptomatic reading
ensures that meaning is produced, in process, but never stable or unitary.
Moreover, misunderstanding and misrecognition belong to the process
as much as or more than their opposites. Hence, in this period Althusser
constantly refers to the project of understanding Marx as incomplete.
The essays in *Lire le Capital* are 'unfinished texts, simple beginnings
of a *reading*' (3), and Marx's *Capital* – and perhaps all texts – are a forest
that may be traversed in any number of ways: 'everyone having taken
his own oblique path through the immense forest of the Book' (4).
So the reader is not set up in the position of a detective who traces
effects to their causes and definitively elucidates the text's lack of self-
understanding. The relationship between text and reader is more complex, less one-sided and stable. Reading is more like a psychoanalytic

encounter in which meaning slides elusively between analyst and analysand; it is potentially interminable because of the limitless potential for fresh associations. We have seen that Althusser's allusions to Freud and Lacan and his use of psychoanalytic vocabulary suggest the importance of psychoanalytic models of (mis)understanding even in his Marxist texts; he explores this aspect of reading and the production of meaning further in his discussion of the relationship between analyst and analysand in his essay 'Sur le transfert et le contre-transfert'.

## Transference and counter-transference

Transference had been identified by Freud at an early stage of the development of psychoanalysis as an important part of the psychoanalytical cure. The rekindling of long-repressed emotions and their direction towards the analyst allows them to be recognized, worked through and liquidated. However, if he wrote at some length about transference, Freud was more reticent in discussion of counter-transference, the analyst's unconscious response to the analysand's transference. Whilst suspicious of the term *counter-transference*, Lacan was bolder in acknowledging the entanglement of desires in the relationship between analyst and analysand. For the analysand, the analyst is 'the subject supposed to know', a projection of the unconscious desire for the Other to have a knowledge of me which I lack; at the same time, the desire which is recognized in the theory of transference is the analyst's own.[12] Analyst and analysand are thus each manifestations of the other's unconscious, each bound up in a drama with the Other in which neither holds the truth. In the analytic situation, then, neither analyst nor analysand has final knowledge of the other, as each is ceaselessly buffeted in the ebb and flow of transference and counter-transference. The question is: who holds the key to the other's desire and the desire of the Other? However, whilst acknowledging that the analyst's desire is made legible in transference, Lacan notes that this is true of all analysts except one: Freud.[13] Freud enjoys a special status here. He is not just the subject *supposed* to know: 'He wasn't only the subject supposed to know. He knew, and he gave us that knowledge in terms that one can call indestructible in as far as, since they were uttered, they bear an interrogation which, up until the present, has never been exhausted'.[14] Unlike any other analyst, Freud was both the subject supposed to know and the subject who really did know.[15] How could Freud occupy this extraordinary position? This is the question which Althusser addresses in 'Sur le transfert et le contre-transfert'.[16]

As we shall see, the problems of textuality and intelligibility will come to dominate Althusser's later work, so that the question of meaning is as much posed by his text as it is discussed thematically. Drafted in 1973 and published posthumously, Althusser's essay on transference is an odd piece of writing. From the opening page of 'Sur le transfert et le contre-transfert', Althusser goes about disrupting the argumentative force of his own text. He warns his reader that its form is modelled on Spinoza's *more geometrico*, a form adopted because 'it made the thought of its author practically unintelligible' (177). Its theoretical and political effectiveness is in direct proportion to its unintelligibility. Accordingly, Althusser insists that he has chosen effectiveness over meaning: 'If by chance the reader had the feeling of understanding, let him be reassured: he will have understood nothing because there is nothing to understand' (177). This reassurance notwithstanding, Althusser builds up an argument of increasing complexity. His premise is that transference is a universal phenomenon. In any relationship between two people, A and B, each operates a transference on to the other. The situation is complicated if A is an analyst. The transference from B to A still occurs, but it is not reciprocated; the analyst must control his or her transference on to the analysand. The control of transference is possible because the analyst has also been analysed, and only those who have been analysed can become analysts. In order to be the Lacanian 'subject supposed to know' the analyst must adopt a stance of neutrality which can be maintained only as the result of a successful analysis.

At this point a major problem arises. Whereas Lacan was content to make of Freud an exceptional figure, not only *supposed to know* but also *knowing*, Althusser allows no such exceptions. In order to control his transference, Freud must himself have been analysed. How could this have happened? Althusser suggests that he might have been analysed without knowing it, perhaps unwittingly by Fliess as Freud was working out the theory of psychoanalysis. But where did Freud learn the theory of psychoanalysis? From his (mostly female) patients. Perhaps Freud recognized in them something which related to his own neurosis and which set his own analysis in motion:

And if we return to the situation in which A is analysed by B, in which someone who has not yet been analysed is analysed by someone who is already analysed, doesn't the situation return us, *mutatis mutandis*, to Freud's situation with his first patients? Can't we say that to a certain extent the analyst may be put on the track of the analysis of his own phantasms by the patient in analysis? And is this situation exceptional, or, on the contrary, the daily bread of analysis? That is what we shall see.

(183)

Althusser's next suggestion, that Freud had analysed himself, leads to a provisional double conclusion:

> We shall retain two provisional conclusions from this: that all analysis is self-analysis, that the analyst A is not the only one to 'work' on and in the transference of the analysand, but that above all it is the analysand who 'works' in the analysis; and that each analyst is pursuing his (interminable) analysis through the 'work' of his patients, therefore that the unanalysed person contributes to the analysis of the analyst.

(184)

The consequence of this is that counter-transference, rather than being a late event in the psychoanalytic process, is actually its founding moment; and through this inaugural counter-transference, the analysand is called upon to make an essential contribution to the analyst's self-understanding. Althusser joins Lacan in seeing the presence of the unconscious as permeating every part of the psychoanalytic situation, but unlike Lacan he makes no exceptions for Freud. The founding gesture of psychoanalysis is Freud's self-analysis through his counter-transference on to his patients, and this is repeated in subsequent analyses. The question of where knowledge comes from is thus twisted out of all recognizable shape. All analysis is self-analysis, yet the self can only be known through the mediation of the Other; meaning comes from the Other-analyst, but the Other-analyst's knowledge comes from the analysand; the subject supposed to know knows nothing other than what the subject supposed not to know has told it. The psychoanalytic situation thus gets bound up in a relay whereby each participant finds in the other, and the Other, a knowledge which is already his own, and attributes to the other, and the Other, a knowledge which cannot be his own. The possession of knowledge is thus simultaneously claimed and disclaimed. What is mine comes from the Other, and what comes from the Other is properly and impossibly mine.

These complexities are further enacted in the material aspects of the text. An earlier version of the essay on transference entitled 'Petites incongruités portatives' had been attributed – by Althusser – to his analyst, René Diatkine, and sent to him to read. Althusser records

Diatkine's response, and his own response to his response, in *L'Avenir dure longtemps*: 'He read the text and coldly told me: these things have been known for a long time. I was horribly vexed and conceived a supplementary grudge against him' (174). The text is clearly already bound up in the analytic process which is also its subject. The analyst is both its (albeit fictive) author and its recipient, Althusser being merely the medium by which the analyst tells himself what he already knows. But the patient is also hurt ('horribly vexed') to have his gift refused, to have his message to the analyst denigrated as self-evident and banal. Althusser sets himself up as being like a child wanting to impress an adult, but who fails pathetically. His plea for approval is turned down, with the analyst repeating the refusal of love which Althusser (according to the account given in *L'Avenir dure longtemps*) also experiences in his relationship with his mother. Everything looks, then, as if the text about transference is also part of the transferential process; its meaning is to be found perhaps more in its material existence as a message sent (fictively) *by* and (really) *to* the analyst than in the arguments it adopts.

The question of the source of knowledge in the analytic situation also takes further the problem of reading discussed at the beginning of *Lire le Capital*. The relationship between analyst and analysand is like that of text and reader, all the more so since the intended reader (or at least one of them) was Althusser's own analyst. As in *Lire le Capital*, the reader-analyst in 'Sur le transfert et le contre-transfert' can never be simply the person who sees and knows the truth of the text-analysand, because s/he is bound up in the process and production of meaning from the very beginning. The reader is thus like Freud faced with his first patient, unaware of quite what it is he knows or is looking for, yet uncannily – and cannily – finding his own answer in the enigma of his patient. But the question of who speaks the truth of the Other must then be left suspended. If Althusser for a period thought that the Marxist theorist could speak the truth of and for the masses or the truth of and for Marx, the innumerable blanks, silence and elisions in any text, the imbrication of text and reader or analyst and analysand, the need for supplementary voices to fill in the gaps that always remain, all this ensures that no one ever speaks the final word for anyone. I only know what the Other tells me, and the Other only knows what I tell it.

All this goes together with a practice of writing which approaches being unreadable and impossible to edit. In the heroic project to publish Althusser's posthumous papers, it is often possible to see the editors' exasperation as they try to establish in legible and intelligible form texts that are on the very edge of sense. The editors fill in gaps, correct mistakes, restore deletions, arbitrate between competing versions of the same passages. Intelligibility is constantly 'compromised',[17] as if a former or future or ideal version of the texts would be free of the frequent blemishes which makes them so disorientating – and exciting – to read. One long typescript has an introduction on numbered pages which do not make sense in the order they are given because some of them refer to an abandoned version of the following text; other parts of the same project are 'fragments with barely any meaning' which the editors decline to publish.[18] Another article is unpublishable in its extant form because it contains several identical passages, sudden breaks or inserted pages in the middle of a sentence.[19] The editors do their best to 'correct' these 'failings'. But they are in a no-win situation, since they must either renounce the prospect of publication or falsify the texts. For the editorial project to be viable, the editors cannot accept Althusser's work in the form he left it, yet something essential to the texts is also lost when they are put into intelligible form.

Althusser struggles both to ground meaning and to destabilize it. Frequently, his texts almost make sense, but not quite; and the compromised intelligibility of his writing is the textual enactment of the madness – linked to the inability to locate and to identify his own voice – which becomes the central issue of his life and thought up until his death in 1990. In effect, he endeavours to make visible and palpable the blanks which he had worked so hard to track down in Marx's writing, not in order for the truth of his text to emerge more clearly, but so that what impedes the production of assured meaning could come to occupy the forefront of his writing. Latent blanks become the manifest content of his texts; and this disrupts the process by which anyone might claim to speak for anyone else: the theorist for the masses, Marx for Smith, Althusser for Marx, the analyst for the analysand, the reader for the text. In the next section, we shall see how the question of who speaks for whom, who holds the key to whose meaning, reaches its most acute point in Althusser's autobiographical writings.

## Meanings/lives

In his posthumously published autobiography L'Avenir dure longtemps, Althusser accounts for his inability ever fully to coincide with himself, his constitutional self-decentring, by reference to his own pre-history.[20] A certain Louis Althusser became engaged to Lucienne Berger around the time of the First World War. After Louis's death at Verdun, his elder brother Charles married Lucienne, and their first child, born on

16 October 1918, was given the name of his father's brother and his mother's first fiancé. The second Louis Althusser attributes his artifice and imposture to the fact of bearing a name which is not his own and being the object of his mother's love which was never truly meant for him. The name Louis contains an affirmation (*oui*, yes) that its bearer refuses, and it also contains the word *lui* (him), making of the self an other and a usurper:

> And especially it [the name *Louis*] said *him* [*lui*], that third-person pronoun which, ringing like a call from an anonymous third person, stripped me of all personality of my own, and alluded to that man behind my back: *He was Louis* [*Lui, c'était Louis*], my uncle, whom my mother loved, not me.
>
> (57)

*L'Avenir dure longtemps* is a sort of detective story in which Althusser attempts to make sense of his own life. Moreover, it is a detective story which begins with a murder (the death of Althusser's wife Hélène) and ends with its explanation. Even if the identity of the murderer is never in doubt, the causes of his act are an enigma that needs explaining. So Althusser's autobiography reconstructs the story which led up to the murder recounted on its opening page, and it ends with the final eluci-dation of the crime. But this gives an altogether too coherent picture of the book and does not account for its repetitions, digressions and incon-sistencies. Much of the problem of the text derives from the narrator's ambiguous speaking position. The dilemma of not having a proper site from which to write, the non-position of imposture, is explicitly raised in the second chapter of the book through Althusser's ruminations on the significance of the legal term *non-lieu* (no-place). After killing his wife, rather than being tried, Althusser was able, according to the French expression, to '*bénéficier d'un non-lieu*', literally, to benefit from a no-place or a non-suit. No trial ever took place because Althusser was deemed not to have legal responsibility for his acts. The *non-lieu* amounts to a state of non-responsibility (36), and Althusser underlines the ambiguity of the benefits this brought. If he escaped trial, he was also interned in a mental institution for an indefinite period, and denied the possibility of defending and speaking for himself. He even lost legal rights over his signature and name: 'considered to be lacking sane judgement and therefore the freedom to decide, the interned mur-derer can lose his juridical personality, which is delegated by the prefect to a "tutor" (man of the law) who holds his signature and acts in his name and place' (37). In writing *L'Avenir dure longtemps* Althusser is reclaiming his signature and voice, but the place from which he is speaking is still a no-place, more a void than a utopia. The issue is how to bear witness to one's own life when you can't even sign your own name. Without a place from which to speak, Alhusser's book is thus almost without precedent (Althusser cites only the confession of the murderer Pierre Rivière published by Foucault as a point of comparison), and it does not belong to any recognized genre: 'I give a warning: what follows is neither a journal, nor memoirs, nor autobiography' (47). Althusser tells us what his book isn't, but doesn't even attempt to tell us what it is.

In light of the no-place from which it is written, *L'Avenir dure longtemps* unsettles the link between the narrator and his account of his life. The madman's sense of the sense of his own story is contaminated from the outset by his sense of the nonsense of stories in general. Stories are lies we tell ourselves about our lives. Althusser gives his definition of materialism as 'Not to tell oneself stories' (*Ne pas se raconter d'histoire*) (247), a refusal to mistake stories for truth. Yet he is also aware that the autobiographical project is an exercise in telling stories which confer a semblance of meaning onto life. He repeatedly alludes to the psychoanalystic term *après coup*, this being the French translation of Freud's *Nachträglichkeit* (deferred action or retroaction), the process by which an event retrospectively acquires a meaning in the light of subsequent occurrences.[21] Being immersed in psychoanalysis, Althusser is aware that events do not simply signify in themselves; they acquire meaning only in relation to other events, so that 'Not to tell oneself stories' is both the materialist's imperative and his impossible dream. This tension between the distrust of and need for stories is reflected in the self-interpretations offered throughout the text. Althusser aims to establish a level of self-understanding which is compelling, leaving readers nothing to work out for themselves. He claims to deliver 'everything that can be known about me' in order to silence those who think they have some understanding of him which he has not himself anticipated:

> For this time all the journalists and other media people will be overwhelmed, but you will see that they won't necessarily be happy about it. First of all because they won't have had anything to do with it, and then because what can they add to what I write? A commentary? But I am doing that myself!!

(236)

This represents Althusser's victory in his struggle with the Other as subject supposed to know. His hatred of having others speak in his place or form ideas about him which he cannot control is overcome through the assertion of his hermeneutic dominance over his own text. He refers to 'the summit of my desire: to be alone right against everyone!' (209). He aspires to be the master of the meaning of his own writing and his own history, and therefore at last the true subject of his own life, no longer a creature of imposture and artifice denied his own proper place. On the other hand, the exhaustive self-interpretation may appear a little *too* compelling, its very excess producing the suspicion that more remains to be said. And whilst excluding the Other's command over meaning, the text also appeals to the Other for collusion and approval. Althusser's proper voice can be achieved only when the interests of self and Other can be brought into alignment. Althusser offers to repay 'what I owe to my reader, because I owe it to myself' (182), and later he acknowledges the same debt: 'On that issue I owe, to myself first of all, but also to all my friends and readers, if not an explanation, at least an attempt at elucidation' (253–4). Meaning is a *debt* which is owed to both self and Other. On the one hand the text looks like a closed circuit in which the narrator addresses only himself ('to myself first of all'); but the closed circuit does not exclude, in fact it requires, the reader's approval if it is to function at all. In the contract of reading implied here, the reader-Other retains a commanding position in the process of meaning despite the narrator's assumptions of hermeneutic control because the reader is called upon, implored, to approve the narrator's interpretation. The debt is owed to the self, but is acquitted only if the Other acknowledges it as such. Despite the relegation of the reader, structurally s/he retains the position of the subject supposed to know through which meaning must pass if it is to be accorded any validity.

In the production of meaning, stories are both distrusted as distortions of truth ('Not to tell oneself stories'), and recognized as the inevitable bearers of meaning. This can be illustrated by comparing the different treatment of two episodes from Althusser's early life in *L'Avenir dure longtemps* and *Les Faits*, his first attempt at an autobiography. Although not published until after Althusser's death, *Les Faits* was drafted in 1976, nine years before *L'Avenir dure longtemps*; so the two autobiographies are separated by the murder of Hélène in 1980. However, just as *L'Avenir dure longtemps* begins with the enigma of Hélène's death, *Les Faits* is also marked from an early stage by unexplained violence, as Althusser recalls two incidents from his childhood. First, for a reason he does not recall ('And I don't know why, I got into a quarrel with a child'), he remembers quarrelling with a child over marbles and striking him. This occasions terror and panic in him; he offers the child all his marbles in exchange for his silence, and he concludes the anecdote by describing its continuing effect on him: 'I admit that I still tremble at the thought of it' (324). This recollection is immediately followed by another which, in comparison, 'was no big deal' (324). He insults the daughter of a friend of his mother, again for reasons he does not recall ('over some trifle'), by using a term of abuse that he does not understand. As the squabble is patched up by the two mothers, Althusser draws a rather tangential conclusion: 'I remained stunned that you can have ideas that you don't have' (324).

In the context of *Les Faits*, neither of these incidents seems to have much broader significance. However, the text was published after Althusser's death under the same cover as *L'Avenir dure longtemps*, and that context throws a very different light on the two memories. Beyond the fact that the first story concerns Althusser losing his literal or metaphorical marbles, both revolve around unexplained acts of aggression in which physical or verbal violence leaves Althusser shocked by his ability to harm others for no apparent reason. The fact that the second incident involves aggression against a female may also be significant, as is perhaps suggested by the memory which immediately follows it; whilst walking with his mother, he observes another act of violence: 'we saw a woman on the ground being dragged by the hair and covered in violent insults by another woman. A man was there, motionless, enjoying the scene and repeating: be careful, she's got a gun' (324). Althusser again concludes that the scene still confounds him: 'I haven't got over it properly' (324). Since *Les Faits* is printed alongside and after *L'Avenir dure longtemps*, it is impossible for us not to read these memories through the lens of Hélène's murder. The enigmas of *Les Faits* retrospectively acquire a significance that Althusser cannot have known they had when we know that he would go on to kill his own wife; or to put it another way, the murder of Hélène is the action which makes sense of the enigma of his childhood recollections. It is as if *Les Faits* were explained by the murder that *L'Avenir dure longtemps* endeavours to explain.

This reading is supported when the two incidents I have been discussing make their reappearance in *L'Avenir dure longtemps*. In the later text the account of the episode with the marbles is more detailed. Althusser now apparently recalls the reasons for his quarrel with the other boy, who had lost all his marbles to Althusser but nevertheless wanted to retain one. The story illustrates Althusser's superiority (if only in the game of marbles), and the other's refusal to accept the proper consequences of that superiority. The violence is thus to some extent provoked. After the blow, Althusser runs after the boy, not this time merely to buy his silence with the gift of marbles: 'And me, I immediately run after him, for ever, in order to repair the irreparable: the harm [or: evil, *le mal*] that I have done him' (71). Here, the stakes are raised. Marbles, once lost, cannot be returned; the childhood anecdote has become an example and foreboding of the irreparable, of evil that cannot be expiated. Several pages later, the second incident is reported. Whereas in *Les Faits* Althusser merely insults the girl, this time he strikes her as well; and whereas the first account ends in some semblance of reconciliation ('The matter was settled by apologies between the mothers', 324), in the second telling Althusser's mother drags him away 'without a single word' (77). This time, Althusser is more lucid about the significance of the incident: 'Another gesture of sudden violence which had escaped me, as in the school courtyard. But this time it was against a girl. I remember not having felt any shame or desire for reparation over it. At least "that" had been gained!' (77).

The two accounts of these incidents bring to the fore the workings of retroaction in the construction of meaning. In the dark light thrown on the past by the murder of Hélène, insignificant memories acquire a more coherent sense, as they become forebodings of the violence to come. The murder is both an enigma to be explained, and also a principle of explanation which makes sense of other enigmas, as it is the most dramatic episode in a pattern of violence which aims to dominate and suppress the Other. *L'Avenir dure longtemps* is thus an exercise in *making sense*, drawing on long years of reflection and psychoanalysis, tracing the murder back to Althusser's feelings of inexistence, artifice and imposture which derive from his substitution for his mother's dead fiancé. However, this account of *L'Avenir dure longtemps* ascribes to the text a coherence which it only ever partly achieves. Earlier, I suggested that the autobiography ends with the explanation of the crime with which it begins. This is in fact true only in a limited way. In chapter 22 Althusser completes his story by describing events following the murder; and apparently by way of conclusion, he offers his own interpretation heavily coloured by years of psychoanalysis: the initial loss of the mother's love produces a feeling of inexistence and a desire to lose or destroy what is most dear; in killing Hélène, the person he loved most, he was also rehearsing his own suicide, his own failure to exist. In this account, Althusser asserts the coherence of his own story: 'I now have reason to think [*J'ai lieu maintenant de penser*] that everything held tightly together [*que tout se tenait étroitement*]' (305). The French expression '*J'ai lieu maintenant de penser*' perhaps suggests that the *non-lieu* has been replaced (re-placed) by the *lieu* (place) of the final summary, the madman now has a position from which to think and to speak for himself.

If *L'Avenir dure longtemps* had ended there, then the explanation offered might have succeeded in holding together the vagaries and difficulties of the preceding text, and of the life that the text reflects upon. But in fact there is another chapter still to come, a further conclusion added to the conclusion that we have already been given. Uniquely, this chapter was also given a title by Althusser, though in the published edition we are only told of this in a footnote. Chapter 23 was to be entitled 'Non-lieu', picking up the *non-lieu* of chapter 2, and negating the place which seemed to have been reconquered in chapter 22. The status of this final chapter is as problematic as its content: the *non-lieu* is both part of the autobiography, but also aside from it, in a place or no-place of its own. With the exception of a short introduction and ending, the entire chapter is occupied by the verbatim report of the words of someone described only as 'an old doctor friend' (308) who has read the preceding twenty-two chapters.[22] This old friend is both reader and supplementary interpreter of the text we have just read. Since the rest of the book is already heavily pre-interpreted by Althusser himself, it is not surprising that to some extent this final voice confirms what we have already been told. Thus, passages from chapter 22 are directly echoed in chapter 23. First of all, Althusser offers his own self-interpretation:

And why this relentless desire for self-destruction? If not because, deep down, unconsciously . . . I wanted to destroy *myself* because, for ever, I did not exist. What better *proof of not existing* than to draw the conclusion *by destroying oneself* after having destroyed all the closest, all my supports, all my recourses?

(305–6)

In the following chapter this is endorsed in very similar terms by the old doctor friend:

you would at the same time have wanted to realize unconsciously your own desire for self-destruction through the death of the person who believed most in you, to be assured that you were just that

> character of artifice and imposture who always haunted you. The best proof that one can in effect give oneself of not existing is to destroy oneself by destroying the one who loves you and above all believes in your *existence*.
>
> (311)

These direct reminiscences have an uncanny effect. The repetition of the same words and phrases creates a sort of excess; rather than simply confirming the truth of what has gone before, it establishes a verbal delirium into which the reader – the old doctor friend – is also drawn. But even this excess is exceeded. The old friend does not merely confirm, he also introduces other possibilities of interpretation, dismissing some as aberrant but leaving others as unprovable and unfalsifiable. Most of all, he insists on the role of ambivalence and chance, or what he repeatedly calls, echoing Althusser's own later vocabulary, the aleatory:[23]

> In truth, it is not a question of 'causal' determination, but of the appearance of an *ambivalent meaning* in the torn unity of desire, which can then only be realized, in the total ambivalence of its ambiguity, in the external 'occasion' which allows it to 'take', as you say of Machiavelli. But this taking itself, which depends terribly on aleatory circumstances (your analyst's letter which didn't reach Hélène, Hélène's total absence of defence, the solitude you shared also – if you had had anyone else around, what would have happened? What do I know?), can occur in objective reality only under highly aleatory circumstances. Those who think that they can give a *causal* explanation understand nothing about the ambivalence of phantasms and internal *meaning, in life and not in the definitive retrospect of death*, they also understand nothing about the role of objective external aleatory circumstances which allow either the fatal 'taking' or else (and this is the great, the immense statistical majority of cases) to escape from it.
>
> (314)

In adding to Althusser's neatly coherent explanation of the murder, the old friend takes interpretation to the point that it has spun completely out of control, as he darkens all previous illuminations and propels the hermeneutic exercise into unchartable waters: 'In truth, to understand the incomprehensible, you must therefore at the same time take account of aleatory imponderables (very numerous in your case) but also of the ambivalence of phantasms which opens the way to all possible contraries' (314).

Althusser's relationship to the Other as source of meaning enacts the ambivalences of the relationship between analyst and analysand in 'Sur le transfert et le contre-transfert'. On the one hand, he wants to be the supremely self-possessed self-analyst, the master of meaning who does not need the Other to reveal his own truth to him. The summit of his desire is to 'to be right alone against all' (*avoir raison seul contre tous*) (209), he violently resists the idea that anyone might 'lay a hand' or 'have ideas' on him (166–7). At the same time, he knows that the truth of the self comes into being only through the mediation of the Other. Throughout *L'Avenir dure longtemps* Althusser frequently refers to what friends or acquaintances have said, and how they provide an illumination that he had not achieved himself.[24] This becomes particularly marked towards the end of the book. Althusser reports the words of 'an analyst friend' (*un ami analyste*) who leaves him 'very astonished, incredulous' (304–5) when he tells him that the murder of Hélène was an unconscious aggression against his analyst; and he also reports the view of a female friend ('What I don't like about you is your desire to *destroy yourself*')[25] which 'opened my eyes' and 'practically incited me to write this little book' (305).

As in the psychoanalytic situation, the subject supposed to know may not have any knowledge other than what the analysand gives to him or her, but that knowledge will not be brought to light without his or her presence. Despite everything, then, the Other emerges in *L'Avenir dure longtemps* as an agent in the production of meaning, even if the meaning that it offers fatally disrupts the understanding that the self had arrived at on its own. And this in turn leads to the closest the text gets to offering the prospect of some sort of ethical relationship; here, the Other appears finally as more like the generous Other of Levinas than Lacan's uncompromising tyrant:

> In the meantime, I think that I have learned what it is to love: to be capable, not of taking those initiatives of escalation or 'exaggeration' on oneself, but to be attentive to the other, to respect his desire and his rhythms, to ask for nothing but to learn to receive and to receive each gift as a surprise from life, and to be capable, without any pretension, of the same gift and the same surprise for the other, without doing him the least violence.
>
> (307–8)

*L'Avenir dure longtemps* comes to us heavily pre-interpreted, pre-psychoanalysed, but rather than closing down further interpretation by effectively pinning the autobiographical subject to a fixed meaning, the profusion of interpretation guarantees that assured knowledge remains elusive. The final chapter of *L'Avenir dure longtemps* constitutes a sort of supplement of interpretation, with *supplement* understood in the Derridean sense: it reiterates, completes, but in the process also shatters the integrity of the interpretation we had already been given.[26] The final word is never the final word; to recall the old doctor friend's metaphor borrowed from Althusser, the explanation never fully 'takes'. Althusser's friend warns him that something more or different always remains to be added: 'That said, you can't prevent anyone from thinking otherwise' (314). And in the closing paragraph of the text, briefly speaking again for himself, Althusser transforms the possibility of the supplementation of meaning into the hope for survival: 'Just one word: let those who think they know and can say more not be afraid to say it. They can no longer do anything except help me to live' (315). At this point the book ends, except for the final initials, L. A., that close the text. These initials are not the full signature denied the man benefiting from a *non-lieu*, perhaps not yet a proper voice or a secure place from which to speak, but they may be at least the sign that some trace of a forgotten voice has survived.

With breathtaking rapidity *L'Avenir dure longtemps* posits, repeats, supplements and sabotages meaning. Perplexity refuses to give way to the urge for knowledge, and the resistance to clarity contains its own kind of insight.[27] Through the supplementation or excess of meaning, the subject holds himself unavailable, for the moment at least, for exhaustive understanding; and in this lies the possibility of a precarious survival in the openness of a still untotalized truth. The text thus echoes the suspension of sense described at the beginning of 'Sur le tranfert et le contre-transfert': 'If by chance the reader had the impression of understanding, let him be reassured: he will have understood nothing, for there is nothing to understand.'[28]

## Hope from Kant to Althusser

In 'L'espérance', written whilst Althusser was a prisoner of war, what possibility of hope there is resides not in the unfurling of historical necessity, but in a view of history as living, not written out in advance:

> There is necessity: it was written. There is life: it is not yet written. Whoever says it is written is giving up. Whoever lives does not say

that. If it is dark all around him, he remains of course in the dark, but have confidence, confidence, he still has a little hope which shines deep down . . .[29]

These words, attributed to a fellow prisoner, strangely anticipate the final lines of *L'Avenir dure longtemps* which appeal for a meaning which has not yet been written, and which will help Althusser to live in an uncertain future. It is essential to Althusser's materialism that history has no direction or end. Althusser effectively refuses the operation of retroaction when it comes to making sense of history. The end does not explain the beginning, and the materialist can have no sense of where he is heading:

> an idealist is a man who knows both from what station the train leaves and what its destination is: he knows in advance, and when he boards a train he knows where he is going because the train is carrying him. The materialist, on the contrary, is a man who takes a train which is already moving without knowing from where it comes or where it is going.
>
> (244)

Althusser's Marxist materialism turns out to be, on this issue at least, surprisingly close to Lyotard's definition of postmodernism as 'incredulity toward metanarratives'. Both refuse any narrative which endows history with meaning and direction. In his later theory of aleatory materialism, echoed in the words of the 'old friend' at the end of *L'Avenir dure longtemps*, Althusser pushes this refusal of teleology to its limit. In the important late essay 'Le Courant souterrain du matérialisme de la rencontre' (1982), he attempts to unearth a suppressed materialist tradition counter to the materialism of necessity and teleology widely attributed to Marx, Engels and Lenin. The latter form of materialism is, he argues, merely a disguised form of idealism; he wants instead 'a *materialism of the encounter*, therefore of the aleatory and of contingency' of which he finds the traces in Epicurus, Spinoza, Hobbes and others.[30] In this tradition, meaning is made through the contingency of the encounter rather than given in advance and pre-inscribed in history. There is no necessary order or direction in history, but this is not to be taken as a counsel of despair:

> From this one can see that we are not, that we do not live in Nothingness, but that, if there is no Meaning to history (an end which

transcends it, from its origins to its completion), there can be meaning *in* history, because that meaning is born from an encounter which is effective and effectively fortunate, or catastrophic, which is also an encounter *of* meaning.[31]

There may be no Meaning, but there is still meaning; indeed meaning is humankind's natural habitat, what it creates or secretes through its contingent encounters as it retroactively transforms them into unavoidable necessities: 'we should think of necessity as the becoming-necessary of the encounter with contingent factors' (566). Crucially, when meaning is not pre-inscribed in the encounter, we cannot be sure that it will be for the better; it may be, as Althusser says, 'fortunate, or catastrophic'. If this is not the most reassuring of prospects, it is at least not desperately bleak. Catastrophe is no more inevitable than triumph. As the 'old friend' underlines, events needed to be only slightly different for the murder of Hélène to have been avoided. The best may not be guaranteed, but at least the worst is not certain.

If this is a form of hope, it is significantly different from its Kantian version. Kantian hope lay in the prospect that the world of sense (*Sinnenwelt*) may be bound to a world of Sense, the intelligible world; in a vast historical sweep, reason and morality may be working towards their own magnificent ends, unbeknownst to individuals and irrespective of the surface vicissitudes of history. Despite everything, reason and history, morality and happiness may be brought together. The alternative to believing this is to see the phenomenal world as nothing more than 'the dismal reign of chance', a possibility too dire to countenance. Hope, then, resides in the coupling of meaning and history. Althusserian hope, on the other hand, resides in their decoupling, in the wresting of individual and collective destiny from the Other's established meanings. Althusser embraces Kant's nightmare of the dismal reign of chance as the best prospect we may have, the only source of hope that everything is not decided in advance. Life may be bleak but it could have been – and could still be – better. A man may after all refrain from murdering his wife. Meaning may still come as a surprise, and not necessarily an unwelcome one; and even a life which has been already written may still be read and reread, and find its meaning transformed.

# Chapter 6

# After identity

## Kristeva's life stories

> Even the most robust amongst us know that a firm identity remains a fiction.[1]

In the initial list of the fundamental questions of philosophy given in his *Critique of Pure Reason*, Kant omitted the one which he would later regard as the most important of all: '*Was ist der Mensch?*' (What is the human being?).[2] According to Kant, this question belongs to the domain of anthropology, but he adds that the other three questions could also be counted as anthropological since they are all ultimately aspects of what it means to be human. With a calm assurance, Kant suggests the predominance of anthropology amongst intellectual disciplines. Influentially, in *Les Mots et les choses* (1966) Foucault traced back the modern conception of man precisely to the moment when Kant established anthropology as the key area of philosophical enquiry.[3] To ask and to privilege the question 'What is the human being?' makes of philosophy pre-eminently an investigation into the nature of man and assigns to it the task of uncovering fixed universals behind surface differences. So Kant's question predetermines the kinds of answers that will be given and thereby constitutes the field of enquiry it purported merely to describe. The question is then a major philosophical event in its own right, since it sets the task of philosophy for future generations. For Foucault though, it is time to wake up from the 'anthropological sleep'. Man is merely 'a recent invention, a figure which is not two centuries old, a simple fold in our knowledge'.[4] Foucault is here trying to set a fresh agenda for thought by pleading for the possibility of finding new questions and new ways of going about answering them. This requires in part that the anthropological conception of man should be dismantled; and for the structuralists and poststructuralists the death of man and the decentring of the subject provided a new, anti-humanist lens for examining the constitution of humanity.

The word used by Kant, *der Mensch*, is grammatically masculine, but unlike the English *man* or the French *l'homme* in normal use it does not refer specifically to the male of the species. Even so, the investigation of man has most commonly been the investigation of men. Kant's own *Anthropologie in pragmatischer Hinsicht*, a work translated into French by Foucault in the early 1960s, devotes barely ten of its nearly 300 pages to women and thereby strengthens a suspicion that men are conceived as somehow more universal than women; men are the norm of which women are the variant. When at the beginning of *Le Deuxième Sexe* (1949) Beauvoir poses the question 'What is a woman?' (*Qu'est-ce qu'une femme?*), she both echoes and significantly modifies Kant's question. Women are no longer to be subsumed under a universal which is modelled on man, and the generalizing definite article of '*der* Mensch' is replaced by the particularizing indefinite article of '*une* femme'. In Beauvoir's wake, even questions in the form 'What is. . .?' became suspect and unacceptable because they seemed to rely upon mystified essentialist premises. In her much-read *Sexual/Textual Politics*, for example, Toril Moi suggested that 'all efforts towards a definition of "woman" are destined to be essentialist'.[5] In contexts such as this, *essentialist* appears as a critical term which requires no further elucidation. However, Moi herself later acknowledged that she had been 'quite insufficiently nuanced about when essentialism is a bad thing and when it doesn't matter';[6] and the adoption of Beauvoir's 'Qu'est-ce qu'une femme?' in the title of her book *What is a Woman?* entails the recognition that questions in the form 'What is. . .?' do not inevitably produce essentializing responses. On the contrary, Moi argues forcefully that Beauvoir's answer to her own question is concrete, situated and materialist, and as such it serves as an invaluable antidote to some of the abstract generalities offered by thinkers who followed her.

So, for the anti-essentialist, anti-universalist, anti-foundationalist and anti-humanist decentred subjects of poststructualist thought, it was not a question of giving new answers to the question 'What is the human being?', and a fortiori its gendered version 'What is Man?'. The questions themselves had to be reframed in order to allow for thought to be liberated. Ironically, whereas Kant had characterized Enlightenment as the escape from self-imposed shackles, the forms of Enlightenment questioning now appeared as precisely the shackles which impeded thought. However, the decentred subject is still a subject *in some sense*, even if it is no longer grounded, secure and self-possessed; and the attacks on poststructuralism which argued that it abolished subjectivity and agency, and in consequence any possibility of political or ethical engagement, were both fatuous and misguided. In this context, Julia Kristeva is an interesting figure. In the 1960s and 1970s her work in semiotics could be taken to epitomize the evacuation of the human from the most abstract, cutting-edge French thought. Her insistence that 'Woman as such does not exist' (La femme comme telle n'existe pas)[7] repudiated at a sweep both Kant's 'Was ist der Mensch?' and Beauvoir's more circumspect 'Qu'est-ce qu'une femme?' by refusing to engage with the terms in which the questions are posed. But Kristeva's work has shown a shift in emphasis from semiotics to psychoanalysis. As both practising psychoanalyst and theorist of psychoanalysis, she has become increasingly concerned with the human being as subject of and subject to its experiences and traumas. Decentred, dispersed, fragmented and elusive, the human subject nevertheless endeavours to reassemble the sense of an existence it continues to perceive as its own. Crucial to this is the subject's ability to construct and to narrate stories. These stories become the vehicle of intersubjective communication, and in particular they establish the possibility of exchange between analyst and analysand in the course of psychoanalytic treatment. Following Hannah Arendt, Kristeva rejects the form of the question 'What is the human being?' and asks instead who it is that the story identifies as the agent of a narrative and a life.[8] This chapter examines Kristeva's conception of the powers and limits of the story and it looks at how her own fiction explores the dynamics of storytelling and its role in human identity. The chapter thus picks up the relationship between narrative and thought explored in previous chapters, but from a different perspective. Whereas Levinas resists stories because of their wayward, disruptive potential, and Althusser is at best sceptical about their ability to make sense of a life, Kristeva is much more positive about the role of storytelling in giving intelligible form to experience, and thereby in ensuring the communication of the subject with its others.

## Narratable lives

At the beginning of Sens et non-sens de la révolte (1996) Kristeva announces one of the central issues at stake in her work and thought in the mid-1990s:

> One of the stakes consists in getting beyond the notion of text, to the elaboration of which I contributed with so many others and

which has become a form of dogma in the best universities of France, not to mention the United States and other even more exotic places. I will attempt to introduce, instead, the notion of *experience* which includes the pleasure principle as well as the principle of rebirth of meaning for the other and which cannot be understood except on the horizon of revolt-experience.[9]

Whilst not quite rejecting her earlier work, Kristeva's words read like something of a *mea culpa*. At the beginning of *Séméiotiké* (1969) Kristeva had described how 'textual practice decentres the subject of a discourse (or meaning, of a structure) and is constructed as the operation of its pulverization into a differentiated infinity'.[10] Here, the focus is on the activity of the text rather than on its subject or meaning. However, as Leslie Hill has observed, in Kristeva's approach to literature the focus on non-signifying semiotic aspects of texts in early works such as *Séméiotiké* and her thesis, published as *La Révolution du langage poétique* (1974), gives way in her later work, so that the thematic dimension increasingly comes to predominate.[11] For the later Kristeva literature is the site of experience and a means of communication with others. Whereas the text decentres and pulverizes the subject, the notion of experience preserves it, at least in some form. Writing is now viewed as an affirmation and exploration of subjectivity, however problematic, endangered or uncertain it may be.

This rehabilitation of experience and meaning is also a rehabilitation of the value of storytelling. If Kristeva's early work tended to privilege avant-garde, non-narrative literature (Artaud, Lautréamont, Mallarmé), her more recent writing emphasizes the desire for and necessity of stories. Her first novel, *Les Samouraïs* begins with the lament, 'There are no more love stories [*Il n'y a plus d'histoires d'amour*]. However, women want them, as do men when they are not ashamed to be tender and sad like women.'[12] In particular in her work on Hannah Arendt, Kristeva develops a view of the story as the essential means for encapsulating the sense of a life. In Arendt, Kristeva finds a thinker for whom narration is a defining human activity:

> In this way, then, the possibility of representing to ourselves birth and death, to think of them in time and to say them to the Other by sharing them with others – in short, the *possibility of recounting* –, founds human life in so far as it is specific, non-animal, non-physiological.

(76)

The crucial distinction here is between *zoe* and *bios*; the first is bare biological life whereas the second is life capable of acquiring meaning, of becoming a biography. The ability to recount one's life, and to live life as recountable,[13] is what lifts humankind above pure animal existence. Moreover, narratability gives purpose to political action by inscribing it in the experience and memory of the broader community. An action, however heroic, is only fully complete when it is recalled, and hence when it is witnessed and recounted by others. The narrator of the story thus plays a necessary role in its realization, ensuring that its significance is made available to others. Kristeva outlines the conditions by which action becomes narration, and hence an essential part of a group's cohesion:

> Here we are at the heart of Arendt's conception: for a true story to become a narrated story, two inseparable conditions are necessary. First of all, the existence of a *being-amongst* [*inter-esse*] in and through which are then formed *memory* and *testimony*. The fate of narrative depends on a situation of being with others out of which arises the resolving logic of memorization as detachment from the lived *ex post facto*. Only under these conditions can the 'fact' be revealed in 'shareable thought' by the verbalization of a 'plot'.
>
> (125)

Humankind, then, derives its specificity from its ability to tell stories. A crucial part of this conception, which is of particular importance for Kristeva, is the co-implication of selves and others in the loop of storytelling. A story cannot just be what a solipsistic subject recounts to itself. It is bound up in history and it implies the existence of a community because it requires agents who act, witnesses who recount, and audiences who listen and recount in their turn. The essential function of the story is to identify a human subject who is the agent of the narrated actions and to find in his or her actions a significance that may not have been visible previously. The pattern or the meaning that may then be found in the life of the subject may be sketched in the story that is told, but it can be realized only in the understanding of the listeners or readers. The life is a sign, and as such it is 'condensed, lacunary, fragmentary: it launches the infinite action of interpretation' (126). It points towards the possibility of a meaning, but requires the involvement of others for its meaning to become explicit.

The necessary involvement of others in the circuit of storytelling is one of the features which link it to Kristeva's view of psychoanalytic treatment. The story identifies an agent, and crucially that agent is revealed and constituted in the story as being *in relation with others*: witnesses, narrators, listeners and readers. Narration prevents an action from being forgotten and also opens it up to interpretation, thereby making its potential for meaning available to a wider community. This focus on storytelling displaces the Kantian question 'What is the human being?' and asks instead about individuals and their relations to others. The Italian philosopher Adriana Cavarero, who also draws heavily on Arendt, identifies this displacement as the demise of a universalizing ethic which excludes the specificity and uniqueness of the individual story. Instead, she proposes a relational account of identity in which storytelling plays a vital role. Without others, there is no story to tell, no one to tell it, and no one to whom it can be told. The relation with others through storytelling is not an optional or accidental extra in an otherwise self-contained life, it is the very condition of human existence:

> Only in the improbable case of a life spent in perfect solitude could the autobiography of a human being tell the absurd story of an unexposed identity, without relations and without world. The existent is the exposable *and* the narratable: neither exposability nor narratability, which together constitute this peculiarly human uniqueness, can be taken away.'[14]

A life is a life in as far as it is a life *story*, with a pattern that emerges as it is told by and to others. Cavarero describes this primary exposure to others as *altruism*: 'Prior to being a generous life-style in the service of others, altruism is indeed the foundational principle of a self that knows itself to be constituted by another: *the necessary other*.'[15]

The importance of the story in the constitution of the self involves privileging specificity and particularity rather than universal or essential characteristics. Where general rules and immutable principles are no longer available, stories offer individual cases and examples for consideration. Moreover, the story is not just a vehicle for reflection, it is also the site where identity is constructed. According to the philosopher Alasdair MacIntyre, the stories our culture passes on to us help to make us what we are. They condition the intelligibility and coherence of our lives, determine how we live, and make our experiences recountable to others. The unity of a life is not explicable in psychological terms; it can be grasped only in so far as a life is narratable, and in so far as individuals can give account of themselves to others. Thus, MacIntyre argues that any attempt to elucidate personal identity which separates it from narrative, intelligibility and accountability is bound to fail.[16] In similar vein, Richard Kearney argues that telling and listening to stories is a major part of what it means to be properly human, and that stories are intimately bound up with our lives: 'there is an abiding recognition that existence is inherently storied. Life is pregnant with stories. It is a nascent plot in search of a midwife.'[17]

So Kristeva's interest in Arendt can be related to a broader philosophical context in both France and the anglophone world. Rather than essences, universals, fixed rules and immutable principles, stories offer a world of discrete instances saved from anarchy and formlessness by the shared project of storytelling. Lives are bound together by the stories that are exchanged between selves and others. However, in this consensus on the role of storytelling, it is striking that little discussion is devoted to the problem of what a story actually is. Its forms and conditions are barely scrutinized. The narration of experience and the recognition of stories are depicted as if they were fairly straightforward. MacIntyre quotes from Sartre's *La Nausée*, in which the protagonist Roquentin declares that 'you have to choose: to live or to recount' (*il faut choisir: vivre ou raconter*).[18] For MacIntyre, however, there is need to choose between living and narrating. Roquentin's suggestion that stories may falsify experience is dismissed as nonsense. In MacIntyre's view, our lives as we live them are already stories, or at least parts of some possible narrative; and as such, although they may be unpredictable, they inevitably have a certain teleological character.[19] Storytelling is unproblematic because stories are our natural medium; we inhabit them and they inhabit us.

For Kristeva, things are not so simple. Her interest in stories derives in large measure from the insight that they are difficult to recount, on the very edge of sense and effability, and their relationship to our experience and lives can never be taken for granted. As we have seen, her first novel *Les Samouraïs* begins by lamenting the shortage of stories: 'There are no more love stories.' At the beginning of her own *Histoires d'amour*, she attempts to explain this shortage in terms of a difficulty with language: 'As far back as I can recall my loves, it is difficult for me to speak of them.'[20] In the contradictions and equivocations of love, there is both too little and too much meaning; the limits of identity are lost, and the sense and reference of language lose their precision.[21] Love puts the ability to communicate to the severest test, so to tell a love story is to attempt the near-impossible: to try to put into words an experience which dislocates language. For Kristeva, the only stories worth telling are ones which seek to cross over the edge between what can and cannot be said and experienced. Literature may be the site of narratable experience, but for Kristeva the key event of modern literature has been what she calls, with a characteristic avant-garde sense of drama, '*the encounter of literature with the impossible*'.[22] Modern literature is a radical exploration of the resources and limits of language: 'what to say? how to say? what does "to say" signify? to make and to unmake meaning?'.[23] It explores the blind spots of consciousness and becomes associated with madness; and the sense it makes is always on the edge of nonsense. In consequence, the notion of the story and the possibility of narration are far more problematic than they appear to be for Cavarero or MacIntyre or Arendt. For them, the notion of the story is relatively unproblematic, whereas for Kristeva its form, meaning and possibility can never be taken for granted.

So, although she learns a great deal from Arendt, Kristeva does not entirely share her interests and emphases, even if she only hints at her differences. If for Arendt the story cannot be naively identified with lived experience, it is nevertheless through the story that such experience is given meaning and made public. Whilst not being merely a straightforward record of lived events, it is not strictly *fiction* either. It is the mode of presentation of life to others. Arendt's conception privileges the writing of biographies or narratives which bear witness to actions of historical, political or social significance. She is not interested in literary experimentation or in problems of narrative or style. Kristeva is struck by Arendt's blindness towards the workings of modern literature, revealed, for example, when she commends Kafka for his 'absence of style'.[24] Even in discussion of Nathalie Sarraute, Arendt bypasses questions of technique in order to focus on the revelation of social mechanisms (154). The kind of story to which Arendt refers is implicitly a straightforward narrative which does not question its own language or structure. Arendt does not look into the reasons why many writers contemporary to her rejected the forms and limits of this sort of narrative. For her, what is specific to human existence is the possibility of narrating, and narrating itself is a relatively unproblematized process. Even when not literally true, the story is the vehicle through which reality becomes meaningful and known in the community of selves and others. With her intense involvement in the avant-garde, as theorist, critic and writer, Kristeva cannot accept Arendt's unquestioning endorsement of a model of narrative which passes so readily from reality to meaning:

It may be regretted that Arendt does not appreciate the intra-psychic, but also historical, need for *revolt* which led the avant-gardes of this century to an unprecedented re-evaluation of the structures of narrative, of the word, and of the Self . . . Art, and especially narrative art, have a history which does not repeat either the stakes or the solutions of the past, and which is today closer to a clinical protocol than a moral judgement. It is our task to uncover the causes and the destiny of this history, not to stigmatize it.

(156–7)

Although Kristeva does not elaborate here, she hints at two related areas in which her interest in narrative departs from Arendt's: Arendt pays scant attention to the forms of narrative or to the reasons why those forms have been brought into question; and largely because of this, she misses what is for Kristeva the crucial link between the stakes of modern fiction and those of psychoanalysis. For Kristeva, the re-evaluation of narrative, self and language are all of a piece, and the invention of psychoanalysis by Freud is the founding event which explains, enables and necessitates the re-invention of selves, of stories, and of the language which connects them.

## Psychoanalysis and the gift of meaning

Whilst rejecting the choice posed in Sartre's *La Nausée* between living and recounting, MacIntyre acknowledges that there are some people who fail to perceive their own lives as a meaningful narrative:

When someone complains – as do some of those who attempt or commit suicide – that his or her life is meaningless, he or she is often and perhaps characteristically complaining that the narrative of their life has become unintelligible to them, that it lacks any point, any movement towards a climax or a *telos*.[25]

Cavarero, quoting Arendt, also concedes that without the meaning conferred by the story, life would be 'an intolerable sequence of events'.[26] For none of these thinkers then, despite their insistence on the essential role of the story as the vehicle of identity, is life always and inevitably meaningful. All envisage a state where the subject is unable to recognize or to construct the meaning of its own narrative, though they suggest that such a state is unbearable. However, none suggests any means by which a story can be supplied when no design or pattern emerges spontaneously or easily. This is the point at which Kristeva's understanding of psychoanalysis comes into its own, because psychoanalysis provides a theory and a protocol for the emergence of stories out of the formless matter of experience. It is concerned precisely with those subjects for whom words and stories are drained of meaning. 'I am trying to get her to recount her story', says the psychoanalyst of her patient in Kristeva's *Les Samouraïs*.[27] Only when the patient begins to recount is the cure under way; recounting entails the acceptance of the story as project, as gesture towards the possibility of meaning, and as link with others. Only through this restored link can the word drained of sense be restored to the process of meaning.

In *Sens et non-sens de la révolte* Kristeva's account of the development of Freud's views on language justifies the central role of storytelling in psychoanalysis. In this account, psychoanalysis comes into its own in *The Interpretation of Dreams* when Freud begins to elaborate what Kristeva calls his optimistic model of language based on the practice of free association. The question which psychoanalysis poses is: how can the unconscious be known? If the unconscious is genuinely alien and inaccessible to consciousness, then the whole project of psychoanalysis falters. But free association permits a seepage of unconscious material into language, and hence into the psychoanalytic process. This is possible, according to this optimistic model of language, because, although the unconscious is not made up of language nor does language belong to the unconscious, the two do not exist independently from one another. Language is on the borders of consciousness and the unconscious, and it enables communication between them. Moreover, Kristeva accepts Lacan's description of the unconscious as 'structured like a language'. The unconscious has a kind of order, as can be seen for example in the interpretation of dreams: the processes of displacement, condensation and overdetermination constitute a grammar and a rhetoric which make the dream available to understanding. Free association unlocks unspeakable, repressed trauma because it relays the structures of the unconscious into those of language. This is why Kristeva describes the early psychoanalytic model of language as optimistic: 'Since the unconscious is articulated like a language, "I" can decipher it, "I" can find rules for it; moreover, because it is situated in an intermediary position between different instances, it will give me access to the unknowable, that is, to trauma.'[28]

Psychoanalysis becomes a narrative therapy because the analyst encourages the analysand, through free association, to seek out the stories which make sense of her illness. On this model, the stories which are discovered point towards the truth behind the symptom; the homology between language and the unconscious allows knowledge of trauma through the mediation of the word. This, however, is not the end of the matter. Psychoanalysis is not just about the discovery of the unconscious. It is also, and crucially, a *relationship* between analysand and analyst, involving transference and counter-transference, and all the accompanying resistance, ambivalence and love. On the positive side, transference is the possibility of a relationship with another, and without transference there can be no cure; yet transference also introduces into psychoanalysis a dynamic which risks getting out of hand, and which makes of language a lure as much as a sign of truth. In Kristeva's account, Freud became increasingly aware of the problems which beset the royal road to the unconscious:

> Not only can words allow *internal* things to become conscious, but also and conversely, they can be the source of *errors* and engender *hallucinations*; they are not as sure as they seem to be for moving between perception and consciousness, and vice versa; from that point, language ceases to be a sure ground for leading to truth.
>
> (77)

Psychoanalysis does not abandon its attempt to turn trauma into narrative; the analyst still invites the analysand to tell her story:

> Recount your phantasms to me, put into narrative the sado-masochism of your drives, of your parents, of your grandparents, transgenerational and primitive stories, and, why not, make yourself into animals, plants, amoebae or stones; make the unrepresentable enter into representation.
>
> (94–5)

But these stories can no longer be taken as true in the same sense as they might have been according to the optimistic model of language.

However, in terms of effectiveness, the truth or falsehood of the emergent story is not of primary importance; the story has real effects because it is able to bridge the divide between trauma and representation and between self and other. Kristeva suggests this through her account of what is in a sense the story of the power of stories, Freud's account of the murder of the primal father at the end of *Totem and Taboo*. Freud describes a patricidal act at the origins of civilization. The primal father expels his sons in order to keep all the women for himself;

the sons subsequently gang together, kill their father and, being canni-
bals, eat him. Freud equivocates over the literal truth or falsehood of
this story, suggesting on the one hand that 'it may safely be assumed'
that events took place as he describes them,[29] but later describing his
narrative more sceptically as a 'Just-So Story'.[30] Subsequent commentators have had little difficulty discrediting Freud's account of the primal
horde.[31] Kristeva, however, is not interested in the historical credentials
of Freud's story, describing it as the '(fictive?) narrative' of an important
stage in the socialization of *homo sapiens* (69); nor does she dismiss
the criticism that Freud's *Totem and Taboo* merely gives expression to
Freud's own patricidal inclinations. However, neither of these issues is
germane to the theoretical interest of the story. For Kristeva, the crucial
stage is not the murder and consumption of the father, but the *repetition*
and *commemoration* of the act in the subsequent totem meal, when the
brothers consume an animal which represents the dead father. Before
the totem meal, the brothers are locked in the guilt and trauma of an
unrepresentable act. In the totem meal, the act is *represented*, it becomes
a symbolic link both to the past and between the brothers. Kristeva
summarizes the significance of the story:

> Allow me to return to the two psychic strategies brought to the fore
> by Freud in *Totem and Taboo*: on the one hand, the unrepresentable
> acts of which the prototypes are the father's murder and coitus . . .
> on the other hand the representations which give structure through
> identification with the father. It is at this point that the notion of
> significance [*signifiance*] emerges; it is not a linguistic matter, as
> Freud is investigating not the structure of language, but the psychic
> dynamics in which it is the dichotomy between *act* and *representa-
> tion*, between the *unrepresentable* and the symbolic *contract around
> authority* which interests him.
>
> (72)

For Kristeva, the question of the literal truth or universal validity of the
story is an irrelevance. Its point is to represent the possibility of overcoming trauma through the process of representation itself. What
Kristeva calls *signifiance* is not an established meaning conveyed in language and susceptible to evaluation in terms of truth or falsehood; it is
rather a process of meaning poised on the tension between an unrepresentable trauma not quite available to memory and a symbolic order
in which meaning, representation and stories are possible. The bril-
liance of Freud's story in *Totem and Taboo* is that it both exemplifies and

theorizes this process of mediating between what cannot be called back to memory and what can be narrated.

In Kristeva's version of it, psychoanalytic treatment entails the endeavour to enable the analysand to reproduce Freud's feat of narration in *Totem and Taboo*. She ends her account of the development of Freud's views on language with an example of the use of free association in her own analytic practice. An analysand subject to bulimia and vomiting reaches the point where her words have become obscure and lacunary like the poems she had written previously.[32] The analyst suggests that her words remind her of a novel by Céline, on whom the analysand had written a dissertation. This suggestion unlocks the possibility of narrative, and the analysand begins to write short stories. The reference to Céline is not the solution to the analysand's problems, it is not the masked truth of her illness, but it enables the transfer of symptoms from the body to language by giving a narrative syntax to her poem-like utterances. As Kristeva puts it, 'language again becomes narrative' (100); and Kristeva is adamant that the narrative, unlocked by free association and the analyst's suggestions, *saves the life* of her patient:

> The symptom without words was deadly. Poetic writing – self-absorbed, phobic and apparently protective – was a mausoleum which proved impotent against destructive attacks. On the other hand, free association for someone – the analyst – to swallow and to vomit first of all put my patient in danger. Then, situated in the context of the cure and in the transsubjective context of cultural history, it made it possible for the word to preserve the life of this woman who was destroying herself in her symptom and by poetry.
> (101)[33]

Kristeva characterizes psychoanalytic interpretation as 'a gift of meaning' (*une donation de sens*).[34] Its aim is not to master or to say the final word about the symptom, but to offer to the patient the possibility of telling the story, or one of the possible stories, of her suffering. On this issue, Kristevan analysis differs crucially from the Lacanian version. For Lacan, as interpreted by Žižek, narrative is a form of occlusion. It emerges 'in order to resolve some fundamental antagonism by rearranging its terms into a temporal succession',[35] it turns the 'meaningless contingency' of destiny into a life-narrative endowed with meaning.[36] The psychoanalytic cure is complete only when the analysand has learnt to recognize meaningless contingency for what it is, namely meaningless and contingent:

Lacan = Narrative ORDERING
Kristeva = Narrative MEANING (S)

at the end of the psychoanalytic cure, the analysand has to suspend the urge to symbolize/internalize, to interpret, to search for a 'deeper meaning'; he has to accept that the traumatic encounters which traced out the itinerary of his life were utterly contingent and indifferent, that they bear no 'deeper message' . . . at the moment of 'exit from transference' which marks the end of the cure, the subject is able to perceive the events around which his life story is crystallized into a meaningful Whole in their senseless contingency.[37]

From a Kristevan perspective, Žižek makes two basic mistakes: he conflates interpretation with the search for a 'deeper meaning', and he implies that it is possible to dwell in contingency without symbolization. The meaning offered by the analyst through Kristeva's 'gift of meaning' aspires to be neither authoritative nor definitive. Psychoanalytic interpretation is, on the contrary, a 'relation which is dynamic, essentially open and perpetually to be remade, undecidable'.[38] By unlocking the possibility of narrative Kristevan analysis does not mask or occlude the fundamental antagonisms which lie behind the analysand's suffering, rather it seeks to give them the only possible language in which they can be communicated to another. It hopes to restore the possibility of *saying something meaningful* to someone else.

Kristeva illustrates this process through her account of Melanie Klein's treatment of Dick, a disturbed four-year-old boy who barely speaks and appears to be indifferent to everything around him.[39] Klein attempts to establish contact by speaking in his place, announcing that two toy trains are Dick and his father. The boy's response suggests that he understands and accepts this identification. He takes the train which Klein had named Dick, rolls it to the window and says 'Station', upon which Klein tells him that the station is his mother.[40] It certainly looks here as if Klein's attempt to speak on behalf of Dick entails imposing her own preoccupations on him. In any case, in therapeutic terms there seems to be a beneficial effect as Klein provides Dick with a primitive form of symbolization which he can now use to express the anxiety and aggression that had been simmering inside him. The analyst's gift of meaning creates a contact between the boy and others, and it makes it possible for him to distance himself from his suffering through words and play. The key moment here is the patient's acquisition, through the intervention of the analyst, of a means by which trauma can be represented. In effect, the aim of analysis is to permit the analysand to repeat the act of symbolization performed by the patricidal brothers from Freud's primal horde, which Freud placed at the origin of civilization; and this also involves providing a language in which to reproduce the act of narration achieved by Freud himself in *Totem and Taboo*, when he realized the necessary imbrication of psychoanalysis and storytelling.

In this version of storytelling in psychoanalysis, the truth of the story is less important than its role in the exchange of meaning, its status as gift from the analyst and its acceptance as such by the analysand. Peter Brooks has described Freud's discovery, in the course of his analysis of Dora,

> that the relation of teller to listener is as important as the content and structure of the tale itself. Or rather: that the relation of teller to listener inherently is part of the structure and the meaning of any narrative text, since such a text (like any text) exists only in so far as it is transmitted, in so far as it becomes part of a process of exchange.[41]

The recounting and interpretation of stories can thus be understood as belonging as much to psychoanalysis as to fiction. Likewise, the transferential and counter-transferential slippages between analysand and analyst reproduce the unstable mix of identification and distance which occurs between narrators and readers. The story is a form of relationship with another, in which the identity of both self and other is in play and at stake. For Kristeva also, there is a direct parallel between fiction and psychoanalysis. Freud called upon his patients to become storytellers: 'What are the stories that Freud asked his patients to recount to him? Narrative full of gaps, silences, confusion . . . kinds of novels deprived of a public'.[42] These psychoanalytic narratives do not emerge as well-made coherent tales. They are full of holes, on the edge or over the edge of coherence, their elaboration is painful and their interpretation often erroneous. Even so, they are a response to the analyst's gift of meaning, and they return that gift in an acknowledgement of the existence of the other. In this context, then, it is not surprising that Kristeva is herself an author of fiction, moreover an author of dark, violent, enigmatic fictions which attempt to trace in words the passage of trauma and desire, and the permeable identities of self and other. We saw in chapter 4 that Levinas's resistance to storytelling is a stumbling block of his thought. In Kristeva's case, on the contrary, it is a direct extension of it.

## Fictions

To date, Kristeva has published three novels. The first, *Les Samouraïs* (1990), recounts in barely veiled form the intellectual and private lives of Kristeva and her friends in Paris from the 1960s to the 1980s. In the present context her second and third novels, *Le Vieil Homme et les loups* (1991) and *Possessions* (1996), are more interesting because they escape the semi-factual constraints of the *roman à clef* and explore the connections between identity, narration and otherness which are also central to her essays on psychoanalytic issues. Both these novels have as their central character a journalist called Stéphanie Delacour, who is also one of the narrators along with an anonymous third-person voice; both novels adopt in part the format of detective stories, and both are set in a place called Santa Barbara, which may recall but should not be entirely identified with the Californian city of the same name. In what follows I concentrate on *Possessions*. Of Kristeva's novels it is the one which adheres most closely to the conventions of detective fiction. It begins with a murder, presents the various suspects and finally pieces together the events which led up to the crime. Within this fairly classical format, it also explores the transferential exchanges between criminal, victim, detective and reader in a way which brings out the psycho-analytic undertones of the detective story.[43]

Why a detective story and why Santa Barbara? The detective novel provides Kristeva with a popular form in which to explore the darker regions of the mind. It also entices its reader with a promise of knowledge; as Kristeva herself puts it, '"You can know", is in substance what the detective novel says to the reader'.[44] On the surface, then, the detective novel is the antithesis of the modernist or postmodern novel in which truth is fragmented or elusive, broken down into its constituent lies. It is no doubt in part in order to display and to confound the promise of meaning in the detective novel that so many modernist and postmodern authors, from Robbe-Grillet and Butor to Modiano and Pennac, have been attracted to the format. In Kristeva's versions, setting the novels in a city called Santa Barbara already hints that the quest for truth may not run smoothly. In *Etrangers à nous-mêmes* Kristeva discusses the word *barbarian* and its possible derivation from the senseless words supposedly spoken by non-Greeks: '*bla-bla, bara-bara*, inarticulate or incomprehensible mutterings'.[45] Barbarians are the strangers or outsiders who speak nonsense, they are alien to the logos which is both the language of the Greeks and the intelligible order of the world. Santa Barbara, then, is sacred (Santa) and senseless (Barbara), a site of inviolable otherness not susceptible to reason's scrutiny. One might even venture that it is the 'other scene' of the unconscious. Small wonder, then, that at the end of *Le Vieil Homme et les loups* Stéphanie returns to France, which in Kristeva's detective novels represents reason, clarity and transparency, complaining that 'Santa Barbara did not reveal its secrets to me'.[46] In Santa Barbara Stéphanie must speak another language, 'santabarbarian' (*santabarbarois*), a sacred babble which will not easily be translated into French, the language of the conscious mind. The detective novel is thus given a setting which is highly unpropitious for the solving of mysteries.

*Possessions* opens with a description of the headless corpse of Gloria Harrison, a translator and mother to the profoundly deaf child Jerry. Stéphanie's response to the sight of the body already raises the possibility and impossibility of bearing witness to a traumatic, apparently senseless scene. Over several pages she reflects upon works by artists such as Caravaggio, Rodin and Degas which depict headless bodies, then finally she explains her manoeuvre: 'But what other point is there in art other than to allow us to look death in the face?'[47] Art protects from horror and makes it possible to face it. It provides a way of looking by not looking, of contemplating the headless body and *seeing it as something else*. Thus, the traumatic instance can only be seen for what it is by being seen *otherwise*. The thing itself – here, trauma or death, or elsewhere identity or sexual difference – cannot be witnessed directly; the witness sees only what she is capable of seeing, the thing in so far as it can be known, mediated by perceptions which make it visible whilst also masking it from sight. From the very beginning, then, Stéphanie's musings parallel the analyst's 'gift of meaning' by offering a way of viewing trauma without claiming to see it for what it is. This is also the role of fiction and, the novel will suggest, the role of detection, and so preeminently the role of detective fiction.

As the investigation gets under way, the police appear ineffective in their search for the truth. The police doctor tries to establish the precise time and cause of death, but fails because of the missing head. The detective Northrop Rilsky seems surprisingly unconcerned to discover the facts of the matter (see 51, 92). So the journalist Stéphanie Delacour turns detective, though she is also a suspect in the crime. The lines between suspect and detective are further blurred, as other suspects turn detective in search for the truth. But the truth appears to exist in different versions. Stéphanie's fellow-journalist Larry Smirnoff seeks the sources of the murder in social and political scandal. Victor Zorine, a psychiatrist with a penchant for psychoanalysis, suggests that the real truth is that of the psyche. Each of the real or surrogate detectives is a story-builder, and each builds a different story. In one of the novel's most self-referential passages, Larry Smirnoff explains to Stéphanie that the detective novel consists precisely in this endeavour to turn a past event into a coherent narrative:

> Besides, that's what the interest of crimes is, surely, and detective novels: the essential has taken place, but it appears that the essential is not there; the death has been filmed, okay, but other films are possible. And at that point everything begins again: the enquiry and therefore the novel. Conclusion: the end of the story wasn't the end of the story. Is there ever an end to the story ?
>
> (144)

Just as, according to Freud, psychoanalysis might prove to be interminable, then so is the work of detection and the writing of the detective story. Stéphanie concurs:

> Everything had already taken place. There remained to find out what, who, when, why. Isn't that why we invent stories in the imperfect? Accomplished in the present, the imperfect puts them into form but they deform it in their turn. Only one story will be the true one. It will not always be known.
>
> (145)

The story deforms what gives it form; in other words its form is uneasy, precarious, and at best provisional, it never entirely accommodates the material which it nevertheless makes intelligible. Other forms, other stories, are always possible. As for the novel itself, to the profusion of detectives it offers us corresponds a profusion of murders. Gloria, it transpires, was killed more than once. She was poisoned by her son's speech therapist Pauline Gadeau, strangled by her lover, stabbed by an escaped serial killer, and finally beheaded by Pauline Gadeau. Poisoned, strangled, stabbed and beheaded, she is indisputably dead.

In all this, the detective's error is not that he weaves a story out of the material at his disposal, but that he halts the story too rapidly: 'From all these puzzles, the Commissioner had chosen the one that was the most spectacular and the least harmful' (192). The story he settles for, involving a tragic mother, a crooked lover and a serial killer is, for all its narrative contortions, too stereotyped to match the complexity of the real. The final story may never be told, indeed it may be untellable.

This is suggested by the fact that Gloria's head is missing, in which it is possible to see an echo of Marguerite Duras's novel *L'Amante anglaise*. In Duras's novel the perpetrator is apprehended, but the victim's head is never recovered, serving to ensure that the puzzle has a missing piece and the crime is never finally resolved. Typically, in the modern and postmodern detective story, the truth is beyond grasp, and the detective's construction or the analyst's gift of meaning to the analysand is as much an index of their own desire as of the mystery with which they are confronted. And so when, hypothetically, Stéphanie finally reconstructs the events leading up to the beheading she concedes that 'This story is mine' (*Cette histoire est de moi*) (235). The story is her own, perhaps in all senses: she has constructed it, it is not a simple reflection of events as they occurred, but perhaps also it is her own story she is telling, the story of her own desire and of her own implication in the crime. Is her version the true one? The question hardly matters: 'True or false? That isn't the question, the question isn't asked, life goes on, that's life' (248).

So whose story is it that is being told in this convoluted detective novel? The open, transferential structure of identity prevents there from being any simple answer to such a question. The gift of meaning, or the gift of a story, is made by one subject to another, analyst to analysand, detective to criminal, author to reader; it is thus in some sense simultaneously the story of both, though it clearly can never be the *only* story of either. This ambiguity is suggested in the title of the novel, *Possessions*, and the use of the word in the text. *Possession* is to be understood in both active and passive senses: it is what the subject possesses and is possessed by. Language, for example, is described as something which possesses and is possessed by the speaker (see 30–1). Love, such as Gloria's love for her son Jerry, is also a possession in this sense, focusing and dispersing the self at the same time: 'The self of being outside oneself' (*Le soi de l'être hors-soi*) (66). It is important also that the title of the novel is in the plural: the possession of what I am possessed by and what possesses me is not singular, unique and definitive. The circulation of desires and identities ensures a susceptibility to others, a permeability and openness to otherness at the centre of the self. The novel builds up a complex network of transferences and substitutions. It turns out that years earlier Pauline had lost a beloved brother, Aimeric. For months she did not speak, and she even tried to cut her own throat. Making a new life for herself, in Santa Barbara she becomes a speech therapist, giving language to those who do not possess it. When she meets Jerry, she recognizes in him both herself, the speechless child she once was, and her lost brother. As she takes over the maternal role of Gloria, she becomes mother both to the child she was and to the beloved sibling who has died. Severing Gloria's head from her lifeless corpse thus in a sense completes the suicide she had earlier attempted and allows her to begin again, in Gloria's place.

Stéphanie, the detective-journalist who solves the mystery, is drawn into this process of transference and substitution. She is also mourning a lost child, a baby conceived but never born; and she is herself a lost child, orphaned by the death of her father recounted in *Le Vieil Homme et les loups*. Like Pauline, she recognizes in Jerry both the child she is and the child she lost, and she feels the maternal attraction to him that has already led Pauline to replace Gloria. In this account, the play of identifications is such that no character occupies a single or stable position. As in the psychoanalytic experience, the transference and counter-transference of desires sets up a merry-go-round which need never stop. The self is the other's possession. The detective story places trauma at the centre of the interminable transferences between subjects. The substitution of Pauline for Gloria, and potentially of Stéphanie for Pauline, ensure that the identities of victim, murderer and detective are separate only contingently. Any character could occupy the position of any other. Stéphanie feels herself being absorbed by Jerry: 'My flesh becomes permeable, the child infiltrates me, I become diffused in him' (234). This then leads to the possible revelation of a new self: 'you will see me as Jerry reveals me in myself' (*vous me verrez telle qu'en moi-même Jerry me révèle*) (234). The *you* implicates the reader and draws her in to the transferential drama. We are the necessary witnesses who make possible the gift of meaning and the construction of new identities. Like the psychoanalyst's patient, Stéphanie is revealed to herself and to others by another; and by revealing herself to us, she perhaps also allows us to become her, revealed to ourselves in turn by and as another, as victim, murderer and detective, as destitute child and loving mother.

According to Peter Brooks, 'It is only through assuming the burdens and risks of the transferential situation that one reaches the understanding of otherness'.[48] In both fiction and psychoanalysis, the dynamics of transference disturb 'the totalitarian foreclosure of interpretation and meaning'.[49] The constructed narrative 'finds its power in its capacity to illuminate the buried history of unconscious desire, to make sense of an otherwise muddled life story'.[50] Through the relation with otherness which constitutes the story, meaning is construed and construed, and identity is constructed and reconstructed. By accepting to enter into transference, the reader or analyst allows the story to recon-figure her desire. But the story is always recountable in different ways, its meaning is never foreclosed. None of the real or surrogate detectives of Kristeva's *Possessions* claims to grasp the final truth behind the con-voluted history of desire buried in the secret recesses of Santa Barbara. Kristeva's novel makes of the detective story a drama of trauma and transference. Its purpose is to stage the devastating force of desire, from which no subject is immune. If transference takes place, the identity of reader or detective is evaporated and remade: 'There is no longer any "you" [*Il n'y a plus de "vous"*]. Possessed, you give way [*Possédée, vous cédez*] in front of what is not a power, but something obvious' (65). The 'you' is obliterated ('There is no longer any "you"'), immediately rein-stated ('*you* give way'), but then slips away again ('you *give way*'). Decentred and reconfigured, it has learned that the other's story may be the story of itself as other. Kristeva's wager is that detection, analysis and reading are all the generous traversal of otherness.

For Kristeva, as the epigraph to this chapter suggests, identity is a fic-tion and fiction is the place where the drama of identity can be played out. Stories, whether they be told between analyst and analysand or in novels, are an endeavour to find sense in broken lives and fractured selves.[51] They are a means of reaching out to the other through the offer of an always fragile meaning. For Kristeva, as for thinkers such as Hannah Arendt, Alistair MacIntyre, Adriana Caverero or Richard Kearney, to be human is to tell stories. The stories we tell constitute who we are and the communities to which we belong. And Kristeva's use of detective fiction is particularly revealing. The free-floating guilt suggests that we are all murderers, at least in our unconscious.[52] But the desire to kill is not the last word here. The profusion of narratives and the effects of transference whereby each story becomes the story of another correspond to the analyst's gift of meaning. Through this gift, something like an understanding of the other can be achieved; and with this comes also the possibility of renewal, rebirth and forgiveness, which Kristeva writes as *par-don* (literally: by-gift) because it is received through and as a gift. In this respect, psychoanalysis and the novel share in the endeavour to give sense to suffering:

> To give meaning to suffering and to open the associative word which will transform pain and death into the narrative of a life, for a new life: that is how it could be possible to define the value of analytical interpretation as for-giveness [*par-don*]. If you prefer, you can call this experience a 'cure'. Without end.[53]

In Žižek's account, the translation of trauma into story is an existential lie, an avoidance of the real of desire. For Kristeva, both as analyst and novelist, the story is the only way in which the real of desire can be encountered without intolerable pain. What fiction and analysis offer is meaning and forgiveness. This is not the final or the only meaning, and forgiveness does not permit us to escape the consequences of our acts;[54] but it does allow the prospect that desire may find a voice, and that entangled in a story which may be our own, or someone else's, or even no one's, we may not be as innocent as we hoped nor as wicked as we feared.

## Conclusion: on stories

Kristeva describes how psychoanalytic experience suggests that a child's earliest experiences may illustrate a pre-disposition to narrative:

> The hypothesis has been suggested that, in humans, *narrative* is as original as *syntax*: as soon as the small child articulates some repetitive sound to its mother, the incantation would be already a phrase (such and such a melody signifies: 'I want mother'), but also a phantasm ('I am eating mother') which betrays a conflict, a trial, the pursuit of a goal, a satisfaction or a frustration. In other words, every phrase is a phantasm, and every phantasm is a narration.[55]

This narrative pre-disposition is at the same time an aspect of the decentring of the subject (the stories we tell about ourselves are never entirely our own) and what makes it possible to present ourselves as agents, not just victims, of our desires and anxieties. Once unlocked, this propensity to narrate also gives us access to the world of others. *Zoe* becomes *bios*, as stories are exchanged and lives acquire significance. Kristeva knows that our stories are shot through with ambiguity and with distress, that they impede and dispel understanding as much as they allow meaning to be condensed. The phantasms that lurk behind what we recount may be violent and frightful; but they provide a means of reaching *back* to something which without them would be inaccessible, and of reaching *out* to others in the prospect of inaugurating some form of dialogue.

Kristeva, then, is more sanguine about the role of stories in configuring experience than the authors discussed in previous chapters. And importantly also, she does not conceive of theory and storytelling as being fundamentally in opposition to one another. As we have seen in previous chapters, theorists of quite different persuasions see dangers inherent in stories: Lyotard rejects the 'grand narratives' which falsely unify human history,[56] Levinas repudiates fiction because of the in-authentic shadow world which it creates, and Althusser's materialist follows the injunction 'Not to tell oneself stories'. These views all in their way echo the ancient quarrel between philosophy and literature and depict stories as potentially opposed to theoretical clear-sightedness because they encourage the spread of falsehood. Kristeva's assessment of the role and value of stories is much more positive. By following Klein in tracing back storytelling to the earliest levels of human development, she makes of it the medium by which our experiences, desires and anxieties can be made known both to ourselves and others. This in turn establishes a connection between storytelling and theory. For Kristeva, the sense of the Freudian revolution does not lie only in the dislodging of consciousness from its position of primacy. 'More radically,' she suggests, 'it consists in inscribing language and thought in the sexual drive, all the way down to its biological substratum.'[57] In this account, then, there is no antagonism between theory and storytelling because they originate together, both emerge from and attempt to name our fundamental experience of what it means to be human.

This does not mean that all distinctions are collapsed and that theory and stories are simply the same as one another. Theory aspires to generality whereas the story points towards specificity; but to understand the difference between them in terms of opposition would be to misapprehend the continuum which links them together. Both theory and story are mired in the ambiguity of being human, they gesture towards the possibility of finding meaning amidst the nonsense, and they imply the viability of a public language which might snatch us from solipsism. And both are haunted by the insight that such a public language may never be fully or finally articulated. The story may temporarily establish a sort of community, as teller and listeners, analysand and analyst, self and other, come together to be instructed, entertained, intrigued or enraged; but such a community may fall apart again at a moment's notice, its unity being only ever provisional. Similarly, the achievements of theory are never definitive. Its characteristic delusion may be that it aspires to find the answer to all its questions; but such hubris is quickly discredited. As the next chapter suggests, the most ambitious claims theory sometimes makes for itself must be counterbalanced by its awareness of its limitations. If it dreams of occupying the place of the master, it also knows that such a position is not available.

# Chapter 7

# Spectres of theory

In 1986, in his presidential address to the Modern Language Association of America, the Yale deconstructive critic J. Hillis Miller announced the 'triumph of theory'. The theory wars which raged in British and North American universities in the 1970s and 1980s had ended in the apparent victory of the theorists, and Hillis Miller could claim that the triumph of theory was 'almost universal'.[1] But where next? What if theory had drawn its momentum and energy from the strength of the opposition to it? The triumph of theory might turn out to be only a hair's breadth from its demise. In fact, in his presidential address Hillis Miller concentrates mostly on what he calls 'a sudden, almost universal turn away from theory in the sense of an orientation toward language as such'.[2] The moment of theory's triumph was also the moment at which it could be consigned to the past. A series of books with titles such as *In the Wake of Theory*, *The Wake of Deconstruction*, *After Theory*, *Reading after Theory* and *What's Left of Theory?* suggest that theory may be dead and gone.[3] We are now 'post-theoretical', even if opinions differ on what this might mean.

In pronouncements of the 'death of theory', what is meant by 'theory' is most often poststructuralism in one of the various forms in which it was represented in anglophone universities in the 1970s and 1980s. It is evidently a simplification to limit theory to one of its particular varieties in this way, thereby implying that other theoretical or theorized practices are in some way not 'theory'. It is also particularly ironic that one of the principal accusations made against theory in the guise of poststructuralism is that it claimed to explain *too much*, that it arrogated for itself total authority over other perspectives and practices. Post-structuralism in general is highly sceptical about any such claims. It denies that theory, including its own, has the sort of final mandate that would allow it rightfully and securely to occupy a position of dominance.

This is one of the points which separates poststructuralism from structuralism. Whereas structuralism aspires to the impartiality of science, poststructuralism shows a predilection for excess, transgression, residue, paradox and aporia. Far from trying to bring everything under the authority of a single reading, it characteristically focuses on what resists totalizing interpretations. So to accuse poststructuralism of attempting to explain too much precisely replicates its own principal objection to structuralism.

This chapter sketches some of the differences between structuralist and poststructuralist conceptions of theoretical practice by contrasting Althusser's use of the term *theory* in the 1960s with Derrida's discussion of the authority of theory in *Limited Inc.*, which brings together three essays written in the 1970s and 1980s. The chapter then discusses accounts of the post-poststructuralist, post-theoretical condition. The final section of the chapter looks more closely at the personification of theory and what this implies about its life, death and ghostly afterlife. What does it mean for theory to die and to return as a ghost?

## The triumph of theory

In a general introduction to structuralism, François Wahl refers to its 'scientific vocation' and states that its work is 'of an order which is not ideological but theoretical'.[4] The suggestion here is that theory aims to achieve a scientific status which allows it to stand outside ideology. Todorov specifies that structuralism is scientific not so much in the degree of precision which it hopes to achieve as in the level of generality on which it operates. Rather than, for example, interpreting an individual literary text, the structuralist seeks to establish the 'general laws of which this text is the product'.[5] Structuralism can be defined in part by reference to its interest in sign systems and signifying processes derived from Saussurean linguistics. Just as importantly, it entails a conception of theory as capable of being uncontaminated by individual perspectives, wilful interpretations and ideological distortions. This conception of theory underpins the association with structuralism of Althusser's texts from the 1960s. Althusser was more influenced by Freudian, and to a lesser extent Lacanian, psychoanalysis than by Saussurean semiotics. But he shares the structuralist attribution of scientific status to theory. In his *Pour Marx* (1965), responding to the conviction in some parts of the Communist movement that concrete action is more important than abstract theorizing, he gives an account of theory which emphasizes its unique ability to understand the mechanisms of ideology and therefore its essential role in the revolutionary cause. In defence of the value of intellectual labour Althusser repeats Lenin's dictum that without theory there is no revolutionary practice. Despite the opposition of less philosophically minded comrades, he argues that theory should play a vital role in the Communist movement.

Althusser distinguishes between three different kinds of theoretical practice which he terms *theory*, *'theory'* and *Theory*. The first of these, theory, is an activity which is part of the complex unity of social practice. Like other forms of labour, it has its own primary material (representations, concepts, facts) and it is concerned with specific areas of enquiry, such as law, aesthetics or the history of science. The product of this theoretical reflection is what Althusser calls 'theory', which is the system of fundamental concepts elaborated in the course of theoretical practice. Both theory and 'theory' are bound to particular fields of investigation. They are constantly prone to ideological distortions, so they require ongoing vigilance and purification. The means for achieving this are provided by Theory, which Althusser defines as

> the general theory, that is, the Theory of practice in general, itself elaborated on the basis of the Theory of existing theoretical practices (of the sciences), which transform into 'knowledge' (scientific truths) the ideological product of existing 'empirical' practices (the concrete activity of men). This Theory is materialist *dialectics* which is the same thing as dialectical materialism.[6]

Althusser identifies Theory with the version of materialist dialectics which he finds in Marx's writing, though he suggests that Marx himself did not adequately theorize it. Althusser attempts to remedy this, and in the process he gives to Theory an overriding role in the purification of existing 'theories' and the elaboration of new ones. In Theory is expressed 'theoretically the essence of theoretical practice in general, and through that the essence of practice in general, and through that the essence of transformations, of the "becoming" of things in general' (170).

In Althusser's terminology philosophy is a practice tied to ideology whereas Theory is not.[7] Indeed, he makes it clear that Theory is uniquely privileged in that it alone makes it possible to examine and to dismantle ideology from the outside. He refers to 'an unceasing struggle against ideology itself, that is, against idealism, a struggle which Theory (dialectical materialism) can illuminate as to its reasons and objectives, and guide like no other method in the world' (171). The urgency of

Theory and of explicating the untheorized Marxian notion of dialectical materialism comes from the unique status attributed to it:

> The only Theory capable of dealing with, if not of posing, the
> underlying question of the validity of these disciplines, of critiquing
> ideology in all its disguises, including the disguises of technical
> practices in science, is the Theory of theoretical practice (as dis-
> tinguished from ideological practice): materialist dialectics, or dia-
> lectical materialism, the conception of Marxist dialectics in its
> *specificity*.
>
> (172–3)

There is a Kantian ring to all this, as Althusser's Theory resembles
Kant's view of philosophy as outlined in *The Conflict of Faculties*. It is
not so much a body of knowledge in itself as a discipline with a regula-
tory role in relation to others. At least at this stage of his career
Althusser can be seen as playing a part in Habermas's unfinished project
of modernity, as he wields the tool of Theory to unmask ideology in the
interests of emancipation.

Althusser's readings of Marx attempt to draw out the Theory which
Marx himself did not make explicit, but which underlies his analyses of
the workings of capitalism. Hence, as I suggested in chapter 5, the title
of *Pour Marx* does not simply imply that Althusser is speaking *in favour
of* Marx, but also *on his behalf*, providing the words to articulate what
Marx *would have* said had he written a full-blown work of Theory.
Althusser assumes the authority to speak in the place of Marx; and as
Theorist tracking down the ruses of ideology, he also speaks on behalf of
the Communist movement and the working classes in general. Because
Theory stands outside ideology it enables the Theorist to speak in the
place of others, to know more than they know about the meaning of
their words and actions.

This theoreticist self-assurance acquires poignancy when seen in the
light of the reversal that Althusser would go on to experience. From
being the mouthpiece of Theory capable of voicing the truth of the
other, after the murder of his wife and his detention on grounds of
mental health Althusser would learn at first hand what it was like to
have others assume the right to speak on his behalf. His case was never
brought to trial, and he lost the right to speak for himself, to defend
himself, and even to sign his own name. The title of his first sketch of an
autobiography, *Les Faits* (The Facts), drafted before the murder of Hélène,
suggests that at this stage Althusser still aspires to speak of things as they

are, describing a reality containable within an authoritative discourse. By the time of *L'Avenir dure longtemps* the autobiographical speech act is no longer so assured and its aim is not so much to assert its interpretative authority as, more modestly, to re-affirm the author's right to speak in his own name: 'I now take my turn to speak: naturally you will believe me when I say that I am speaking only for myself.'[8] Yet, even as he reclaims his own voice, he finds the meaning of his story slipping away from him. The book ends with him appealing to 'those who think they know and can say more'[9] to speak out, in order to complete or to restore the truth which still eludes him.

It may be fanciful to see the difference between the self-assurance of Theory in *Pour Marx* and the self-questioning, self-doubting erosion of hermeneutic control in *L'Avenir dure longtemps* as illustrating some of the changes in French thought from the structuralist 1960s to the post-structuralist 1970s and 1980s. To make Althusser's life into an allegory of Theory's self-dismantling may merely repeat the process by which his own voice was wrested from him. In any case, Althusser's theoreticist confidence in *Pour Marx* now seems quaintly outdated. Both the scientific status of Theory and the sharp distinction between facts and their interpretation would come under extreme theoretical pressure.[10] In retrospect the authority of Theory seems theoretically shaky. Althusser asserts that there is a distinction between Theory and theory, or between science and ideology, but he cannot properly refute the suspicion that these distinctions are ideological rather than scientific, and therefore not as objective as Althusser requires them to be. It remains unclear *how* Althusser expects Theory to escape ideology and what grounds its overarching authority. Its privileged status derives from the discourses and the texts which instantiate it, from Marx's under-theorized analyses to Althusser's own work. So it looks as if Theory draws its unique prestige from the acts of language which assert it. Althusser wanted Theory to be a practice not a performance; post-structuralism represents the acute awareness that theory draws its effects from its performative dimension rather than from any transcendental, non-ideological, or non-discursive grounding.

## The demise of theory

Poststructuralism can be understood as the heavily theorized dismantling of the privilege of theory in the structuralist sense. Theory, as it were, turns against itself and begins to consume its own tail. As we saw in chapter 3, in 'Apathie dans la théorie' (first published in 1975) Jean-

François Lyotard announced that 'The big issue for us now is to destroy theory'.[11] This does not mean simply abandoning theory, but rather fundamentally altering the kinds of claim that are made on its behalf. Lyotard gives an example of a self-questioning theoretical practice by quoting from the end of section 6 of Freud's *Beyond the Pleasure Principle*. Here, Freud directly addresses the epistemological status of his speculations:

> It may be asked whether and how far I am myself convinced of the truth of the hypotheses that have been set out in these pages. My answer would be that I am not convinced myself and that I do not seek to persuade other people to believe in them. Or, more precisely, that I do not know how far I believe in them. There is no reason, as it seems to me, why the emotional factor of conviction should enter into this question at all. It is surely possible to throw oneself into a line of thought and to follow it wherever it leads out of simple scientific curiosity, or, if the reader prefers, as an *advocatus diaboli*, who is not on that account himself sold to the devil.[12]

According to Lyotard, this is much more than a disarming, modest disclaimer through which Freud concedes that he might be wrong. Freud is adumbrating a different kind of theoretical practice uncoupled from claims of mastery and truth. Conviction plays no role, as the theorist becomes someone who speculates rather than someone who knows or believes or seeks to convince others. In 'Spéculer – sur "Freud"' (published in *La Carte postale*) Derrida shows an interest in *Beyond the Pleasure Principle* similar to Lyotard's, as he analyses its dazzling and disorientating textual elaboration rather than assessing the truth or falsehood of its theses. What intrigues both Derrida and Lyotard is the possibility of a theoretical text severed from claims of epistemological mastery. In this view, theory is denied its authority over other practices of language. Destroying theory thus means continuing to practise theory, but in self-parodic, self-subverting forms:

> what we are lacking is a devilry or an apathy such that the theoretical genre could itself undergo subversions from which its pretentions would not rise up again; that it should become simply a genre amongst others and be dismissed from its position of mastery or domination which it has occupied at least since Plato; that the true should become a matter of style.[13]

It is possible to see here some of the characteristic moves of post-structuralist thought at its most ambitious. Lyotard identifies a defining feature of Western thought which can be traced back 'at least' to Plato; he endorses Freud, or a certain – in some ways very un-Freudian – reading of Freud as marking an important hiatus in the otherwise monolithic tradition (elsewhere, Nietzsche, or Marx, or Spinoza, or Heidegger will fulfil the same role); he rejects truth as the guiding criterion of all worthwhile intellectual enquiry; and he anticipates a possible and even imminent moment when thought may venture into hitherto unexplored territories. So Lyotard's call for the destruction of theory is far from the anti-intellectual slogan it might appear to be. It entails a thorough reconceptualization of the role and status of philosophy which is both modest and outrageously ambitious: modest, because philosophy loses its power to legislate over other disciplines; ambitious, because in depriving itself of its legislative function it also liberates itself from its most distinctive fallacy – its belief in its own special status – and makes it possible to think what had never been thought before. Lyotard describes his problem in Le Différend as saving the honour of thought,[14] and he destroys theory in order to make possible new ways of thinking. This cannot mean 'doing theory' with the same mind set as Althusser's self-confident Theorist. Parody and self-doubt are to be incorporated into the forms and fabric of theoretical writing. Postmodern philosophy entails thought without assured knowledge, investigation without a pre-established sense of where it is heading or what it might discover.

This is clearly no longer 'theory' in the same sense as the term was understood by structuralists. In this context Derrida's Limited Inc. is of particular interest since it is a text which analyses and brings about theory's dispossession of its dreams of authority whilst also instituting the novel theoretical and textual practice which emerges in the wake of this dispossession. Limited Inc. consists of three essays written by Derrida at different times in different contexts. The first, 'Signature événement contexte', deals in part with J. L. Austin's speech act theory, and was published in Derrida's Marges de la philosophie in 1972. The second, 'Limited Inc a b c. . .', was first published in 1977 in response to fierce criticisms of Derrida's reading of Austin made by the American philosopher John Searle. The final piece, 'Vers une éthique de la discussion', is a postface for Limited Inc. which looks back at the Searle–Derrida controversy with over a decade's hindsight. Derrida's initial interest in Austin comes from Austin's notion of the performative, defined as those utterances which perform what they state, such as 'I name this ship the Queen Elizabeth', 'I promise to meet you at six o'clock', 'I bet you sixpence', and so on. The details of Austin's discussion are of relatively little interest to Derrida. Rather, he is drawn to Austin's performative for a range of interconnected reasons: it is an act embedded within a context which produces or transforms the situation in which it occurs, it has no referent, it does not describe anything which preexists it outside language, and it is not subordinate to the value of truth or falsehood.

On this latter point, though, Derrida makes a fascinating slip. He writes that 'Austin had to remove the *analysis* of the performative from the authority of the *value of truth*, from the true/false opposition'.[15] This is nearly, but not quite, true. Whilst Austin certainly does endeavour to unsettle the truth/falsehood fetish, the *analysis* of the performative remains firmly under its authority. In other words, the performative is not true or false in the same way as a constative utterance, but Austin's theorization of the performative is still maintained as being or at least aspiring to be constative, i.e. susceptible to proof or disproof by established procedures of argumentation. The crucial shift in Derrida's account is that it is not only the performative which escapes evaluation in terms of its truth or falsehood, but also the analysis of the performative. So Derrida's discourse on the performative is itself drawn into, fatally imbricated with, performativity.

This tiny slip on Derrida's part indicates a faltering of the theoretical project. In the appropriation of Austin's performative, a sort of recognition scene occurs in which the poststructuralist discovers something fundamental about the nature of his own theoretical activity. Performativity is both the mode and the object of analysis. Much of the subsequent exchange with Searle is concerned with Derrida's manner of practising philosophy, and in particular with what Searle charmingly calls Derrida's 'distressing penchant for saying things that are obviously false' (quoted by Derrida, 83). Searle alleges that Derrida cannot be serious. Derrida retorts with one of his most unserious, playful or perverse texts in which what is at stake, in large measure, is the value of seriousness itself. According to Derrida, theory in its classic, traditional sense demands speech acts which are serious, literal and strictly policed in order to achieve proper theoretical impartiality. Yet this impartiality is necessarily impugned when what is being analysed is the value of serious or literal utterances. To claim that only a *serious* analysis of the serious/non-serious opposition is valid entails a prior decision in favour of one side of the opposition, so that the theorist's discourse is predetermined by the hierarchy of values which it purports to stand outside and to theorize dispassionately. But Derrida insists that, from a theoretical perspective, the serious analysis of seriousness cannot be taken seriously because it is so entangled with its object. The theorist is thus knocked off his impartial pedestal because his prior options disqualify him from neutrality.

Through this analysis of seriousness, Derrida both diagnoses and performs the theorist's exclusion from the position of knowledge; he is no longer, and for theoretical reasons cannot be, an impartial judge who sees things as they are. In consequence, the claims of theory must be reined in: 'This does not imply that all "theorization" is impossible. It merely de-limits a theorization that would want *to incorporate* totally its object and can only do it in a *limited* way' (136). Theory is deprived of its overarching vision. And this inevitably has consequences for the status of the theoretical text, which can no longer unambiguously occupy the 'serious' side of the serious/non-serious opposition. Derrida plays with his readers by asking them to decide for themselves how to assess the seriousness of his text: 'I had (very) sincerely promised to be serious. Have I kept my promise?' (197). Should we take Derrida seriously in his non-serious assault on seriousness? What is the nature of his speech act in *Limited Inc.*, is it felicitous or infelicitous, serious or non-serious, literal or metaphoric, performative or constative? Derrida's practice does not simply offer an alternative to Searle's views which would be susceptible to discussion according to shared standards of academic debate. Instead, Derrida questions those standards and their indebtedness to an unquestioned preference for the serious and the literal, a preference which simultaneously validates and limits the validity of theory. Without simply opposing the injunction to be 'serious', Derrida subjects it to extreme theoretical pressure which brings its authority into question.

Derrida's demonstration of the way in which theory is complicit with the object it is theorizing is, in my view, decisive. From the perspective of poststructuralism, Althusser's notion of Theory as the sole agency capable of telling the truth of others looks self-deluded in the extreme. So *Limited Inc.* provides the theoretical explanation for theory's self-dispossession of its own most cherished claims and privileges. Deconstruction, according to Derrida, resembles a theory (271), but it is also theory's other (135–6), a practice which accepts that theory is always in some way ironic, parasitic, metaphoric, citational, cryptic, fictive, literary, deceitful (137). Derrida acknowledges that his speech-act opponents may not be happy to learn that their seriousness cannot be taken seriously, but he advises that it is 'Up to them to take this opportunity or to transform this infelicity into rapture [*jouissance*]' (137). *Jouissance* is as much pleasure as pain, and here it is the exquisite and distressed

insight into the dissipation of the claims of theory. *Limited Inc.* diagnoses the delusion of grandeur from which theory draws its authority; at
the same time, in large measure through its own playful, irritating and
brilliant textual practice, it gestures towards the recognition of theory as
something other than an impartial, authoritative discourse. In this key
moment when poststructuralism grasps its own activity, theory's defining claims of abstraction and universality are knowingly renounced.
Poststructuralism gestures towards the possibility of opening up thought
to something unheard, and in the process theory is itself *othered*, made
unrecognizable to itself.

However the importance of Derrida's *Limited Inc.* is not exhausted by
the power of its theoretical dismantling of theory. The account I have
given of *Limited Inc.* so far emphasizes the break between structuralist
and poststructuralist conceptions of the theoretical enterprise. This has
also sometimes been depicted as the collapse of a certain Enlightenment project to dominate the real and to domesticate thought. But just
as the othering of theory derives from an appropriative misreading of
Austin's notion of performativity, the designation of theory as emanci-
pated from Enlightenment mystification entails a further misreading. For
poststructuralism to identify itself as unfettered from the illusions of
theory would be a further illusion, an important element in the self-
misrecognition which makes it what it is. The interest of *Limited Inc.* in
this context is that, whilst performing its departure from the normative,
regulative fallacies of theory, it knows full well that those mechanisms
inevitably continue to regulate its performative flouting of them. In the
final essay of *Limited Inc.*, 'Vers une éthique de la discussion', Derrida's
style shifts abruptly, as he himself indicates: 'In addressing you in as direct
a manner as possible, I am returning to a very classical, *straightforward* [in
English in original] form of discussion' (206–7). Now, in response to
questions posed by Gerald Graff rather than to Searle's more oppositional
polemic, Derrida writes in a manner much closer to the philosophical
style he had previously parodied. This goes together with statements of
intention which suggest that deconstruction, as the other of theory, is
nevertheless within theory, contained by its practices and norms, rather
than in some unlocatable other place. Deconstruction turns out, after all,
to be regulated and contained by the frameworks it calls into question:

> I have never put 'radically in question concepts like truth, reference
> and the stability of interpretative contexts', if 'putting radically in
> question' means contesting that there is and that there must be
> truth, reference and stable contexts of interpretation. I have, which

is a quite different matter, asked questions which I hope are necessary about the possibility of these things, of these values, of these
norms, of this stability (which is by essence always provisional and
finite). This questioning and the discourse which goes with the possibility of these questions (indeed the discourse on the possibility
and the limits of the questioning attitude in general) obviously no
longer belong, no longer simply, in a homogeneous way, to the
order of truth, reference, contextuality. But they don't destroy them
or contradict them.

(277–8)

Here is a statement in which the theorist's interest in generality and
conditions of possibility is explicitly upheld. Even the aside that makes
the possibility of norms always provisional and finite addresses the issue
in terms of essentiality ('by essence') and universality ('always'). Derrida
acknowledges that asking questions about the conditions of possibility
of concepts such as truth and reference is a move embedded within
the philosophical tradition, even if it also seems to weaken some of the
privileged terms of that tradition. This places him in an ambiguous
relationship to the project of theory, but one which certainly cannot be
characterized as outright rejection. Deconstruction, like Kantian critique, does not purport simply to stand outside the objects of its
scrutiny. It knows itself to be part of what it strives to question. And
this means that some of the aspirations of theory are retained even as
they are subjected to the work of deconstruction. Habermas's allegation
that Derrida breaks with the Enlightenment project entails, as we saw
in chapter 2, a false radicalization of deconstruction which may mask its
truly radical insight: its knowledge that the errors and illusions of the
past are now *inescapable*.

One of the consequences of all this is that the privileged status
implied and conferred in Althusser's capitalization of Theory is dismantled. Theory can never get sufficiently outside what it is analysing
to enable it to maintain a pure descriptive, legislative or regulative
function. In the terms Lyotard adopts from Kant, its judgements must
be reflective rather than determinant because its grounding concepts
are not known in advance. Deleuze and Guattari go even further in
*Qu'est-ce que la philosophie?* by insisting that concepts are not found
ready-made by philosophers, but that they 'must be invented, fabricated
or rather created, and they would be nothing without the signature of
those who create them'.[16] It would be a mistake to impose a false unity
on the various thinkers who can be broadly grouped together as post-

structuralist. Even so, one feature they have in common is a scepticism about the claims of theory which both restricts and opens up the possibilities of thought. The ambition of mastering the whole domain of the knowable is discredited, and at the same time it is suggested that the reach of thought might be extended beyond the barriers which hitherto have kept it in check.

When Hillis Miller announced the 'triumph of theory' in 1986, he was highlighting an *institutional* dominance which *theoretically* post-structuralism is ill-equipped to maintain. It renounces the ambition of constituting anything like a Kantian philosophy faculty, which might judiciously arbitrate in border disputes between academic disciplines. Instead, it willingly undermines the authority of theory without renouncing all theoretical endeavour. With an ambiguous fidelity to what went before and excited bewilderment as to what might come after, post-structuralism heralds a new understanding of what it means to do theory. In this conception the situation of theory is strictly untenable as it endeavours to speak of generalities without succumbing to the illusion that it is possible to occupy the position of the master. The final section of this chapter explores the ambiguities of this situation as they are encapsulated in the image of theory as a ghost which has somehow survived its own demise; the next section looks at some responses to the 'death of theory' in discussions of what it means to be 'post-theoretical'.

## Post-theory

The term 'post-theory' has been adopted in the title of two collections of essays, *Post-Theory: Reconstructing Film Studies* (1996) and *Post-Theory: New Directions in Criticism* (1999), though the suggestion that the moment of theory may be passed is now a well-established commonplace.[17] The subtitles of the two post-theory volumes indicate the different disciplinary fields covered by the essays (film studies and literary criticism), and they also suggest significant differences in approach. In the earlier volume, what comes 'after theory' is a process of *reconstruction*, as film studies can get back to what it should have been doing all along; for the editors of the later volume, the demise of theory opens up the possibility of *new* directions. The first book repudiates theory whereas the second seeks to go beyond it. A similar discrepancy emerges between Docherty's *After Theory* and Cunningham's *Reading after Theory*. In the first case, the end of theory entails the liberation of thought from Enlightenment shackles; in the second it means that we can finally get back to close reading of literary masterpieces.

These different versions of post-theory have at least one thing in common: they rely on a depiction of theory as monolithic, ossified and oppressive so that their own post-theoretical practice can then be figured as a liberation. The post-theorists follow Althusser in giving Theory an initial capital. This implies that Theory is a single phenomenon which can be broadly identified, though it turns out to refer to quite different practices. For Docherty in *After Theory*, Theory refers to the drive towards abstract theorization 'as it came to be practised in the twentieth century';[18] for Cunningham in *Reading after Theory* it is 'the modern kind [of theory] which took over from the 1960s on'.[19] The opening paragraphs of *Post-Theory: Reconstructing Film Studies* acknowledge the diversity of theoretical movements, but nevertheless lump them all together:

> Our title risks misleading you. Is this book about the end of film theory? No. It's about the end of Theory, and what can and should come after.
>
> What we call Theory is an abstract body of thought which came into prominence in Anglo-American film studies during the 1970s. The most famous avatar of Theory was that aggregate of doctrines derived from Lacanian psychoanalysis, Structuralist semiotics, Post-Structuralist literary theory, and variants of Althusserian Marxism. Here, unabashedly, was Grand Theory – perhaps the first that cinema studies had ever had. The Theory was put forth as the indispensable frame of reference for understanding all filmic phenomena: the activities of the film spectator, the construction of the film text, the social and political functions of cinema, and the development of film technology and the industry.
>
> (xiii)

The 'most famous avatar of Theory' turns out to be an 'aggregate of doctrines' of which the underlying identity is never justified. The capitalization of Theory is an enabling gesture which confers false unity and totalizing pretensions on an otherwise bewildering diversity. It is much easier to combat and to defeat a single monolithic Theory than it is to contend with the various branches of psychoanalysis, semiotics, post-structuralism and Marxism. Even so, in the Introduction to *Post-Theory: Reconstructing Film Studies* it soon emerges that the principal theoretical opponent is Lacanian psychoanalysis, and the essays in the volume all exemplify 'the possibility of scholarship that is not reliant upon the psychoanalytic framework that dominates film academia' (xvi). This raises what Žižek, in a telling dissection of post-theory, calls 'The Strange Case of the Missing Lacanians'.[20] With a few exceptions including himself, Žižek claims to know of no film theorists who effectively accept Lacan as their ultimate background.[21] The evil Lacanians are like the reds under the bed who serve as the target of hysterical denunciation, but who don't actually exist; and Theory, complete with its threatening initial capital, is to a significant extent a creation of its opponents, at least in as far as it is depicted as a unified field.

The key objections to Theory echo to an uncanny degree those made by Picard to *la nouvelle critique*: it is totalizing, it employs unintelligible jargon, it distorts the films or texts it purports to explain by finding in them reflections of its own prejudices, through its institutional dominance it has become a complacent *doxa* rather than challenging or instructive, it is biased against truth.[22] Theory purports to explain everything, but in fact it merely allows its practitioners to say anything they like.[23] Cunningham argues that 'at its most rampant Theory happily eschewed the idea of any interpretative stop'.[24] Theory endorses the view that 'anything goes', that one can say absolutely anything, even if the theorists themselves do not endorse such a view:

> Once they're installed, what I. A. Richards called *stock notions* – and the idea that 'anything goes' because Derrida, or whoever, says so is one of the most persistent stock notions of Theory – stay firmly in place even when denied by those masters believed to uphold them.[25]

The fudge and obfuscation here are quite shocking. It is implied that Derrida 'or whoever' say that 'anything goes', though no supporting evidence is provided. And anyway, however vigorously or repeatedly 'those masters' might deny that anything goes, the notion is persistent and firmly in place. No amount of denial could dislodge it, because Cunningham knows it is there. This is all the more astonishing because Cunningham advocates careful and close reading, whereas 'Theorists are, as a class, bad readers'.[26] Proper reading requires a 'readerly *tact*' which involves not only respecting literary texts, but also 'listening to what *Theorists* really say as well'.[27] So Cunningham knows what Theorists 'really' say, even if they don't actually say it. From this position of 'tact', it is established that even if no particular theorist is cited as arguing that 'anything goes', this is nevertheless the view that Theory persistently endorses.

These caricatures of theory are opposed by values such as tact and patience which appear to be quite temperate but which in practice also rely on a dogmatic arrogation of the interpretative authority which poststructuralism calls into question. The post-theorists reclaim for themselves the comfortable superiority of a privileged, unbiased perspective. Their readings of texts or films are deemed better to represent what they really mean, rather than making them comply to some pre-established theoretical framework. They even purport to speak on behalf of the poststructuralists, since they claim to know what it is the poststructualists are saying even when they don't say it. Žižek suggests in relation to the film studies version of post-theory that the post-theorists' show of modesty allows them to claim a much more immoderate position of enunciation, as they set themselves up as observers exempted from the object of study and therefore able to survey it with a neutral gaze.[28] Žižek suggests that the way to counter statements of modesty is by taking them literally: "'Actually, what you're saying *is* just a modest contribution!'", or, to paraphrase Freud, "Why are you saying that you're only giving a modest opinion, when what you're giving is only a modest opinion?'".[29] So when, for example, Carroll concedes that he was probably naïve in confessing that he couldn't make sense of the scepticism of 'one of these sophisticated postmodernist film Theorists', we might agree that he is indeed naïve, and exhort him to try to do better in the future.[30]

If the sense that the moment of Theory is passed is shared in the different texts I have mentioned, there is less consensus about what should come next. Cunningham advocates 'a rational, proper, moral even, respect for the primacy of text over all theorizing about text'.[31] For Bordwell and Carroll, the end of Theory is not the end of theory, but an opportunity to return to a better form of theoretical reflection:

> What is coming after Theory is not another Theory, but *theories* and the activity of *theorizing*. A theory of film defines a problem within the domain of cinema (defined nondogmatically) and sets out to solve it through logical reflection, empirical research, or a combination of both. *Theorizing* is a commitment to using the best canons of inference and evidence available to answer the question posed. The standards ought to be those of the most stringent philosophical reasoning, historical argument, and sociological, economic, and critical analysis we can find, in film studies or elsewhere (even in science).
>
> (xiv)

They defend cognitivist 'middle-level research' and 'piecemeal theorizing' over the grand abstractions of Theory.[32] If theorizing continues, it should be in more modest, empirical and pluralistic vein, for, as Bordwell concludes, 'Grand Theories will come and go, but research and scholarship will endure'.[33] Once again, it is easy to hear in this the echo of Picard's appeal for modest, scholarly research and rational, responsible standards of argumentation.

This version of post-theory as *return* to former standards contrasts with the aspiration in Docherty's *After Theory* and in *Post-Theory: New Directions in Criticism* to look beyond the demise of Theory. Docherty rejects pragmatism as just another theoretical position, and concludes that it is 'only in the refusal to be answerable to a governing theory that thought, and above all theoretical thought, becomes possible once more'.[34] The editors of *Post-Theory: New Directions in Criticism* describe post-theory as

> a state of thinking which discovers itself in a constant state of deferral, a position of reflexivity and an experience of questioning which constantly displaces itself in the negotiation with the aporias of Theory. Post-Theory speaks to the Other to whom it must be addressed.[35]

In these versions, what comes after Theory is not a return to older certainties. Rather, it entails trying to find 'new directions' to think through the 'post-' of post-theory and to discover new possibilities for thought by seeking to explore otherness. In similar vein, Docherty argues that Enlightenment rationality 'must be countered with a postmodern orientation towards alterity and heterogeneity, such as we have it in, for example, the ethics of Levinas or the psychoanalysis of Kristeva or Lacan'.[36] These versions of post-theoretical thought are, then, still closely allied to the theoretical concerns and prestigious thinkers repudiated in Bordwell and Carroll's version.

The editors of *Post-Theory: New Directions in Criticism* suggest that 'the monolith of Common Sense' is a fantasy of Theory, constructed as a fictive reactionary force which shores up Theory's self-perception as radical (ix–x). If this is true, it is also the case that Theory is a fantasy figure which doesn't quite correspond to the characterizations of it. Žižek is right to describe post-theoretical attacks on Theory as 'a comically simplified caricature'.[37] Even so, this non-dialogue between imaginary adversaries may mark a significant shift in the theoretical agenda. In his short Preface to *Post-Theory: New Directions in Criticism* Ernesto Laclau neatly reassesses the contemporary status of theory:

On the one hand we are certainly witnessing the progressive blurring of the classical frontiers which made 'theory' a distinctive object: in an era of generalized critique of the metalinguistic function, the analysis of the concrete escapes the rigid straitjacket of the distinction theoretical framework/case studies. But, on the other hand, precisely because we are living in a *post*-theoretical age, theory cannot be opposed by a flourishing empiricity liberated from theoretical fetters. What we have, instead, is a process of mutual contamination between 'theory' and 'empiria' – the former having abandoned its aspiration to constitute a 'superhard transcendality' and the latter having lost the innocence associated with pure 'data'. So, although we have entered a post-theoretical universe, we are definitely not in an a-theoretical one.

(vii)

Laclau does not give theory an initial capital nor does he set it up as a sclerotic monolith to be righteously vanquished. His account roots post-theory in the self-questioning of theory which was discussed in the previous section. In his account, the need for the reorientation of theory stems from an internal dynamic by which it discovers its own limitations. The demise of theory comes in part from its inability to keep itself rigorously separate from non-theory. Theory, in for example its psycho-analytic or deconstructive forms, is often associated with a practice of interpretation or close reading, so that at its best it is elaborated through exchange with a person or text rather than just 'applied' from the outside. In consequence the boundaries between theory and reading, or as Laclau puts it between theoretical framework and case study, are hard or even impossible to draw. This does not result in a simple abolition of the distinction. Laclau talks instead of 'a process of mutual contamination', so that theory cannot be conceived as independent of the data and the data cannot be accessed separately from the theory. As a result, there can be no question of simply saying farewell to theory and getting back to 'a flourishing empiricity liberated from theoretical fetters'. However, it is important that in Laclau's version this mutual contamination produces a distinct agenda. If theory is not quite Theory, and data are never entirely given, Laclau's programme for post-theory nevertheless comes down clearly on the side of the latter. He refers to 'a new sophistication in the analysis of the concrete, which can no longer be conceived in terms of an unproblematic empiricity' (vii). Our conception of 'the concrete' might need re-thinking, but the concrete is nevertheless placed before theoretical frameworks as the prime subject for analysis.

Laclau makes two important moves here. He suggests that post-theory evolves out of developments in theory rather than simply breaking with it, and he prioritizes the concrete over the theoretical, however slippery the terms of the distinction might be. At least for the moment, the time for grand abstractions seems to be over. This can be seen for example in the current flourishing of different forms of identity politics and corresponding critical practices. Whereas poststructuralism broadly rejects stable identities, subject areas such as queer theory and postcolonial studies respond to the fact that in many circumstances we do identify ourselves as situated, embodied, gendered, sexual and racial beings. This is not necessarily in blunt denial of poststructuralism, even if it is sometimes presented and perceived as such. There is no necessary contradiction between believing that identity is radically unstable and that our sexual, national, or racial identifications are important to us. Even so, the renewed focus on human diversity and specificity entails the displacement of theory in favour of the more empirically based work of cultural studies, with its fertile sub-disciplines: the critique of Orientalism, subaltern studies, the investigation of minority discourses, and the study of culture as hybridity.[38] By contrast to cultural studies, with its interest in all forms of particularity, theory has been depicted as highbrow, elitist, and grounded in white, male, Eurocentric assumptions. However, as Rey Chow convincingly argues, despite the opposition between proponents of theory and cultural studies, the mutual implications between them are in fact tenacious.[39] Similarly, rejecting the simple choice between theoretical abstraction and empirical data, Laclau's Preface to *Post-Theory: New Directions in Criticism* astutely suggests that the analysis of the concrete is bound up with theoretical reflection, even if it also represents a shift in emphasis and a more explicit politicization of intellectual practices.

The work of Toril Moi illustrates the turn from theoretical abstractions to concrete particularities. Moi's early, much-read book on feminist theory *Sexual/Textual Politics* (1985) is sympathetic to poststructuralist theory and heavily indebted to it. Her more recent *What is a Woman?* (1999) is in part a work of self-critique in which poststructuralist work on sex and gender is described as reaching 'fantastic levels of abstraction without delivering the concrete, situated, and materialist understanding of the body it leads us to expect'.[40] Drawing on the thought of Stanley Cavell, Moi now argues for a return to 'the sphere of the ordinary, that is to say the sphere in which our political and personal struggles actually take place' (120). The excessive abstractions of poststructuralist theory can now be seen as neglecting the familiar, the concrete and the everyday. However, this does not entail a wholesale rejection of theory, as Moi argues in a lengthy engagement with Jane Tomkins's appeal for the inclusion of the personal in literary criticism. Although Moi does not dismiss out of hand the characterization of theory as patriarchal, alienating, cold and inherently oppressive, she argues against the implication that it *must always* have these qualities. If the postmodern 'return to the personal' simply meant abandoning theory, it would also be necessary to give up the claim that what one writes might have validity for others: 'Like other theorists, I have no wish to write in a way that is falsely universalizing, exclusionary, arrogant, and domineering. Yet the fact remains that it is impossible to write theory without generalizing and universalizing' (123). Moi's repudiation of the excesses of high poststructuralism still entails a commitment to theory, understood as the search for a discourse capable of broad validity and applicability.

One of the principal reasons for turning against theory is the belief that it is insufficiently political, that either it is irrelevant to or else it positively undermines meaningful political practice. Habermas objected to poststructuralism on the grounds that it could provide no norms to govern and to justify political action. Edward Said reflects this view in *Culture and Imperialism* when he describes the work of Foucault and Lyotard in the 1970s and 1980s as a curtailing of their earlier political radicalism.[41] Foucault turned away from the study of oppositional forces in society to focus on the cultivation of the self; and Lyotard's rejection of grand narratives left no room for global revolutionary politics. In both cases, all that remains is a watered-down activism restricted to local issues. Said expresses a suspicion towards poststructuralism with which many would agree. In its difficulty and abstraction it can appear elitist and politically numbing, and its suspicion towards agency undercuts the possibility of effective political intervention. The return to the political in the humanities thus becomes bound up with a turn away from theory. Already in his address of 1986, Hillis Miller related this to 'a demand to be ethically and politically responsible in our teaching and writing, to grapple with realities rather than with the impalpabilities of theoretical abstractions and barbarous words about language, such as the names of figures of speech'; and he listed the subjects which were replacing theory as 'history, culture, society, politics, institutions, class and gender conditions, the social context, the material base in the sense of institutionalization, conditions of production, technology, distribution, and consumption of "cultural products", among other products'.[42] Questions of history, context and human specificity underpin the re-politicization of work in the humanities.[43] Even a prominent theorist such as Judith Butler suggests that what she does should be called *politics* rather than *theory*:

> I do not understand the notion of 'theory', and am hardly interested in being cast as its defender . . . If the political task is to show that theory is never merely *theoria*, in the sense of disengaged contemplation, and to insist that it is fully political (*phronesis* or even *praxis*), then why not simply call this operation *politics*, or some necessary permutation of it?[44]

This may be part of the ebb and flow of intellectual and institutional fashion rather than a permanent realignment.[45] The collective volume written by Butler together with Ernesto Laclau and Slavoj Žižek, *Contingency, Hegemony, Universality* (2000), demonstrates that the question of universality is still a pressing concern in theory and politics. Moreover, it is clearly a simplification to envision theory and politics as directly in opposition to one another. Butler's comment quoted in the previous paragraph insists that theory is not merely 'disengaged contemplation'; and the ambiguous title of the book co-edited by Butler, *What's Left of Theory?* neatly implies the ambivalence towards theory inherent in the politicized wing of the humanities: the title suggests that political criticism is simultaneously *outside* theory (what is *to the left* of theory?) and still *inside* it (what *remains* of theory?). Theory survives, if only as a remnant or a ghost. As Moi indicates, its forms may be variable, but it is hard to dispense with its aspiration to make general and communicable validity claims. Such claims may be ultimately deluded, but without them we might have little to say to one another beyond fragments of autobiography formulated in largely private languages. And the repudiation of theory on the grounds that it claims to know too much is merely part of the caricature wheeled out to discredit it.

Discussions of post-theory tend to have at least two features in common: the creation of an imaginary opponent (theory is transmogrified into Theory, despite the reluctance to attribute Theory's most outrageous claims to any particular theorist), and a desire to set the agenda for others to follow. Bordwell and Carroll introduce their collection by saying it is about 'the end of Theory, and what can and *should* come after' (xiii; my emphasis); Cunningham describes what reading 'should do' after Theory;[46] the editors of *Post-Theory: New Directions in Criticism* tell the younger generation of critics that it is 'their task not to re-enact old paradigms and operations' and that they 'must be in a constant state of rediscovery of the conditions of Post-Theory' (xvi). The contents of these normativities may be different, but the impulse to produce them is commonplace. Such comments betray the new authoritarianism which lurks behind the rejection of the allegedly authoritarian discourse of theory. The place of the master is apparently available once again, and the post-theorists are eager to occupy it. They know what's best for us, and it certainly isn't theory. And in any case, there is no point in continuing with theory, with or without a capital, because it is dead or dying. References to the death of theory are now so frequent that they may be treated as a cliché or a joke.[47] The final section of this chapter examines the personification of theory which endows it with life, and therefore condemns it to death but also allows for its ghostly return to haunt the banquet of post-theory.

## Conclusion: spectres of theory

Theory provokes a quite remarkable amount of figural language, as those who write about it fumble around for some way of characterizing this elusive entity. In the space of one paragraph Noel Carroll has theory 'on the wane', 'out of gas', 'exhausted' and 'dead'.[48] So theory is like the moon, an automobile or a living creature. The figuration of theory in living terms, particularly through the trope of personification, is by far the most persistent source of metaphors.[49] This can reach comic proportions, perhaps intentionally in *Post-Theory: New Directions in Criticism*, in which theory (described at one moment as a 'sausage machine')[50] is attributed with various desires, self-perceptions and emotions. It is 'only too happy' to witness its own passing; when attacked it 'reacts with righteous indignation' and 'redoubles its efforts'; it wishes to retain the 'right to write its own epitaph'.[51]

It is striking that the personification of theory most frequently leads to references to its death, as if its trajectory could be understood as a life cycle which must inevitably come to an end. References to the 'wake' of theory are now commonplace, for example in the titles of Paul Bové's *In the Wake of Theory* and Barbara Johnson's *The Wake of Deconstruction*, and numerous passages of other recent works.[52] Johnson explains her title as a triple pun: the wake is a service held for the not-yet-buried dead, the trace on the water left by the passage of a ship or whale, and (less grammatically) a state of nonsleep.[53] I assume that at least the first two of these are evoked in other references to the wake of theory. The addition of the third sense, at the cost of stretching grammar to breaking point, brings an important extra element, or rather it makes clearer

a problem which was already implicit in the other senses. If deconstruction, or theory more generally, is dead, how can it be awoken, how can
what has passed away somehow still be present, or return, how can it be
that its influence has not simply vanished? The other senses of wake
also suggest that what has gone has nevertheless not yet fully departed:
the wake which precedes a burial occurs whilst the dead are still
amongst us; the wake left on the water is the visible trace of something
which is still not yet far away. In all cases, what has gone has not quite
gone, its presence can still be felt. Johnson traces rumours of the death
of deconstruction to at least 1980. Deconstruction is dead, though at its
own wake it has not yet finished dying. As Bennington reports Derrida
as saying, 'nothing seems so clearly to indicate the vitality of deconstruction as announcements of its imminent demise';[54] or even, one
might add, announcements of its recent death.

The labour of figuration to which theory gives rise is an attempt to
pin it down, to identify what sort of entity it is and to understand how
its effects occur. The personification of theory treats it as a being capable of life and agency, and therefore of death; and once its death has
been announced, a line can be drawn under the ignorance which it
exposes and it is possible to return in confidence to the certainties and
structures of authority which it endangers. Theory is dead, and can now
be forgotten. The persistence of claims of its death suggests that it was
given life *only so that* it could then be proclaimed as dead. But in so far
as we are still present at its wake it has not yet gone away, it is still
amongst us despite its demise. Death implies the termination of agency
and influence, but to talk of its wake, or alternatively in terms of its
legacy or afterlife, suggests that in some sense its agency continues, even
if it is now uncertain how and to whom that agency should be attributed. Theory is dead, but it won't quite lie down. As Johnson says of
deconstruction, like Finnegan it might wake up at its own wake.[55]

In this book I have argued that attacks on theory and on poststructuralism in particular follow predictable patterns and rely on
consistent claims which result from poor or non-existent readings of the
texts being attacked. The chapters on Lyotard, Levinas, Althusser and
Kristeva indicate through detailed accounts of some of their work how
their texts deal with the great philosophical issues of knowledge, ethics,
meaning and identity. At its simplest my point has been that these
thinkers have important things to say about important matters, and we
shouldn't foreclose discussion by declaring their work to be 'dead'.
Indeed, part of their interest derives from the complex ways in which
they negotiate the prospects and limits of their own theoretical projects,

and of the project of theory more generally. Only when theory is defined in a ridiculously narrow way, for example when it is identified
uniquely with French and French-inspired work from the 1970s and
1980s or more restrictively still with a particular phase of deconstruction, does it make any sense to announce its demise. Jean-Michel
Rabaté concludes his informed and splendidly polemical book *The
Future of Theory* by listing seven thinkers who are engaged in innova-
tive theoretical work, ten schools which are mapping out the main
projects for contemporary theory and six agendas or special projects
which are particularly relevant to current interests in theory.[56] These
lists are not intended to be limiting, and the fact that any one of us
might want to add or to substitute different names and projects testifies
to the vitality of the theoretical enterprise, even if it is momentarily
unfashionable to name it as such.

So it is (always) too early to say that theory is dead. In its wake it is
still with us, through the traces on the water which are still visible, or
the corpse in the coffin which will not lie still. The image of theory
trying to write its own epitaph used by the editors of *Post-Theory: New
Directions in Criticism* nicely encapsulates the paradoxical survival of
theory even after its own death. In this reference we can see the personification of theory getting tangled up in its own figural web, undermining its logic of life, agency and death, and affirming the survival of
something not quite identifiable despite the employment of a figure
which aims to identify and to kill it. If the personification of theory
allows it to live and to die, it also suggests its capacity to return as a
ghost.[57] As Rabaté puts it, 'If Theory is reduced to the ghost of itself,
then this is a very obtrusive ghost that keeps walking and shaking its
chains in our old academic castles'.[58] The notion that theory survives in
spectral form is taken further in the editors' Preface to *What's Left of
Theory?*, which considers the extent to which theory has yet to be laid
to rest. Whilst the title suggests that theory may be gone, the Preface
implies that it is still with us, as a ghost:

> Thus, a number of questions remain: Is there a specter of 'high
> theory' that continues to inform the left work in cultural studies
> and new historicism that cannot be eradicated from its operations,
> and on which it remains fundamentally dependent? Has 'theory'
> post-de Man been repudiated only to emerge as the animating spec-
> ter of contemporary literary analysis, whereby 'theory' is both dis-
> avowed and preserved in the reaction formation that has followed?
> Is theory still 'poststructuralism' or has that very term become

meaningless precisely as its dissemination and contamination in cultural and political analysis establishes a set of unanticipated meanings for the term? In a sense, the value of poststructuralism no longer forms the pivot of contemporary debate, but, rather, its place in new forms of cultural and political analysis is both inchoate and central. Although there are leftist positions that seek a full purging of the poststructuralist trace, panicking at the slightest trace of 'jargon', they still contend with its specter as one of the ghostly conditions of their own emergence.[59]

In a passage dominated by the question of *remains* ('a number of questions remain', 'on which it remains fundamentally dependent', 'the left work', implying both work done on the political left and the work which is left to do), it turns out that what remains is a spectre. It confounds attempts to repudiate it or pin it down, as it is both 'disavowed and preserved', 'inchoate and central'. It is present and absent, alive and dead, evanescent and foundational, the elusive condition of everything that follows. Its haunting presence in this passage is felt in the accumulation of questions and in the suspicion that the terms being used may no longer be meaningful, as if the presence of the spectre undercuts the ability of language to affirm anything with confidence whilst also being one of the 'ghostly conditions' of saying anything at all. And since this Preface is multi-authored, even its questions cannot be attributed to a single voice or source. There is only a rumbling of voices trying to emerge into sense and to acquire the power of assertion. Moreover, in the final paragraph of the Preface, the spectre of theory turns out to be even more difficult to pin down. Politicized critics reject theory because of its formalism, but the editors of *What's Left of Theory?* argue that this is an unfair reading of the work of thinkers such as Derrida, de Man and Foucault. So the repudiation of theory may be addressed to an imaginary entity, raising the possibility that the ghost which continues to haunt us is the trace of something that never existed.[60] By this point, the process of figuration which justifies the claim that theory is dead has become hopelessly snarled, revealing that theory is not so easy to grasp, and therefore not so easy to kill, as some may have hoped. The figuration which seemed designed to pin it down ends up making it all the more elusive. Neither alive nor dead, the ghost of theory does not speak from any position which we can easily repudiate.

So what future does this leave for theory? In an account tinged with nostalgia, Antoine Compagnon concedes that the glory days of theory in the 1960s and 1970s are now well gone. In Compagnon's account the original impetus theory is oppositional and subversive, but it is destined to be institutionalized and turned into a method which is as dull and as unself-questioning as what it initially aimed to challenge.[61] Malcolm Bowie has expressed a similar sense of disappointment when describing how some critics have turned to theory in order to blot out the perplexity haunting the critical act:

> In certain cases, their commodified 'theory' has been attractive simply because it could still the rage of a literary text, or reduce to diagrammatic form a mobile and over-determined cultural field. Theory, in this incarnation, is a system of brakes, chocks, and mooring ropes applied to a semantic mechanism that might otherwise – oh calamity! – run wild or fly free; such writing remains safe and normative even as it pays tribute to difficulty, excess, transgression, and catastrophe. Much of the critical language that theory inspires has gone stale, and the time that it occupies is as flat, characterless, and future-bereft as that of a Rotary Club luncheon.[62]

Anyone who has ploughed through mechanical, turgid, opaque, theory-driven prose is likely to share Bowie's exasperation; and those of us who use theory live in constant fear that we will be next to be caught out for replicating its worst traits. However, Bowie contrasts this commodified theory with a theoretical impetus which seeks out 'as yet unrealized zones of meaning', generating 'flexed, tensed, desirous, and prospective critical performances' which are 'restlessly inventive in their diction'.[63] It is through these performances – amongst other examples Bowie cites Freud on Michelangelo, Derrida on Plato, and Lacan on Poe – that fresh, startling questions are asked and new possibilities of meaning are opened up. This implies that to set out a future programme for theory would be to destroy in advance any possibility it might have of significantly restructuring the intellectual fields in which we work. No one could predict the innovations of a Derrida or a Žižek; the best we can hope is that we still have the openness of vision to recognize their importance when we have the good fortune to encounter them. Currently, in public debate fuelled by half-baked, ill-informed and hysterical critiques, it is still, and increasingly, respectable to decry theory on the grounds that there are some (or many) bad theorists. A danger inherent in this situation is that we stultify our and our students' ability to engage with new ideas and emerging realities. We also risk impeding the core function of theoretical reflection, which is to join in the ongoing endeavour to understand as best we can what is common and communicable about our disparate lives.

If theory returns in spectral form after its apparent death, it is because we have not entirely given up on it. This book has traced some of the ways in which theory gestures towards the possibility of heightened understanding even as it becomes entangled in the difficulties of achieving it. Stories have played an important role here because they both promote and impede the anticipation of intelligibility. Indeed, this may be why theory is attracted and rebutted by stories in equal measure. Telling and reading stories turn out to be not so far removed from practising and reading theory, at least to the extent that all of these can be seen as the attempt to find or to forge some comprehensible pattern which unites bewildering data. The pattern, though, does not fully or finally come to light, so the work of theory continues. It may be that theory's ambition to speak of general truths is its inaugural, defining fallacy, but it is a fallacy that could only be dispelled at a great cost. Without it, there would be no prospect of achieving a shareable discourse in which we could speak meaningfully to one another. Theory emerges out of the possibly deluded project of making sense of ourselves and others. It is haunted, and driven, by the inevitability of its failure and the necessity of carrying on.

# Notes

## Introduction

1 For an informative account of repeated misreadings of theory, specifically of deconstruction, see Rapaport, *The Theory Mess*, especially 5–34. It would be wrong to suggest that antagonism towards French poststructuralism is found only outside France. For hostility in France, see Ferry and Renaut, *La Pensée 68*, and the warm reception given in some quarters to Sokal and Bricmont's *Impostures intellectuelles*, to be discussed in chapter 1. Full references to works cited are given in the Bibliography. All translations from French and German are my own except where English-language editions are cited. In quotations emphasis is as in the original unless indicated otherwise.
2 Habermas, *The Philosophical Discourse of Modernity*, 192.
3 For analysis of the disavowal of theory in cultural studies, see Chow, *Ethics after Idealism*, 7–11.
4 Gadamer, *Lob der Theorie*, 43.
5 For discussion of this in relation to the etymology of *theoria*, see Rabaté, *The Future of Theory*, 113–15.
6 Rabaté, *The Future of Theory*, 9.
7 Kant, *Critique of Pure Reason*, 7–35; *Logik*, 25.
8 On the afterlife of theory, with reference to the work of Paul de Man, see Cohen *et al.* (eds), *Material Events: Paul de Man and the Afterlife of Theory*. See especially the discussion in the opening paper of that volume, Cohen, Hillis Miller and Cohen, 'A "Materiality without matter"?', xiv–xvii.
9 Derrida, *Du Droit à la philosophie*, 83; see 81–9 for Derrida's explanation of the continuing need to read Kant.
10 Derrida, *Du Droit à la philosophie*, 81.
11 Derrida, *Du Droit à la philosophie*, 83.
12 Derrida, *Spectres de Marx*, 40. For further discussion of the ambiguity of the Kantian legacy, see chapter 2.
13 Rabaté, *The Future of Theory*, 140.

## 1 Impostures of French theory

1 Sokal and Bricmont, 'Préface à la deuxième édition', *Impostures intellectuelles*, 28. Subsequent references, given in the text, are to the English-language

edition of the book, *Intellectual Impostures*, except (as in the current case) where the passage appears only in the French edition.

2   On the use of this topos in the Sokal affair, see Jeanneret, *L'Affaire Sokal ou la querelle des impostures*, 188–9.

3   Picard, *Nouvelle Critique ou nouvelle imposture*, 51–2. Subsequent references are in the text.

4   Picard, *La Carrière de Jean Racine*, 14.

5   For a more detailed account of the controversy, see Thody, *Roland Barthes: A Conservative Estimate*, 54–89. Useful accounts, largely from Barthes's point of view, are also given in Moriarty, *Roland Barthes*, 59–72, and Culler, *Barthes*, 61–9. The polarized response of academics to the dispute can be seen by comparing Doubrovsky's *Pourquoi la nouvelle critique*, which takes a new critical standpoint, and Bonzon's *La Nouvelle Critique et Racine*, which patiently analyses new critical readings of Racine, but finds little merit in them.

6   See Picard, *Nouvelle Critique ou nouvelle imposture*, 11: 'A little disorientated, and more scandalized than amused, I thought it was mainly a commercial venture, in which the author had amused himself by throwing himself, with all the talent we know him to have, into the risky and the preposterous.'

7   Goldmann, *Le Dieu caché*, 349.

8   Mauron, *L'Inconscient dans l'oeuvre et la vie de Racine*, 17–18.

9   Barthes, *Sur Racine*, 29. Subsequent references are in the text.

10   See Barthes, *Critique et vérité*, 10–11.

11   In 'La Pharmacie de Platon', first published in 1968 and reprinted in *La Dissémination*, Derrida explicitly denies that the critic can say *n'importe quoi*: 'And anyone who thought they were authorized to add more, that is, to add anything at all, would have understood nothing' (*La Dissémination*, 72). It is clear that those who accuse Derrida of authorizing *n'importe quoi* have not read him any more closely than the opponents of *la nouvelle critique* had read the works of Barthes, Mauron, Goldmann and others.

12   Sokal, 'Transgressing the boundaries: toward a transformative hermeneutics of quantum gravity', reprinted in Sokal and Bricmont, *Intellectual Impostures*, 200.

13   See Sokal, 'A physicist experiments with cultural studies'.

14   See Sokal and Bricmont, *Intellectual Impostures*, ix, referring to an article in *The Guardian* by Jon Henley.

15   See Raymond Tallis, 'Sokal and Bricmont: Is this the beginning of the end of the dark ages in the humanities?'

16   Barthes, *Critique et vérité*, 10. Jeanneret uses this quotation as an epigraph to his *L'Affaire Sokal ou la querelle des impostures*, a book which has proved invaluable in the preparation of this chapter. For some connections between the Barthes–Picard controversy and the Sokal affair, see 185, 194.

17   Sokal and Bricmont, *Impostures intellectuelles*, 13; not in the English edition.

18   See Picard, *Nouvelle critique ou nouvelle imposture*, 63–4, and Sokal and Bricmont, *Intellectual Impostures*, 5.

19   For Sokal and Bricmont's explanation of their choice of authors who are not postmodernists, see *Intellectual Impostures*, 11–12.

20   The problem of defining postmodernism is further discussed in chapter 3.

21 Quoted in Jeanneret, *L'Affaire Sokal ou la querelle des impostures*, 203. A useful history of the word *postmodern* is given in Perry Anderson, *The Origins of Postmodernity*, especially 3–46.

22 Jeanneret, *L'Affaire Sokal ou la querelle des impostures*, 198.

23 For detailed refutations of Sokal and Bricmont by qualified specialists in physics and mathematics, see the essays collected by Jurdant in *Impostures scientifiques*. See for example 'Mathématiques avec Lacan' by Nathalie Charraud, a mathematician and psychoanalyst who flatly repudiates Sokal and Bricmont's particularly virulent attack on Lacan: 'Lacan's mathematical knowledge is never "superficial" . . . the properties he used are never false' (248).

24 Jean-Michel Salanskis gives a pertinent account of Sokal and Bricmont's approach in 'Pour une épistémologie de la lecture', in *Impostures scientifiques*, 174: 'The general "method" of denunciation in the book, which is notably used to an excessive degree in relation to Deleuze, consists in quoting long passages of the authors in question, calling on readers to witness the grotesqueness and absurdity of the discourse which the quotation brings out, and then to pronounce by way of commentary that a given phrase or succession of phrases is strictly devoid of meaning and to pick out the use of mathematical or physical notions in order to stigmatize their non-validity in a footnote.

   In this way, any real reading is evaded: Sokal and Bricmont do not construct a thesis or a meaning from the texts they read in order to argue that the scientific contents on which that thesis or that meaning rely are inexact or wrongly used (giving no support to that thesis or that meaning). They are content either to affirm that there is no meaning, or else that they do not find, in the quoted text, their usual understanding of a certain number of scientific terms.'

25 Barthes, *Critique et vérité*, 42.

26 For evidence, see the analysis based on nearly 300 texts in Jeanneret, *L'Affaire Sokal ou la querelle des impostures*, 144. For Derrida's reaction to Sokal and Bricmont, see his article 'Sokal et Bricmont ne sont pas sérieux'; and for Sokal and Bricmont's response, 'Les Critiques de Derrida et de Dorra ratent leur cible'.

27 Sokal and Bricmont, *Impostures intellectuelles*, 374; the corresponding passage in the English-language edition is rather different.

28 Joan Fujimura, 'L'Autorité du savoir en question', in *Impostures scientifiques*, 218–19. In *Impostures intellectuelles* Sokal and Bricmont describe Fujimura's argument as using 'a confused discourse on non-Euclidean geometry' (374).

29 Žižek, *The Fright of Real Tears*, 4.

30 For further articles on the affair by Sokal and Bricmont, see links on Sokal's web page which can be found at http://www.physics.nyu.edu/faculty/sokal.html.

31 On this aspect of the controversy, and for an astute and detailed account of its various phases in general, see Jeanneret, *L'Affaire Sokal ou la querelle des impostures*.

32 See Bourdieu, *Homo academicus*, 151–5.

33 Bourdieu, *Homo academicus*, 151.

34  Bourdieu, *Homo academicus*, 152.
35  Bouveresse observes the predictability of these counter-accusations in relation to the Sokal–Bricmont affair, in *Prodiges et vertiges de l'analogie*, 143–4:
'Anyone who writes a book like the one by Sokal and Bricmont could also,
I think, all but for a few details, write in advance most of the replies which
he might expect and which have become so predictable for such a long
time that they are no longer of any interest. It would be nice to be surprised
from time to time, but it never happens.'
36  Thody, *Roland Barthes: A Conservative Estimate*, 91.
37  For these and other insults directed by Picard against Barthes, see *Critique et
vérité*, 15–16.
38  See Sokal and Bricmont, *Intellectual Impostures*, 5, 12, 176.

## 2  Enlightenment/poststructuralism

1  On the Enlightenment as totalitarian, see Adorno and Horkheimer, *Dialectic of Enlightenment*, 6. On the critique of the Enlightenment more generally,
see Docherty, 'Postmodernism: An introduction', in Docherty (ed.), *Postmodernism: A Reader*, especially 5–14, and 13 for the description of reason as
racist and imperialist.
2  Derrida, *Limited Inc.*, 261. For further evidence of the importance of Kant
and the Enlightenment for Derrida, see also the essays in *Du Droit à la
philosophie*, especially 'Mochlos – ou le conflit des facultés' and 'Les Pupilles
de l'Université. Le Principe de raison et l'idée de l'Université'.
3  Derrida, *Spectres de Marx*, 149.
4  On the unfinished project of modernity, see Habermas, 'Modernity – an
incomplete project'.
5  Norris, *What's Wrong With Postmodernism*, 70. Norris has consistently
argued for a distinction between Derrida's version of poststructuralism or
deconstruction and the postmodernism of thinkers such as Baudrillard and
Lyotard. In Norris's account, postmodernism rejects the Enlightenment
heritage, whereas Derrida's work is squarely part of it. See for example the
essays collected in *What's Wrong With Postmodernism* and *Deconstruction and
the 'Unfinished Project of Modernity'*.
6  Rorty, *Contingency, Irony, and Solidarity*, 137. For the phrase 'at his best', see
126. Norris concedes that Rorty is correct to see an aspect of Derrida's work
which breaks with received forms of philosophical practice. However,
whereas for Rorty this is the best part of Derrida's work, for Norris, Derrida
is at his best when he writes as a 'philosopher' in a more traditional sense.
For discussion, see for example Norris, *Deconstruction and the 'Unfinished
Project of Modernity'*, 48–51.
7  Habermas, 'Modernity – an incomplete project', 103.
8  Quoted from Hegel's *The Philosophy of History*, in Habermas, *The Philosophical Discourse of Modernity*, 7. Subsequent references to Habermas's book
are given in the text.
9  Rorty, 'Philosophy as a kind of writing: An essay on Derrida', in *Consequences of Pragmatism*, 89–109.
10  For discussion of Habermas's criticisms of Foucault, see the essays collected

in Kelly (ed.), *Critique and Power: Recasting the Foucault/Habermas Debate* and Ashenden and Owen (eds), *Foucault contra Habermas: Recasting the Dialogue between Genealogy and Critical Theory*.

11  One of Habermas's translators, Thomas McCarthy, quotes a commentator who praises Habermas's written style. McCarthy demurs, noting that 'Readers should be forewarned that this last remark is an exaggeration' (Translator's Introduction, in Habermas, *Legitimation Crisis*, viii). Norris cites Habermas's lack of sensitivity to style as one of the reasons for his inability to appreciate the philosophical pertinence of Derrida's work: 'he (Habermas) clearly does not have much concern for the fine points of style, writing as he does in a manner that surpasses even Hegel in its heavyweight abstractions, its relentless piling up of clause upon clause, and the sense it conveys that strenuous thinking is somehow incompatible with "literary" arts and graces' (*What's Wrong with Postmodernism*, 64).

12  For the observation that Habermas either subsumes or rejects the arguments of others depending on how closely they fit with his own, see Ashenden and Owen, Introduction to *Foucault contra Habermas*, 7. On Lyotard and grand narratives, see chapter 3.

13  Habermas's discussion is based on a different essay from the one later published as 'Qu'est-ce que les Lumières?'. In the last decade of his life Foucault in fact wrote about Kant's 'What is Enlightenment?' on three separate occasions. For analysis of these three discussions, including the one to which Habermas's memorial address refers, see Schmidt and Wartenberg, 'Foucault's Enlightenment: Critique, revolution, and the fashioning of the self', 283–314. On Foucault's reading of 'What is Enlightenment?', see also Norris, '"What is Enlightenment?": Kant and Foucault', 159–96, 'Postscript: "The undefined work of freedom" – Foucault and philosophy', in *Truth and the Ethics of Criticism*, 121–8; 'Ethics, autonomy and self-invention: Debating Foucault', in *Deconstruction and 'the Unfinished Project of Modernity*, 119–35; see also Hayes, *Reading the French Enlightenment*, 9–14, and Hubert Dreyfus and Paul Rabinow, 'What is maturity?: Habermas and Foucault on "What is Enlightenment?"', 109–21.

14  Habermas, *The New Conservatism*, 173. Subsequent references are given in the text.

15  Schmidt and Wartenberg, 'Foucault's Enlightenment', 283.

16  Foucault, *Les Mots et les choses*, 352.

17  Owen, 'Orientation and Enlightenment: An essay on critique and genealogy', 37.

18  Kant, 'An answer to the question: What is Enlightenment?', in *Political Writings*, 54.

19  Foucault, 'Qu'est-ce que les Lumières?', 567. Subsequent references are in the text.

20  See Hayes, *Reading the French Enlightenment*, 12–14.

21  This does not mean that Kant was the first to try to answer the question. As Foucault acknowledges, Moses Mendelssohn had already written an article on the same topic for the *Berlinische Monatsschrift*, in which Kant's essay first appeared. In a footnote to his essay Kant says that he had not read Mendelssohn's article at the time when he wrote his own.

22  For this point, see Hayes, *Reading the French Enlightenment*, 11, citing Bonfiglio, 'The patrilineal discourse of Enlightenment: Reading Foucault reading Kant', 111.
23  Norris, '"What is Enlightenment?"': Kant and Foucault', 170–1.
24  Norris, *Deconstruction and the 'Unfinished Project of Modernity'*, 131.
25  Kant, 'What is Enlightenment?', 57; translation modified.
26  Kant, 'What is Enlightenment?', 58.
27  Kant, 'What is Enlightenment?', 54.
28  In his essay 'On the common saying: "This may be true in theory, but it does not apply in practice"', Kant argues that progress 'may at times be *interrupted* but never *broken off*' (*Political Writings*, 88); if it cannot be broken off, it follows that it also cannot be completed.
29  Ashenden and Owen, Introduction to *Foucault contra Habermas*, 3. For further discussion of the differences between Foucault's and Habermas's interpretation of Kant and the Enlightenment, see Dreyfus and Rabinow, 'What is maturity?', 110–12.
30  Hayes, *Reading the French Enlightenment*, 4.
31  See Kelly, Introduction to *Critique and Power*, 2–3.
32  On the decisive role of missed encounters in theoretical discussions over the past thirty years, see Rapaport, *The Theory Mess*, for example 2–5.
33  See Dreyfus and Rabinow, 'What is maturity?', 109–10: 'Both see society as in some way primary but they differ profoundly as to what a modern society is and could be. They both acknowledge that an understanding of critical reason is an essential task of contemporary philosophy but they understand critique and reason in radically different ways. And finally both agree with Kant that *maturity* is the task of the modern age, but Habermas's and Foucault's concepts of *modernity* and *maturity* stand in clear opposition.'
34  See Derrida, *Mémoires pour Paul de Man*, 225–7, and *Limited Inc.*, 244–7.
35  Derrida, *Limited Inc.*, 245.
36  Derrida, *Limited Inc.*, 245.
37  Habermas, *The Philosophical Discourse of Modernity*, 184.
38  Derrida, *Limited Inc.*, 247; see also *Mémoires pour Paul de Man*, 226.
39  See Derrida, *Limited Inc.*, 247, and *Mémoires pour Paul de Man*, 226–7.
40  See Rapaport, *The Theory Mess*, xiv–xv.
41  Derrida, *Mémoires pour Paul de Man*, 225.
42  See Foucault, *Les Mots et les choses*, 255, 256.
43  Schmidt and Wartenberg, 'Foucault's Enlightenment', 303.
44  Schmidt and Wartenberg, 'Foucault's Enlightenment', 287.
45  See Derrida, *Du droit à la philosophie*, 81–9. Subsequent references are in the text.
46  See Norris, 'Deconstruction, postmodernism and philosophy: Habermas on Derrida', in *What's Wrong with Postmodernism*, 49–76; see also in the same book 'Derrida and Kant', 194–207.
47  Derrida, *Spectres de Marx*, 40.

## 3 After knowledge: Lyotard and the postmodern condition

1 Sokal and Bricmont, *Intellectual Impostures*, 173.
2 See Kant, *Anthropologie in pragmatischer Hinsicht*, 229.
3 Kant, *Political Writings*, 99.
4 See Hans Reiss, Introduction to Kant, *Political Writings*, 29.
5 On the problems of translating Kant's *Vermögen* as *faculties*, see *Critique of Pure Reason*, 8, note 16. Kant uses different words for faculty in the sense of the 'doctrine of faculties' (*Vermögen*) and in reference to sections of a university (*Facultäten*, as in *Der Streit der Facultäten*, the Conflict of the Faculties). The fact that English and French translators often use the same word for both cases has been the cause of some confusion. In this chapter I use *faculty* in both senses, despite the risks involved, because it is still the most widely recognized translation.
6 Kant, *Critique of Pure Reason*, 5. Subsequent references are in the text.
7 Cavell, *In Quest of the Ordinary*, 30.
8 Cavell, *In Quest of the Ordinary*, 31.
9 On the collaboration of the faculties in each of Kant's three Critiques, see Deleuze, *La Philosophie critique de Kant*.
10 See Kant, 'Perpetual peace: A philosophical sketch', in *Political Writings*, 93–130
11 Kant, *Anthropologie in pragmatischer Hinsicht*, 229.
12 Lyotard, 'Apathie dans la théorie', in *Rudiments païens*, 28.
13 Lyotard, 'Sur la théorie', in *Dérive à partir de Marx et Freud*, 210. On the difficulties of 'doing theory', see also 'Economie de cet écrit', the final part of Lyotard's *Economie libidinale*; for discussion of the relationship between this text and 'Apathie dans la théorie', see Bennington, *Lyotard: Writing the Event*, 48–51.
14 For Lyotard's account of his involvement in *Socialisme ou barbarie*, see 'Mémorial pour un marxisme: à Pierre Souyri', in *Pérégrinations*, 89–134.
15 Lyotard, 'Apathie dans la théorie', 29.
16 For discussion, see Hillis Miller, *On Literature*, 94–5.
17 Lyotard, *Le Différend*, 12.
18 Jameson, *Postmodernism*, xi, 59–61.
19 Lyotard's account of modern science is discussed later in this chapter. For criticism of Lyotard's view of narrative as reactionary, see Eagleton, *Against the Grain*, 136.
20 See Eagleton, *The Illusions of Postmodernism*, 69: 'Indeed from Bakhtin to the Body Shop, Lyotard to leotards, the body has become one of the most recurrent preoccupations of postmodern thought.'
21 Williams, *Lyotard*, 134.
22 Anderson, *The Origins of Postmodernity*, 26.
23 Bennington, *Lyotard: Writing the Event*, 1.
24 Quoted in Anderson, *The Origins of Postmodernity*, 26.
25 See Anderson, *The Origins of Postmodernity*, 30.
26 Quoted in Anderson, *The Origins of Postmodernity*, 26.
27 See Lyotard, *La Condition postmoderne*, 85. Subsequent references are given in the text.

28   See Lyotard, 'Réponse à la question: Qu'est-ce que le postmoderne', in *Le Postmoderne expliqué aux enfants*; 'Appendice svelte à la question postmoderne', in *Tombeau de l'intellectuel et autres papiers*; and 'Une fable postmoderne', in *Moralités postmodernes*.

29   See Jameson, *Postmodernism*, xi.

30   Lyotard, *Tombeau de l'intellectuel et autres papiers*, 84.

31   Lyotard and Thébaud, *Au juste*, 34.

32   Lyotard, 'Réponse à la question: Qu'est-ce que le postmoderne?', in *Le Postmoderne expliqué aux enfants*, 23–4. For discussion of this, see Bennington, *Legislations*, 174–80.

33   Lyotard, *Moralités postmodernes*, 77.

34   Lyotard, *Moralités postmodernes*, 91–3.

35   Anderson, *The Origins of Postmodernity*, 34–5.

36   Eagleton, *The Illusions of Postmodernism*, vii.

37   Eagleton, *The Illusions of Postmodernism*, viii.

38   Eagleton, *The Illusions of Postmodernism*, viii.

39   Eagleton, *The Illusions of Postmodernism*, viii. For criticism of this view referring to Eagleton's earlier article on postmodernism, see Bennington, *Legislations*, 178: 'most of Eagleton's attacks on Lyotard are either unargued, or aimed at positions Lyotard does not in fact hold'.

40   Jameson, *Postmodernism*, xxii.

41   On 'paralogisms', see Lyotard, *La Condition postmoderne*, 98–108.

42   Bennington, *Legislations*, 172.

43   Lyotard, *Dérive à partir de Marx et Freud*, 5. On the difficulties of introducing or writing about his own work, see also Lyotard's Foreword to *The Lyotard Reader*, reprinted in French as 'Directions to servants' in *Moralités postmodernes*, 131–41; see also 'Economie de cet écrit', in *Economie libidinale*.

44   See chapter 7 for discussion.

45   See for example Eagleton, *Against the Grain*, 136, 138.

46   See Rorty, *Essays on Heidegger and Others*, 165–6; Sokal and Bricmont, *Intellectual Impostures*, 125–8; Bouveresse, *Rationalité et cynisme*, 25–30.

47   Lyotard, *Le Différend*, 207.

48   Kant, *Logik*, 134–5.

49   For wide-ranging discussions of Kant, see for example *Au juste*, *Le Différend*, *L'Enthousiasme*, *Pérégrinations*.

50   Lyotard, *Au juste*, 141.

51   Lyotard, *Le Différend*, 11.

52   See Lyotard, *Le Différend*, 96–101.

53   See Lyotard, *Le Différend*, 96, 101.

54   For discussion of the violence of imagination in Kant, see Žižek, *The Ticklish Subject*, 41–3.

55   Kant, *Political Writings*, 93.

56   See also Bennington, *Legislations*, 267: 'Perpetual peace turns out to be possible only as the perpetual postponement of its own perpetuity.'

57   Kant, *The Conflict of Faculties*, 55.

58   Kant must also have known at first hand how knowledge could become a matter of public performance. As a *Privatdozent* he lectured for a minimum average of sixteen hours a week, giving 268 lecture courses in his career, on

logic, metaphysics, mathematics, physical geography, ethics, the mechanical sciences, natural law, the history of philosophy, anthropology, natural
theology, pedagogy and mineralogy. For these details, see Caygill, *A Kant
Dictionary*, 19–20.

## 4 After ethics: Levinas without stories

1  Hillis Miller, *The Ethics of Reading*, 3.
2  Norris, *Truth and the Ethics of Criticism*, 108–9.
3  The first two articles are reprinted in Derrida's *L'Ecriture et la différence* and
   *Psyché: Inventions de l'autre* respectively.
4  Badiou, *L'Ethique*, 5.
5  Critchley, *The Ethics of Deconstruction: Derrida and Levinas*, xi.
6  Robbins, *Altered Reading: Levinas and Literature*, xiii.
7  Llewelyn, *Emmanuel Levinas: The Genealogy of Ethics*, xi.
8  Derrida, *Adieu à Emmanuel Levinas*, 14.
9  However, for a dissenting view of Levinas, see Badiou, *L'Ethique*, 19–23.
10 Levinas, *Totalité et infini*, 11. For a persuasive account of the continuing
   interest in the subject in modern French thought, see Williams, *Contemporary French Philosophy: Modernity and the Persistence of the Subject*.
11 Levinas, *Humanisme de l'autre homme*, 95.
12 Levinas, *Totalité et infini*, 12.
13 On the terms *hôte* and *otage*, see Derrida, *Adieu à Emmanuel Levinas*, and
   the discussion in Howells, *Derrida: Deconstruction from Phenomenology to
   Ethics*, 146.
14 For a fuller introduction to Levinas, see Davis, *Levinas*.
15 On the problems of understanding the notion of face, see Davis, *Levinas*,
   132–5.
16 See for example Llewelyn on recurrence, in *Emmanuel Levinas*, 184–5:
   'Recurrence is difference intruding upon the same as non-indifference. It is
   the re-identification of identity. Double identity, a doubling of the count-
   able one with which one starts counting by the one understood as the
   incommensurably unique prior to understanding, unless understanding
   (*entendre*) is pre-original obedience (*entendre*), obedience before one starts,
   hypostasis before hypostasis.' I should say that Llewelyn is a very brilliant
   reader of Levinas, and I have no doubt at all that he knows exactly what
   this means; but such writing does little to help readers who (like myself) are
   struggling to come to terms with Levinas at a very basic level.
17 See Derrida, *Adieu à Emmanuel Levinas*, 45–6, 64, 91, 162.
18 Derrida, *Adieu à Emmanuel Levinas*, 197.
19 Derrida, *Adieu à Emmanuel Levinas*, 199.
20 Derrida, *Adieu à Emmanuel Levinas*, 200. This is in accordance with the
   most common interpretation of the command in the Hebrew Bible. The
   command equivalent to Levinas's 'Tu ne tueras pas' is not normally taken as
   forbidding killing in all circumstances, including, for example the killing of
   animals or enemies on a battlefield. I am grateful to Gary Mole for his
   patient explanation of the Hebrew text and its possible meanings.
21 See for example Baumann, *Postmodern Ethics*, 84.

22   This paragraph is based on my *Ethical Issues in Twentieth-Century French Fiction*, 48, which discusses Kant's examples in relation to Lacan and Sartre. On the use of examples in Kant, see David Lloyd, 'Kant's examples', and Cathy Caruth, 'The force of example: Kant's symbols'. The following discussion only considers the example as *Beispiel* (a particular instance), not as *Muster* (a model to be followed). For a full comparison of the thought of Kant and Levinas, see Chalier, *Pour une morale au-delà du savoir: Kant et Levinas*. There is little sustained discussion of Kant in Levinas's writing. The notable exception is in the course of lectures published as *La Mort et le temps*, in which Levinas gives a sympathetic reading of Kant's views on the question of hope, which is discussed in chapter 5; see *La Mort et le temps*, 63–73.

23   Žižek, *Tarrying with the Negative*, 70–1.

24   See Kant, *Grundlegung zur Metaphysik der Sitten*, 27–8. Subsequent references are in the text.

25   See Levinas, *Hors sujet*, 183; see also *Entre nous*, 232–3.

26   See Chalier, *Pour une morale au-delà du savoir*, 82: 'in effect the Kantian subject identifies the other as an *alter ego* and from that point, according to Levinas, despite its vigilance, that subject misses alterity'. See also David-Ménard, *Les Constructions de l'universel*, 28.

27   The idea of the example as 'unruly' is taken from the title of Gelley (ed.), *Unruly Examples*.

28   For further formulations, see *Grundlegung*, 61; *Critique of Practical Reason*, 30; *Critique of Pure Reason*, 738.

29   For objections to Kant's position here, see Chalier, *Pour une morale au-delà du savoir*, 37–9. See also the fascinating discussion of the problem of lying to the murder in Zupančič, *Ethics of the Real: Kant, Lacan*, 43–63. More generally, on objections to the categorical imperative, see David-Ménard, *Les Constructions de l'universel*, 7–8, 22–3.

30   Kant, 'On a supposed right to tell lies from benevolent motives', 362–3.

31   Kant, 'On a supposed right to tell lies from benevolent motives', 363.

32   Kant, 'On a supposed right to tell lies from benevolent motives', 362.

33   See respectively Zupančič, *Ethics of the Real: Kant, Lacan*, 43, and Smyth, *The Habit of Lying*, 18.

34   Davis, *Ethical Issues in Twentieth-Century French Fiction*, 48.

35   See Robbins, *Altered Reading*, xxiii.

36   See Robbins, *Altered Reading*, 72.

37   Herman Rapaport, 'Of the eye and the law', 306.

38   Hand, 'Shadowing ethics: Levinas's view of art and aesthetics', in Hand (ed.), *Facing the Other*, 67.

39   Levinas, 'La Réalité et son ombre', in *Les Imprévus de l'histoire*, 140–1.

40   Levinas, 'La Réalité et son ombre', 147–8.

41   See Hand, 'Shadowing ethics', 81, 84; see also Llewelyn, *The Middle Voice of Ecological Conscience*, 89–113.

42   Robbins, *Altered Reading*, xxi.

43   Levinas, 'L'Autre dans Proust', in *Noms propres*, 118.

44   Levinas, *Noms propres*, 123. For discussion of the ambivalence suggested by this sentence, see Robbins, *Altered Reading*, 82.

45   Levinas, 'Poésie et résurrection: Notes sur Agnon', *Noms propres*, 15.

46 Robbins, *Altered Reading*, 139.
47 Levinas, *Noms propres*, 56.
48 See also Hand, 'Shadowing ethics', 86, on Levinas's 'silent obliteration' of other possible readings of the art works he discusses; Hand's explanation, however, is rather more generous than mine.
49 *Quatre lectures talmudiques* (1968), *Du sacré au saint* (1977), some of the texts collected in *Difficile liberté* (1963 and 1976), *L'Au-delà du verset* (1982) and *A l'heure des nations* (1988), and the posthumously published *Nouvelles lectures talmudiques* (1996).
50 For discussion of the Talmud and Levinas's commentaries, see my *Levinas*, 106–19.
51 Levinas, *Quatre lectures talmudiques*, 14.
52 Levinas, *L'Au-delà du verset*, 7.
53 Levinas, *L'Au-delà du verset*, 9.
54 Levinas, *L'Au-delà du verset*, 8.
55 Levinas, *L'Au-delà du verset*, 8.
56 Levinas, *L'Au-delà du verset*, 136–7.
57 Levinas, *L'Au-delà du verset*, 137.
58 Levinas, *L'Au-delà du verset*, 9.
59 Levinas, *L'Au-delà du verset*, 127.
60 Levinas, *Nouvelles lectures talmudiques*, 17–18.
61 Levinas, *Totalité et infini*, 11.
62 Levinas, *Autrement qu'être*, 262–3. Subsequent references are given in the text.
63 Ricoeur, *Autrement*, 26; Ricoeur is referring in particular to the violent, distressing nature of some of Levinas's language.
64 Eaglestone, *Ethical Criticism: Reading after Levinas*, 139.
65 Chanter, *Time, Death, and the Feminine*, 224.
66 Critchley, *The Ethics of Deconstruction*, 8.
67 Eaglestone, *Ethical Criticism*, 161.
68 Davis, *Levinas*, 92.
69 Critchley, *The Ethics of Deconstruction*, 8.
70 Eaglestone, *Ethical Criticism*, 162.
71 See Derrida, 'Le Mot d'accueil', in *Adieu à Emmanuel Levinas*, 37–211.
72 The notable exception here is Levinas's revision of his thought in response to Derrida's 'Violence et éthique'; for discussion, see my *Levinas*, 63–9.
73 See Tom Driver, 'Beckett by the Madeleine', 22.

## 5 After hope: Althusser on reading and self-reading

1 Althusser, *Lire le Capital*, 3. Subsequent references are in the text.
2 Althusser, *et al.*, *L'Avenir dure longtemps*, 252. Subsequent references are in the text.
3 Elliott, 'Further adventures of the dialectic: Merleau-Ponty, Sartre, Althusser', 213.
4 See Balibar, *Ecrits pour Althusser*, 62–4.
5 Žižek, *The Ticklish Subject*, 127.
6 Žižek describes this view as 'the old liberal slander', whilst also insisting that

'there *is* a direct lineage from Christianity to Marxism'; see *The Fragile Absolute*, 2.

7  Kant, *Critique of Pure Reason*, 738. Subsequent references are in the text.

8  Kant, *Political Writings*, 41, emphasis in original. Subsequent references are in the text.

9  See 'L'Espérance' and 'Leur espérance', both first published in the 1943 Christmas edition of *Le Lien*, the journal of Stalag XA, and reprinted in Althusser, *Journal de captivité*, 345–52, 353–4.

10  Žižek, *The Ticklish Subject*, 127–8. Althusser's notion of Theory will be discussed in more detail in chapter 7.

11  On the 'double science', see Derrida, 'La Double Séance', in *La Dissémination*.

12  See Lacan, *Les Quatre Concepts fondamentaux de la psychanalyse*, 176–9.

13  Lacan, *Les Quatre Concepts fondamentaux de la psychanalyse*, 178.

14  Lacan, *Les Quatre Concepts fondamentaux de la psychanalyse*, 258.

15  However, this evaluation of Freud does not prevent Lacan from criticizing Freud's treatment of actual cases; Freud, it seems, did not always know what it was that he knew.

16  Althusser, *Ecrits sur la psychanalyse*. Subsequent references are given in the text.

17  See for example the notes in *L'Avenir dure longtemps*, 182, 210, 233.

18  See Althusser, *Ecrits philosophiques et politiques* II, 434.

19  See Althusser, *Ecrits philosophiques et politiques* I, 533–4.

20  My reading of Althusser's autobiography has been informed and focused by Marty's book *Louis Althusser, un sujet sans procès*. For a more psychoanalytical account of Althusser's autobiography, see Pommier, *Louis du néant: La Mélancolie d'Althusser*.

21  See for example *L'Avenir dure longtemps*, 105: 'It was only much later, in the well-known retroaction [*après-coup*] of affects, that I could see clearly into these episodes, their affinity and their re-composition: in the course of my analysis.' See also 58, 69, 233, 313, 314.

22  On this 'old doctor friend' and some of the problems raised by the final chapter, see Marty, *Louis Althusser, un sujet sans procès*, 42–51.

23  For Althusser's late ideas on aleatory materialism, see for example *Sur la philosophie*, 34–44, and the final section of this chapter.

24  Althusser's ability to respond to the singularity of others is attested by Balibar; see *Ecrits pour Althusser*, 120: 'I would almost dare to say that Althusser was a different man with everyone he knew. It would not be sufficient to explain it by saying that he could adapt to his interlocutors and to circumstances, it would be necessary to say that he had an extraordinary capacity to listen to and to arouse the singularity of everyone. The true Althusser, if this expression has any meaning, is first of all that capacity.'

25  This is quoted in slightly different form on pages 115 and 175.

26  On the supplement, see Derrida, *De la grammatologie*, 203–34.

27  Here I am drawing on Nagel, *The View from Nowhere*, 4: 'Certain forms of perplexity – for example, about freedom, knowledge, and the meaning of life – seem to me to embody more insight than any of the proposed solutions to those problems.'

28  Althusser, *Ecrits sur la psychanalyse*, 177.
29  Althusser, *Journal de captivité*, 350; ellipsis in original.
30  Althusser, *Ecrits philosophiques et politiques* I, 540.
31  Althusser, *Ecrits philosophiques et politiques* I, 567.

## 6  After identity: Kristeva's life stories

1   Kristeva, *Soleil noir*, 263.
2   Kant, *Logik*, 25.
3   See Foucault, *Les Mots et les choses*, 352.
4   Foucault, *Les Mots et les choses*, 15.
5   Moi, *Sexual/Textual Politics*, 148.
6   Moi, *What is a Woman?*, xiv.
7   Quoted in Moi, *Textual/Sexual Politics*, 165.
8   See for example Kristeva, *Le Génie féminin* I: *Hannah Arendt*, 275–93. Subsequent references to this book are in the text.
9   Kristeva, *Pouvoirs et limites de la psychanalyse* I: *Sens et non-sens de la révolte*, 15–16.
10  Kristeva, *Séméiotiké*, 17.
11  See Leslie Hill, 'Julia Kristeva: theorizing the avant-garde?', 149.
12  Kristeva, *Les Samouraïs*, 9. Although this chapter does not deal with the question of sexual difference, it is worth noting that here and elsewhere Kristeva associates storytelling and the love for stories particularly with women. Cavarero makes a similar point in *Relating Narratives*: 'Women tell stories: there is always a woman at the origin of the *enchanting* power of every story' (122). For Kristeva's views on female specificity, see the conclusion to her three-volume study of female genius, *Le Génie féminin* III: *Colette*, 537–66.
13  On this point, Kristeva interprets a sentence from Arendt in exactly the opposite way from Cavarero. Kristeva quotes the French translation of Arendt's essay on Isak Dinesen (Karen Blixen), which suggests that 'life could be, even should be, lived like a story' (*la vie pourrait être, devrait être même, vécue comme une histoire*) (151). Quoting a truncated version of the English original, Cavarero concludes on the contrary that 'Life cannot be lived like a story, because the story always comes afterwards, it results; it is unforeseeable and uncontrollable, just like life' (*Relating Narratives*, 3).
14  Cavarero, *Relating Narratives*, 36.
15  Cavarero, *Relating Narratives*, 84.
16  MacIntyre, *After Virtue*, 218. For an excellent account of the importance of stories in MacIntyre's work, see Bruns, *Tragic Thoughts at the End of Philosophy*, 71–92.
17  Kearney, *On Stories*, 130.
18  Sartre, *La Nausée*, 62.
19  MacIntyre, *After Virtue*, 214–15.
20  Kristeva, *Histoires d'amour*, 9.
21  Kristeva, *Histoires d'amour*, 10.
22  Kristeva, *Sens et non-sens de la révolte*, 165.
23  Kristeva, *Sens et non-sens de la révolte*, 166.

24  Kristeva, *La Genie féminin* I, 148. Subsequent references to this book are in the text.
25  MacIntyre, *After Virtue*, 217.
26  Cavarero, *Relating Narratives*, 2, 129.
27  Kristeva, *Les Samouraïs*, 372.
28  Kristeva, *Sens et non-sens de la révolte*, 63. Subsequent references are in the text.
29  Freud, *Totem and Taboo*, 224.
30  Freud, *Group Psychology and the Analysis of the Ego*, in *Civilization, Society and Religion*, 154.
31  On the greater importance of *Totem and Taboo* in French psychoanalysis than in other countries, see John Lechte, 'Art, love, and melancholy in the work of Julia Kristeva', 26.
32  The description of the patient's words being like poems is echoed in *Les Samouraïs* in the account of the treatment of Carole; see for example 372, where the analyst Joëlle expresses the view that if she cannot wrest Carole from her poems and get her to recount, the patient will kill herself.
33  For further examples of the 'gift of meaning' in Kristeva's analytic practice, see 'Forgiveness: an interview', 281–2, and *Pouvoirs et limites de la psychanalyse* I: *La Révolte intime*, 38–9.
34  Kristeva, *La Révolte intime*, 21.
35  Žižek, *The Plague of Fantasies*, 10–11.
36  Žižek, *The Indivisible Remainder*, 94.
37  Žižek, *The Indivisible Remainder*, 94–5.
38  Kristeva, *Histoires d'amour*, 25.
39  Kristeva, *Le Génie féminin* II: *Melanie Klein*, 257–73.
40  Kristeva, *Le Génie féminin* II: *Melanie Klein*, 262.
41  Brooks, *Psychoanalysis and Storytelling*, 50.
42  Kristeva, *Sens et non-sens de la révolte*, 103; ellipsis in original.
43  For an astute account of some of the connections between psychoanalysis and detective fiction, see ffrench, 'Open letter to detectives and psychoanalysts: analysis and reading'.
44  Kristeva, *La Révolte intime*, 9.
45  Kristeva, *Etrangers à nous-mêmes*, 75.
46  Kristeva, *Le Vieil Homme et les loups*, 268.
47  Kristeva, *Possessions*, 17–18. Subsequent references are given in the text.
48  Brooks, *Psychoanalysis and Storytelling*, 70.
49  Brooks, *Psychoanalysis and Storytelling*, 71.
50  Brooks, *Psychoanalysis and Storytelling*, 71.
51  See also the reference to the paintings of Picasso copied by Jerry which represent our broken lives and fractured selves: 'crushed faces, identities which are mocked, shots and angles that attack or flee, shifting perspectives, turning consciousnesses – where are you, reference points of yesteryear?' (192).
52  Žižek refers to 'the "inner" truth that each one in the group might have been the murderer (i.e. that we *are* murderers in the unconscious of our desire, in so far as the actual murderer realizes the desire of the group constituted by the corpse)' (*Looking Awry*, 59).

53  Kristeva, *La Révolte intime*, 39.
54  For discussion of this point, and the distinction between private forgiveness and public punishment, see Kristeva, 'Forgiveness: an interview', 282–3.
55  Kristeva, *Le Génie féminin* III: *Colette*, 268. For discussion, see *Le Génie féminin* II: *Melanie Klein*, 236–45.
56  Lyotard does also consider the possibility of postmodern or 'pagan' forms of storytelling which do not share the delusions of 'grand narratives'; see for example *Au juste*, 62–84, and 'Une fable postmoderne' in *Moralités post-modernes*.
57  Kristeva, *Le Génie féminin* II: *Melanie Klein*, 244.

## 7  Spectres of theory

1  Hillis Miller, 'The triumph of theory, the resistance to reading, and the question of the material base', 284.
2  Hillis Miller, 'The triumph of theory, the resistance to reading, and the question of the material base'. 283.
3  See Bové, *In the Wake of Theory*; Johnson, *The Wake of Deconstruction*; Docherty, *After Theory*; Cunningham, *Reading after Theory*; Butler *et al.* (eds), *What's Left of Theory?*.
4  François Wahl, 'Introduction générale', in Todorov, *Qu'est-ce que le structuralisme? II Poétique*, 7.
5  Todorov, *Qu'est-ce que le structuralisme? II Poétique*, 18.
6  Althusser, *Pour Marx*, 169. Subsequent references are given in the text.
7  For the distinction between philosophy and Theory, see *Pour Marx*, 33, where Althusser points out that subsequently he will replace *Theory* by *Marxist philosophy* because the distinction between Theory and theory is not apparent in spoken language.
8  Althusser, *L'Avenir dure longtemps*, 46–7.
9  Althusser, *L'Avenir dure longtemps*, 315.
10  For discussion of this in the context of Marxism, see Docherty, *After Theory*, especially chapter 9, 205–19.
11  Lyotard, 'Apathie dans la théorie', in *Rudiments païens*, 28.
12  Freud, *Beyond the Pleasure Principle*, 332, quoted in Lyotard, 'Apathie dans la théorie', 10–11.
13  Lyotard, 'Apathie dans la théorie', 9–10.
14  Lyotard, *Le Différend*, 10.
15  Derrida, *Limited Inc.*, 37; my emphasis on *analysis*. Subsequent references are in the text.
16  Deleuze and Guattari, *Qu'est-ce que la philosophie?*, 11.
17  *Post-Theory: Reconstructing Film Studies*, edited by Bordwell and Carroll, and *Post-Theory: New Directions in Criticism*, edited by McQuillan *et al.*; references to these volumes are in the text.
18  Docherty, *After Theory*, 2.
19  Cunningham, *Reading after Theory*, 1.
20  Žižek, *The Fright of Real Tears: Krzysztof Kieślowski between Theory and Post-Theory*, 1–9.
21  Žižek, *The Fright of Real Tears*, 2.

22  For these criticisms and others, see Carroll, 'Prospects for film theory: A personal assessment', in *Post-Theory: Reconstructing Film Studies*, 37–68. On the tendencey of Theory to become the doxa it set out to subvert, see McQuillan *et al.* (eds), *Post-Theory: New Directions in Criticism*, xiv.

23  See Žižek, *The Fright of Real Tears*, 14, on the 'mutually exclusive deficiencies' with which Theory is reproached.

24  Cunningham, *Reading after Theory*, 82.

25  Cunningham, *Reading after Theory*, 86.

26  Cunningham, *Reading after Theory*, 59.

27  Cunningham, *Reading after Theory*, 86.

28  Žižek, *The Fright of Real Tears*, 15–16.

29  Žižek, *The Fright of Real Tears*, 15.

30  Carroll, 'Prospects for film theory', 52.

31  Cunningham, *Reading after Theory*, 169.

32  For an account of what is meant by 'cognitivism', see Carroll, 'Prospects for film theory', 61–7.

33  Bordwell, 'Contemporary film studies and the vicissitudes of grand theory', 30.

34  Docherty, *After Theory*, 219.

35  McQuillan *et al.*, *Post-Theory: New Directions in Criticism*, xv.

36  Docherty, *After Theory*, 212. For the importance of alterity in Docherty's work, see also his later book *Alterities: Criticism, History, Representation*.

37  Žižek, *The Fright of Real Tears*, 4.

38  On these branches of cultural studies, see Chow, *Ethics after Idealism*, 2–4.

39  Chow, *Ethics after Idealism*, 7.

40  Moi, *What is a Woman?*, 31. Subsequent references are in the text.

41  Said, *Culture and Imperialism*, 28–9.

42  Hillis Miller, 'The triumph of theory, the resistance to reading, and the question of the material base', 283.

43  For analysis of the political turn in the humanities and the 'eclipsing' of deconstruction, see Rapaport, *The Theory Mess*, for example 89–146.

44  Butler speaking in 1989, quoted in Rabaté, *The Future of Theory*, 1–2.

45  De Man refers to the waning of interest in theory in these terms in *The Resistance to Theory*, 5. Rabaté also refers to the history of theory as cyclical, in *The Future of Theory*, 2. For discussion of competing ways of narrating the recent history of theory, as either its death or 'a partial regression . . . a relapse, in a narrative anything but linear or progressive', see Cohen, Hillis Miller and Cohen, 'A "materiality without matter?", in Cohen *et al.* (eds), *Material Events: Paul de Man and the Afterlife of Theory*, xiv–xv.

46  Cunningham, *Reading after Theory*, 142.

47  See for example the opening lines of the editors' introduction entitled 'The joy of theory', in McQuillan *et al.* (eds), *Post-Theory: New Directions in Criticism*, ix.

48  Carroll, 'Prospects for film theory', 38.

49  On the personification of theory, specifically of deconstruction, see Johnson, 'Double mourning and the public sphere', in *The Wake of Deconstruction*, 16–51.

50  McQuillan *et al.* (eds), *Post-Theory: New Directions in Criticism*, x.

51 McQuillan *et al.* (eds), *Post-Theory: New Directions in Criticism*, ix.
52 For other examples, see Docherty, *After Theory*, 1; Cunningham, *Reading after Theory*, 1.
53 Johnson, *The Wake of Deconstruction*, 16–17; see also 101–3.
54 Bennington, 'Inter', in *Post-Theory: New Directions in Criticism*, 105.
55 Johnson, *The Wake of Deconstruction*, 17.
56 See Rabaté, *The Future of Theory*, 146–9. Rabaté's seven thinkers are Giorgio Agamben, Alain Badiou, Hans Blumenberg, Jean-Luc Nancy, Dorothea Olkowsky, Arkady Plotnisky, Peter Solterdijk; his ten schools are the New Arcades Projects, technological criticism, diasporic criticism, ethical criticism, testimonial studies, new textual studies, science-and-text studies, spectral criticism, hybridity studies and translation studies; the six important agendas are a renewed dialogue between Lacanian and Levinasian ethics, Badiou's critique of historicism, re-readings of the Nietzsche–Heidegger controversy; a rethinking of technology as science and/or art, an assessment of the legacy of Blanchot and Bataille, and a systematic confrontation between Eastern and Western thought.
57 On the relation between theory and ghosts, see 'Introduction: A Future for Haunting', in Buse and Stott (eds), *Ghosts: Deconstruction, Psychoanalysis, History*, especially 5–6. On post-theory as a ghost, see Nicholas Royle's discussion of the Freudian uncanny in the light of Derrida's discussion of ghosts in *Spectres de Marx*, in '*Déjà vu*', 3–20. For theoretically-oriented discussions of ghosts, see Rabaté, *The Ghosts of Modernity*, and Wolfreys, *Victorian Hauntings*.
58 Rabaté, *The Future of Theory*, 10.
59 Butler *et al.* (eds), *What's Left of Theory?*, xi.
60 See Butler *et al.* (eds), *What's Left of Theory?*, xii: 'Are we, as a profession, ghosted by a formalism that never was?'
61 See Compagnon, *Le Démon de la théorie*, 16.
62 Bowie, *Psychoanalysis and the Future of Theory*, 48.
63 Bowie, *Psychoanalysis and the Future of Theory*, 47.

# Bibliography

Adorno, Theodor W., and Horkheimer, Max, *Dialectic of Enlightenment*, trans. John Cumming, New York and London: Verso, 1979.

Althusser, Louis, *Pour Marx*, Paris: Maspero, 1965.

—— *Journal de captivité: Stalag XA, 1940–1945*, Paris: Stock/IMEC, 1992.

—— *Ecrits sur la psychanalyse: Freud et Lacan*, Paris: Stock/IMEC, 1993; Livre de poche edition.

—— *Ecrits philosophiques et politiques* I, Paris: Stock/IMEC, 1994.

—— *L'Avenir dure longtemps, suivi de Les Faits*, Paris: Stock/IMEC, 1994; Livre de poche edition.

—— *Sur la philosophie*, Paris: Gallimard, 1994.

—— *Ecrits philosophiques et politiques* II, Paris: Stock/IMEC, 1995, 1997.

Althusser, Louis, Balibar, Etienne, Establet, Roger, Macherey, Pierre, and Rancière, Jacques, *Lire le Capital*, Paris: Quadrige/Presses Universitaires de France, 1996; first edition 1965.

Anderson, Perry, *The Origins of Postmodernity*, London and New York: Verso, 1998.

Ashenden, Samantha, and Owen, David (eds), *Foucault contra Habermas: Recasting the Dialogue between Genealogy and Critical Theory*, London: Sage, 1999.

Austin, J. L., *How to Do Things with Words*, Oxford: Oxford University Press, 1962.

Badiou, Alain, *L'Ethique: Essai sur la conscience du Mal*, Paris: Hatier, 1993.

Balibar, Etienne, *Ecrits pour Althusser*, Paris: Editions la Découverte, 1991.

Barthes, Roland, *Sur Racine*, Paris: Seuil, 1963; Points edition.

—— *Essais critiques*, Paris: Seuil, 1964.

—— *Critique et vérité*, Paris: Seuil, 1966.

Baumann, Zygmunt, *Postmodern Ethics*, Oxford: Blackwell, 1993.

Bennington, Geoffrey, *Lyotard: Writing the Event*, Manchester: Manchester University Press, 1988.

—— *Legislations: The Politics of Deconstruction*, London and New York: Verso, 1994.

—— 'Inter', in McQuillan, Martin, MacDonald, Graeme, Purves, Robin, and Thomson, Stephen (eds), *Post-Theory: New Directions in Criticism*, Edinburgh: Edinburgh University Press, 1999, 103–19.

—— *Frontières kantiennes*, Paris: Galilée, 2000.

Bonfiglio, Thomas P., 'The patrilineal discourse of enlightenment: Reading Foucault reading Kant', *Bulletin de la société américaine de philosophie française* 6 (1994), 104–15.

Bonzon, A., *La Nouvelle Critique et Racine*, Paris: Nizet, 1970.

Bordwell, David, 'Contemporary film studies and the vicissitudes of grand theory', in Bordwell, David, and Carroll, Noël (eds), *Post-Theory: Reconstructing Film Studies*, Madison, WI: The University of Wisconsin Press, 1996, 3–36.

Bordwell, David, and Carroll, Noël, *Post-Theory: Reconstructing Film Studies*, Madison, WI: The University of Wisconsin Press, 1996.

Bourdieu, Pierre, *Homo academicus*, Paris: Minuit, 1984.

Bouveresse, Jacques, *Rationalité et cynisme*, Paris: Minuit, 1984.

—— *Prodiges et vertiges de l'analogie: De l'abus des belles-lettres dans la pensée*, Paris: Raisons d'agir, 1999.

Bové, Paul, *In the Wake of Theory*, Hanover, NH, and London: Wesleyan University Press, 1992.

Bowie, Malcolm, *Psychoanalysis and the Future of Theory*, Oxford: Blackwell, 1993.

Bricmont, Jean, 'La Vraie Signification de l'affaire Sokal', *Le Monde*, 14 January 1997, 15.

Brooks, Peter, *Psychoanalysis and Storytelling*, Oxford: Blackwell, 1994.

Bruns, Gerald L., *Tragic Thoughts at the End of Philosophy: Language, Literature, and Ethical Theory*, Evanston, IL: Northwestern University Press, 1999.

Buse, Peter, and Stott, Andrew (eds), *Ghosts: Deconstruction, Psychoanalysis, History*, Basingstoke: Macmillan, 1999.

Butler, Judith, Guillory, John, and Thomas, Kendall (eds), *What's Left of Theory? New Work on the Politics of Literary Theory*, New York and London: Routledge, 2000.

Butler, Judith, Laclau, Ernesto, and Žižek, Slavoj, *Contingency, Hegemony, Universality: Contemporary Dialogues on the Left*, London and New York: Verso, 2000.

Carroll, Noel, 'Prospects for film theory: A personal assessment', in Bordwell, David, and Carroll, Noël (eds), *Post-Theory: Reconstructing Film Studies*, Madison, WI: University of Wisconsin Press, 1996, 37–68.

Caruth, Cathy, 'The force of example: Kant's symbols', in Gelley, Alexander (ed.), *Unruly Examples: On the Rhetoric of Exemplarity*, Stanford, CA: Stanford University Press, 1995, 277–302.

Cavarero, Adriana, *Relating Narratives: Storytelling and Selfhood*, trans. Paul A. Kottman, London and New York: Routledge, 2000.

Cavell, Stanley, *In Quest of the Ordinary: Lines of Skepticism and Romanticism*, Chicago and London: University of Chicago Press, 1988.

Caygill, Howard, *A Kant Dictionary*, Oxford: Blackwell, 1995.

Chalier, Catherine, *Pour une morale au-delà du savoir: Kant et Levinas*, Paris: Albin Michel, 1998.

Chanter, Tina, *Time, Death, and the Feminine: Levinas with Heidegger*, Stanford, CA: Stanford University Press, 2001.

Charraud, Nathalie, 'Mathématiques avec Lacan', in Jurdant, Baudouin (ed.), *Impostures scientifiques: Les Malentendus de l'affaire Sokal*, Paris and Nice: Editions la Découverte/*Alliage*, 1998, 237–49.

Chow, Rey, *Ethics after Idealism: Theory–Culture–Ethnicity–Reading*, Bloomington and Indianapolis, IN: Indiana University Press, 1998.

Cohen, Tom, Hillis Miller, Joseph, and Cohen, Barbara, 'A "materiality without matter?"', in Cohen, Tom, Cohen, Barbara, Hillis Miller, Joseph, and Warminski, Andrzej (eds), *Material Events: Paul de Man and the Afterlife of Theory*, Minneapolis, MN, and London: University of Minnesota Press, 2001, vii–xxv.

Cohen, Tom, Cohen, Barbara, Hillis Miller, Joseph, and Warminski, Andrzej (eds), *Material Events: Paul de Man and the Afterlife of Theory*, Minneapolis, MN, and London: University of Minnesota Press, 2001.

Compagnon, Antoine, *Le Démon de la théorie: Littérature et sens commun*, Paris: Seuil, 1998.

Critchley, Simon, *The Ethics of Deconstruction: Derrida and Levinas*, Oxford: Blackwell, 1992.

Culler, Jonathan, *Barthes*, London: Fontana, 1983.

Cunningham, Valentine, *Reading after Theory*, Oxford: Blackwell, 2002.

David-Ménard, Monique, *Les Constructions de l'universel: Psychanalyse, philosophie*, Paris: Presses Universitaires de France, 1997.

Davis, Colin, *Levinas: An Introduction*, Cambridge: Polity Press, 1996.

—— *Ethical Issues in Twentieth-Century French Fiction: Killing the Other*, Basingstoke: Macmillan, 2000.

De Man, Paul, *The Resistance to Theory*, Manchester: Manchester University Press, 1986.

Deleuze, Gilles, *La Philosophie critique de Kant*, Paris: Presses Universitaires de France, 1963.

Deleuze, Gilles, and Guattari, Félix, *Qu'est-ce que la philosophie?*, Paris: Minuit, 1991.

Derrida, Jacques, *De la grammatologie*, Paris: Seuil, 1967.

—— *L'Ecriture et la différence*, Paris: Seuil, 1967.

—— *La Dissémination*, Paris: Seuil, 1972.

—— *La Carte postale de Socrate à Freud et au-delà*, Paris: Aubier-Flammarion, 1980.

—— *Psyché: Inventions de l'autre*, Paris: Galilée, 1987.

—— *Mémoires pour Paul de Man*, Paris, Galilée, 1988.

—— *Du droit à la philosophie*, Paris: Galilée, 1990.

—— *Limited Inc.*, Paris: Galilée, 1990.

—— *Spectres de Marx*, Paris: Galilée, 1993.

—— *Adieu à Emmanuel Levinas*, Paris: Galilée, 1997.

—— 'Sokal et Bricmont ne sont pas sérieux', *Le Monde*, 20 November 1997, 17.

Docherty, Thomas, *After Theory: Postmodernism/Postmarxism*, London and New York: Routledge, 1990.

—— *Alterities: Criticism, History, Representation*, Oxford: Oxford University Press, 1996.

—— (ed.), *Postmodernism: A Reader*, Brighton: Harvester Wheatsheaf, 1993.

Doubrovsky, Serge, *Pourquoi la nouvelle critique: Critique et objectivité*, Paris: Mercure de France, 1966.

Dreyfus, Hubert, and Rabinow, Paul, 'What is maturity? Habermas and Foucault on "What is Enlightenment?"', in Hoy, David Couzens (ed.), *Foucault: A Critical Reader*, Oxford: Basil Blackwell, 1986, 109–21.

Driver, Tom, 'Beckett by the Madeleine', *Columbia University Forum* 4 (Summer 1961), 21–5.

Eaglestone, Robert, *Ethical Criticism: Reading after Levinas*, Edinburgh: Edinburgh University Press, 1997.

Eagleton, Terry, *Against the Grain: Essays 1975–1985*, London: Verso, 1986.

—— *The Illusions of Postmodernism*, Oxford: Blackwell, 1996.

Elliott, Gregory, 'Further adventures of the dialectic: Merleau-Ponty, Sartre, Althusser', in A. Phillips Griffiths (ed.), *Contemporary French Philosophy*, Cambridge: Cambridge University Press, 1987, 195–214.

Ferry, Luc, and Renaut, Alain, *La Pensée 68: Essai sur l'anti-humanisme contemporain*, Paris: Gallimard, 1988.

ffrench, Patrick, 'Open letter to detectives and psychoanalysts: Analysis and reading', in Chernaik, Warren, Swales, Martin, and Vilain, Robert (eds), *The Art of Detective Fiction*, Basingstoke: Macmillan, 2000, 222–32.

Fletcher, John, and Benjamin, Andrew (eds), *Abjection, Melancholia and Love: The Work of Julia Kristeva*, London and New York: Routledge, 1990.

Foucault, Michel, *Les Mots et les choses: Une archéologie des sciences humaines*, Paris: Gallimard, 1966.

—— 'Qu'est-ce que les Lumières?', in *Dits et écrits 1954–1988*, IV: *1980–1988*, Paris: Gallimard, 1994, 562–78.

Freud, Sigmund, *Beyond the Pleasure Principle*, in *On Metapsychology: The Theory of Psychoanalysis*, The Pelican Freud Library volume 11, Harmondsworth: Penguin Books, 1984.

—— *Totem and Taboo*, in *The Origins of Religion*, The Pelican Freud Library volume 13, Harmondsworth: Penguin Books, 1985.

—— *Civilization, Society and Religion: Group Psychology, Civilization and its Discontents and Other Works*, The Pelican Freud Library volume 12, Harmondsworth: Penguin Books, 1985.

Fujimura, Joan, 'L'Autorité du savoir en question', in Jurdant, Baudouin (ed.), *Impostures scientifiques: Les Malentendus de l'affaire Sokal*, Paris and Nice: Editions la Découverte/Alliage, 1998, 214–36.

Gadamer, Hans-Georg, *Lob der Theorie*, Frankfurt am Main: Suhrkamp Verlag, 1983.

Gelley, Alexander (ed.), *Unruly Examples: On the Rhetoric of Exemplarity*, Stanford, CA: Stanford University Press, 1995.

Goldmann, Lucien, *Le Dieu caché: Etude sur la vision tragique dans les 'Pensées' de Pascal et dans le théâtre de Racine*, Paris: Gallimard, 1959; first edition 1956; Tel edition.

Gutting, Gary (ed.), *The Cambridge Companion to Foucault*, Cambridge: Cambridge University Press, 1994.

Habermas, Jürgen, *The Philosophical Discourse of Modernity*, trans. Frederick Lawrence, Cambridge: Polity Press, 1987.

—— *Legitimation Crisis*, trans. Thomas McCarthy, Cambridge: Polity Press, 1988.

—— *The New Conservatism*, trans. Shierry Weber Nicholsen, Cambridge, Polity Press, 1989.

—— 'Modernity – an incomplete project', in Docherty, Thomas (ed.), *Postmodernism: A Reader*, Brighton: Harvester Wheatsheaf, 1993, 98–109.

Hand, Seán (ed.), *Facing the Other: The Ethics of Emmanuel Levinas*, Richmond, Surrey: Curzon Press, 1996.

Hayes, Julie Chandler, *Reading the French Enlightenment: System and Subversion*, Cambridge: Cambridge University Press, 1999.

Hill, Leslie, 'Julia Kristeva: Theorizing the avant-garde?', in Fletcher, John, and Benjamin, Andrew (eds), *Abjection, Melancholia and Love: The Work of Julia Kristeva*, London and New York: Routledge, 1990, 137–56.

Hillis Miller, Joseph, *The Ethics of Reading: Kant, de Man, Eliot, Trollope, James, and Benjamin*, New York: Columbia University Press, 1987.

—— 'The triumph of theory, the resistance to reading, and the question of the material base', *Publications of the Modern Language Association of America* 102 (1987), 281–91.

—— *On Literature*, London and New York: Routledge, 2002.

Howells, Christina, *Derrida: Deconstruction from Phenomenology to Ethics*, Cambridge: Polity Press, 1999.

Hoy, David Couzens (ed.), *Foucault: A Critical Reader*, Oxford: Basil Blackwell, 1986.

Jameson, Fredric, *Postmodernism, or, The Cultural Logic of Late Capitalism*, London and New York: Verso, 1991.

—— *The Cultural Turn: Selected Writings on the Postmodern, 1983–1998*, London and New York: Verso, 1998.

Jeanneret, Yves, *L'Affaire Sokal ou la querelle des impostures*, Paris: Presses Universitaires de France, 1998.

Johnson, Barbara, *The Wake of Deconstruction*, Oxford: Blackwell, 1994.

Jurdant, Baudouin (ed.), *Impostures scientifiques: Les Malentendus de l'affaire Sokal*, Paris and Nice: Editions la Découverte/Alliage, 1998.

Kant, Immanuel, 'On a supposed right to tell lies from benevolent motives', in *Kant's Critique of Practical Reason and Other Works on the Theory of Ethics*,

trans. Thomas Kingsmill Abbott, London, New York and Bombay: Long-
mans, Green and Co, 1898, 361–5.

—— Critique of Practical Reason, trans. Lewis White Beck, London and New
York: Macmillan, 1956.

—— Grundlegung zur Metaphysik der Sitten, Hamburg: Felix Meiner Verlag,
1965.

—— Logik and Pädagogik, in Kants Werke IX, Berlin: Walter de Gruyter, 1968.

—— Political Writings, trans. H. B. Nisbet, Cambridge: Cambridge University
Press, 1970.

—— The Conflict of Faculties/Der Streit der Facultäten, trans. Mary J. Gregor,
Lincoln, NE, and London: University of Nebraska Press, 1979.

—— Anthropologie in pragmatischer Hinsicht, Stuttgart: Philipp Reclam Jun.,
1983.

—— Critique of Pure Reason, trans. Werner S. Pluhar, Indianapolis, IN: Hackett
Publishing Company, 1996.

Kearney, Richard, On Stories, London and New York: Routledge, 2002.

Kelly, Michael (ed.), Critique and Power: Recasting the Foucault/Habermas Debate,
Cambridge, MA, and London: The MIT Press, 1994.

Kristeva, Julia, Séméiotiké: Recherches pour une sémanalyse, Paris: Seuil, 1969;
Points edition.

—— La Révolution du language poétique, Paris: Seuil, 1974; Points edition.

—— Histoires d'amour, Paris: Denoël, 1983; Folio edition.

—— Pouvoirs et limites de la psychanalyse II: La Révolte intime, Paris: Fayard,
1987; Livre de Poche edition.

—— Soleil noir: Dépression et mélancolie, Paris: Gallimard, 1987.

—— Etrangers à nous-mêmes, Paris: Fayard, 1988; Folio edition.

—— Les Samouraïs, Paris: Gallimard, 1990; Folio edition.

—— Le Vieil Homme et les loups, Paris: Fayard: 1991.

—— Possessions, Paris: Fayard, 1996; Livre de Poche edition.

—— Pouvoirs et limites de la psychanalyse I: Sens et non-sens de la révolte, Paris:
Fayard, 1996; Livre de Poche edition.

—— Le Génie Féminin I: Hannah Arendt, Paris: Fayard, 1999.

—— Le Génie féminin II: Melanie Klein, Paris: Fayard, 2000.

—— Le Génie féminin III: Colette, Paris: Fayard, 2002.

—— 'Forgiveness: an interview', in Publications of the Modern Language Association of America, 117, 2 (2002), 278–95.

Lacan, Jacques, Les Quatre Concepts fondamentaux de la psychanalyse, Paris:
Seuil, 1973; Points edition.

Lechte, John, 'Art, love, and melancholy in the work of Julia Kristeva', in
Fletcher, John, and Benjamin, Andrew (eds), Abjection, Melancholia and
Love: The Work of Julia Kristeva, London and New York: Routledge, 1990,
24–41.

Levinas, Emmanuel, Totalité et infini: Essai sur l'extériorité, The Hague: Martinus
Nijhoff, 1961; Livre de Poche edition.

—— *Difficile liberté: Essais sure le judaïsme*, Paris: Albin Michel, 1963 and 1976.

—— *Quatre lectures talmudiques*, Paris: Minuit, 1968.

—— *Humanisme de l'autre homme*, Montpellier: Fata Morgana, 1972; Livre de Poche edition.

—— *Autrement qu'être ou au-delà de l'essence*, The Hague: Martinus Nijhoff, 1974; Livre de Poche edition.

—— *Noms propres*, Montpellier: Fata Morgana, 1976; Livre de Poche edition.

—— *Du sacré au saint: Cinq nouvelles lectures talmudiques*, Paris: Minuit, 1977.

—— *L'Au-delà du verset: Lectures et discours talmudiques*, Paris: Minuit, 1982.

—— *Hors sujet*, Montpellier: Fata Morgana, 1987.

—— *A l'heure des nations*, Paris: Minuit, 1988.

—— *Entre nous: Essais sur le penser-à-l'autre*, Paris: Grasset and Fasquelle, 1991.

—— *La Mort et le temps*, Paris: Editions de l'Herne, 1991; Livre de Poche edition.

—— *Les Imprévus de l'histoire*, Montpellier: Fata Morgana, 1994.

—— *Nouvelles lectures talmudiques*, Paris: Minuit, 1996.

Llewelyn, John, *The Middle Voice of Ecological Conscience: A Chiasmic Reading of Responsibility in the Neighbourhood of Levinas, Heidegger and Others*, Basingstoke: Macmillan, 1991.

—— *Emmanuel Levinas: The Genealogy of Ethics*, London and New York: Routledge, 1995.

Lloyd, David, 'Kant's examples', in Gelley, Alexander (ed.), *Unruly Examples: On the Rhetoric of Exemplarity*, Stanford, CA: Stanford University Press, 1995, 255–76.

Lyotard, Jean-François, *Dérive à partir de Marx et Freud*, Paris: Union Générale d'Editions, 1973; 10/18 edition.

—— *Economie libidinale*, Paris: Minuit, 1974.

—— *Rudiments païens*, Paris: Union Générale d'Editions, 1977; 10/18 edition.

—— *La Condition postmoderne*, Paris: Minuit, 1979.

—— *Le Différend*, Paris: Minuit, 1983.

—— *Tombeau de l'intellectuel et autres papiers*, Paris: Galilée, 1984.

—— *L'Enthousiasme: La Critique kantienne de l'histoire*, Paris: Galilée, 1986.

—— *Le Postmoderne expliqué aux enfants*, Paris: Galilée, 1988; Livre de Poche edition.

—— *The Lyotard Reader*, ed. Andrew Benjamin, Oxford: Blackwell, 1989.

—— *Pérégrinations*, Paris: Galilée, 1990.

—— *Moralités postmodernes*, Paris: Galilée, 1993.

Lyotard, Jean-François, and Thébaud, Jean-Loup, *Au juste*, Paris: Christian Bourgois, 1979.

MacIntyre, Alasdair, *After Virtue*, London: Duckworth, 1981, 1985; second edition.

McQuillan, Martin, MacDonald, Graeme, Purves, Robin, and Thomson, Stephen (eds), *Post-Theory: New Directions in Criticism*, Edinburgh: Edinburgh University Press, 1999.

Marty, Eric, *Louis Althusser, un sujet sans procès: Anatomie d'un passé très récent*, Paris: Gallimard, 1999.

Mauron, Charles, *L'Inconscient dans l'œuvre et la vie de Racine*, Aix-en-Provence: Ophrys, 1957.

Moi, Toril, *Sexual/Textual Politics: Feminist Literary Theory*, London: Methuen, 1985.

—— *What is a Woman?*, Oxford and New York: Oxford University Press, 1999.

Moriarty, Michael, *Roland Barthes*, Cambridge: Polity Press, 1991.

Nagel, Thomas, *The View from Nowhere*, New York: Oxford University Press, 1986.

Norris, Christopher, *What's Wrong with Postmodernism: Critical Theory and the Ends of Philosophy*, Baltimore, MD: The Johns Hopkins University Press, 1990.

—— *Truth and the Ethics of Criticism*, Manchester: Manchester University Press, 1994.

—— '"What is Enlightenment?": Kant and Foucault', in Gutting, Gary (ed.), *The Cambridge Companion to Foucault*, Cambridge: Cambridge University Press, 1994, 159–96.

—— *Deconstruction and the 'Unfinished Project of Modernity'*, London: The Athlone Press, 2000.

Owen, David, 'Orientation and Enlightenment: An essay on critique and genealogy', in Ashenden, Samantha, and Owen, David (eds), *Foucault contra Habermas: Recasting the Dialogue between Genealogy and Critical Theory*, London: Sage, 1999, 21–44.

Picard, Raymond, *La Carrière de Jean Racine*, Paris: Gallimard, 1961; second edition.

—— *Nouvelle Critique ou nouvelle imposture*, Paris: Jean-Jacques Pauvert, 1965.

Pommier, Gérard, *Louis du néant: La Mélancolie d'Althusser*, Paris: Aubier, 1998.

Rabaté, Jean-Michel, *The Ghosts of Modernity*, Gainesville, FL: University Press of Florida, 1996.

—— *The Future of Theory*, Oxford: Blackwell, 2002.

Rapaport, Herman, *The Theory Mess: Deconstruction in Eclipse*, New York: Columbia University Press, 2001.

—— 'Of the eye and the law', in Gelley, Alexander (ed.), *Unruly Examples: On the Rhetoric of Exemplarity*, Stanford, CA: Stanford University Press, 1995, 303–23.

Ricoeur, Paul, *Autrement: Lecture d''Autrement qu'être ou au-delà de l'essence' d'Emmanuel Levinas*, Paris: Presses Universitaires de France, 1997.

Robbins, Jill, *Altered Reading: Levinas and Literature*, Chicago and London: University of Chicago Press, 1999.

Rorty, Richard, *Consequences of Pragmatism*, Brighton: Harvester Wheatsheaf, 1982.

—— *Contingency, Irony, and Solidarity*, Cambridge: Cambridge University Press, 1989.

—— *Essays on Heidegger and Others*, Cambridge: Cambridge University Press, 1991.

Royle, Nicholas, '*Déjà vu*', in McQuillan, Martin, MacDonald, Graeme, Purves, Robin, and Thomson, Stephen (eds), *Post-Theory: New Directions in Criticism*, Edinburgh: Edinburgh University Press, 1999, 3–20.

Said, Edward, *Culture and Imperialism*, London: Chatto and Windus, 1993; Vintage edition.

Salanskis, Jean-Michel, 'Pour une épistémologie de la lecture', in Jurdant, Baudouin (ed.), *Impostures scientifiques: Les Malentendus de l'affaire Sokal*, Paris and Nice: Editions la Découverte/*Alliage*, 1998, 157–94.

Sartre, Jean-Paul, *La Nausée*, Paris: Gallimard, 1938; Livre de poche edition.

Schmidt, James, and Wartenberg, Thomas E., 'Foucault's Enlightenment: Critique, revolution, and the fashioning of the self', in Kelly, Michael (ed.), *Critique and Power: Recasting the Foucault/Habermas Debate*, Cambridge, MA, and London: The MIT Press, 1994, 283–314.

Smyth, John Vignaux, *The Habit of Lying: Sacrificial Studies in Literature, Philosophy, and Fashion Theory*, Durham, NC, and London: Duke University Press, 2002.

Sokal, Alan, 'Transgressing the boundaries: Toward a transformative hermeneutics of quantum gravity', *Social Text* 46/47 (1996), 217–52.

—— 'A physicist experiments with cultural studies', *Lingua Franca* 6, 4 (1996), 62–4.

—— 'Pourquoi j'ai écrit ma parodie', *Le Monde*, 31 January 1997, 15.

—— 'What the *Social Text* affair does and does not prove', in Noretta Koertge (ed.), *A House Built on Sand: Exposing Postmodernist Myths about Science*, New York: Oxford University Press, 1998, 9–22.

Sokal, Alan, and Bricmont, Jean, *Impostures intellectuelles*, Paris: Odile Jacob, 1997.

—— 'Les Critiques de Derrida et de Dorra ratent leur cible', *Le Monde*, 12 December 1997, 23.

—— *Intellectual Impostures: Postmodern Philosophers' Abuse of Science*, London: Profile Books, 1998.

Tallis, Raymond, 'Sokal and Bricmont: Is this the beginning of the end of the dark ages in the humanities?', *PN Review* 128 (1999), 35–42.

Thody, Philip, *Roland Barthes: A Conservative Estimate*, Chicago and London: University of Chicago Press, 1977 and 1983.

Todorov, Tzvetan, *Qu'est-ce que le structuralisme? II: Poétique*, Paris: Seuil, 1968; Points edition.

Wahl, François, 'Introduction générale' in Todorov, Tzvetan, *Qu'est-ce que le structuralisme? II: Poétique*, Paris: Seuil, 1968; Points edition, 7–13.

Williams, Caroline, *Contemporary French Philosophy: Modernity and the Persistence of the Subject*, London and New York: The Athlone Press, 2001.

Williams, James, *Lyotard: Towards a Postmodern Philosophy*, Cambridge: Polity Press, 1998.

Wolfreys, Julian, *Victorian Hauntings: Spectrality, Gothic, the Uncanny and Literature*, Basingstoke: Palgrave, 2002.

Žižek, Slavoj, *Looking Awry: An Introduction to Jacques Lacan through Popular Culture*, Cambridge, MA, and London: The MIT Press, 1991

—— *Tarrying with the Negative: Kant, Hegel, and the Critique of Ideology*, Durham, NC: Duke University Press, 1993.

—— *The Ticklish Subject: The Absent Centre of Political Ontology*, London and New York: Verso, 1999.

—— *The Fragile Absolute, or, Why is the Christian Legacy Worth Fighting For?*, London and New York: Verso, 2000.

—— *The Fright of Real Tears: Krzysztof Kieślowski between Theory and Post-Theory*, London: BFI Publishing, 2001.

Zupančič, Alenka, *Ethics of the Real: Kant, Lacan*, London and New York: Verso, 2000.

# Index